D1131521

A HISTORY OF

FRENCH DRAMATIC LITERATURE

IN

THE SEVENTEENTH CENTURY

PART V

RECAPITULATION

1610-1700

A HISTORY OF
FRENCH DRAMATIC LITERATURE
IN
THE SEVENTEENTH CENTURY

PART V

RECAPITULATION
1610-1700

BY

HENRY CARRINGTON LANCASTER

Professor of French Literature in the Johns Hopkins University

GORDIAN PRESS, INC.
NEW YORK, MCMLXVI

PART
V
IS DEDICATED TO
VICTORY

CONTENTS

INTRODUCTION

When I published Part IV, I proposed to add a ninth volume of general conclusions and of supplementary indices. In the eight preceding volumes are given the facts and arguments on which these conclusions are based. If the latter had been published sooner, they might have suffered from what Racine called " la trop grande proximité des temps " of the investigation. It has been my desire to watch the dramatists at work, to see them as their contemporaries saw them. It is now my purpose to sum up my impressions of their work and to emphasize the more valuable parts of it, while asking specialists to return with the help of the indices to my earlier discussions of details.

I originally hoped that, to constitute such indices, a listing of books, actors, authors, and other persons would be sufficient, but I came to realize that certain topics of interest to the public would not be included in this type of index. I have consequently added a Subject Index of the five parts. As I discovered that there were readers interested in plays whose authors were unknown to them, I have prepared a Finding List that gives the plays alphabetically, according to their titles and sub-titles, rather than under the names of their authors. Finally, in order to spare the reader the task of looking into five indices for each author or book, I have made a General Index of the nine volumes, the items of which are selected according to the principles followed in the indices of earlier parts. It includes the index of Part V and, for the first time, that of the supplements to Parts I, II, III, and IV. It repeats in full minor items given in the indices of earlier parts. In the case of longer items, it refers the reader to the index or indices in which the person or book has been mentioned, according to the method explained at the beginning of the General Index. To have reproduced these longer items in full would have been expensive and would have made many of them too long for easy consultation.

Added after the main portion of the structure has been completed, the chapters of this ninth volume will serve as an entrance to the building, while the indices will direct the inquirers to the special office they may wish to visit.

For financial assistance in publishing Part V, I am indebted to the Johns Hopkins Press, which, as in the case of Parts II, III, and IV, has paid half the expenses with the understanding that it would receive half the returns from sales. For supplying a portion of the other half I must thank the Rockefeller Fund for Research in the Humanities and my friend and colleague, David M. Robinson.

CHAPTER I

THE BACKGROUND

It was during the seventeenth century that France regained the leadership in European literature it had held for a while in the Middle Ages and had lost to Italy in the time of the Renaissance. This triumph of the French spirit, which was to become especially obvious in the eighteenth century, was to a considerable extent the accomplishment of the dramatists whose work has been described in my earlier volumes. Let me sum up the circumstances that made it possible.

The reign of Henri IV, though it brought peace after the Wars of Religion, did not bring about sufficient recovery to permit much development of drama. His murder was followed by so many disturbances that prosperity returned only after Richelieu had taken charge. While the Cardinal was crushing the Protestants in 1628, a new generation of dramatists was beginning to produce a large number of plays, an activity that continued briskly for twenty years and achieved important results. The most notable work in this period is, of course, that of Corneille in tragedy. It is true that Richelieu took his country into a great war, but, as much of the fighting was done on foreign soil, it did not seriously affect the life of the capital, while it even was beneficial to drama, as Richelieu favored the production of plays in order to impress his allies and to divert his officers during their stay in winter quarters. The military spirit of *Horace* and of some other plays must have been due to this war, as may have been much of the confidence in human exertion that is expressed in plays of the time.

The Fronde of 1649-53, however, closed for a while Parisian theaters, discouraged Corneille and other dramatists from continuing to write plays, and demonstrated the fact that heroism may prove quite ineffective. When this civil strife was over and the nation had sufficiently recovered, a new generation arose that preferred comedy to tragedy and, in the latter *genre,* the analysis of emotion rather than the exaltation of patriotism. The period from 1659 to 1672, largely one of peace, is the most important in the whole history of the French stage.

In less than a year after Louis XIV invaded the Netherlands, Molière died. In less than five years Corneille and Racine had given up dramatic composition. Drama seemed to be doomed, but a new period of peace enabled Campistron in tragedy, Baron and Dancourt in comedy, to start their careers with success, though no new Racine or Molière appeared and the war was soon renewed.   In the last decade of the century, it is true, comedy gained some advantage from this state of affairs, for the social changes produced by war enabled dramatists to vary their study of manners and, with an altered audience, to produce, more extensively than their predecessors, short plays, prose plays, and those that introduced dancing and music.   Other *genres* were less fortunate.   Louis XIV's imperialistic wars did not inspire patriotism as Richelieu's efforts to save his country from the menace of the House of Austria had done.   The "machine" play, first undertaken on a large scale just before the Fronde, flourished especially in the period of peace that followed the war with Spain, but was suppressed during the last war of the century.

Under Richelieu, Mazarin, and Louis XIV France wrested from Spain the position of most powerful European country.   During much of the period the errors of the government were not apparent.   Corneille pointed out in *Cinna* the blessings of benevolent and authoritative rule.   He and others slipped into later tragedies praise of Louis XIV.   When he condemned war and exalted peace, as he did in *la Toison d'or*, he allowed himself to do so because a war had just ended.   Campistron, to be sure, warned the king in 1691 against disaster that might come if the fighting continued, but his case was unique.   As a rule, dramatists left the politics of their country to their government, though they introduced it extensively into plays dealing with other lands.

The stratification of society affected French drama as it did that of other peoples.   French tragedy is eminently aristocratic, both because the aesthetics of an aristocratic society demanded heroes of lofty birth and because a king or a noble was freer to act than a less powerful man would have been.   This does not mean that humanity was sacrificed, or that a king necessarily had an admirable rôle, for some are weaklings, others victims of their errors.   There is no *tragédie bourgeoise* after the *Scédase* of Alexandre Hardy, though we occasionally find in tragedies minor persons who are not aristocrats.   There is no reason for condemning in French dramatists a usage that is approved when Sophocles and Shakespeare are discussed.   One should object only when decorum deprives the play of warmth, as it does in Genest's *Pénélope*, but there is compensation even for good manners, for Racine was able to draw tragic effects from the contrast between decorous expression and murderous passion that it veiled.

Comedy, on the other hand, is usually a middle-class affair, though the society of *le Misanthrope* and of certain plays by Baron is aristocratic. Molière made of the young marquis a comic type.   Like many other writers, he held up to ridicule the country nobleman.   He did not plead for one class or another, but sought comic material in them all.   His successors often portrayed the selfishness and impudence of the aristocracy and at times suggested the causes that were to produce its decay. The bourgeois may be presented as sympathetically as Mme Jourdain or as unsympathetically as Mme Patin. Their lives are treated in greater detail than those of members of other classes. Peasants appear from time to time throughout the century. Often they are farcical figures, but, especially towards the end of the century, they may be taken quite seriously. Peasant heroines appear in short plays by Baron, Dancourt, Regnard, and Dufresny, though in five-act comedies they do not have rôles of great importance. One finds, too, members of the city proletariat, but they are presented as individuals, not as groups aspiring to power. Occasional remarks in the mouths of valets show some discontent, some hope of rising to a higher social stratum, but not a desire to destroy the system. In other words, authors of seventeenth-century plays were dramatists rather than preachers of social theories.

If the situation had been otherwise, they might have received greater approval from more modern reformers, but it is doubtful if they would have improved their art. As it was, their acceptance of the social system in which they lived secured for the actors who interpreted them the patronage of Richelieu, Louis XIV, and many nobles. Such patronage brought the troupes substantial revenues, helped at times to add interest to their public entertainments, and was of assistance when they were attacked. Improved policing, too, doubtless rendered service, but there were times when plays were kept off the stage by governmental interference and when the authorities took upon themselves decisions that might better have been left to actors. Louis XIV suppressed the Marais theater, gave Lully a monopoly of professional musicians, drove out the Italian actors. His daughter-in-law forced several actors of the Comédie Française to retire. At times the theater was closed because of a royal death. Royal protection may have seemed a blessing, but it was not unmixed.

It must not be supposed that the lure of such protection persuaded dramatists to write only for an élite. In 1682-3, for instance, over 150,000 admissions were paid to the Comédie Française, and other persons attended performances without paying. Many spectators, of course, went a number of times in the year, but there must have been well over 100,000 different individuals who attended. It is impossible that so large a number did not include persons of all classes. Subligny's reference to a *porteuse d'eau* who discussed *Andromaque* would hardly be found in a play acted at the Palais Royal if such persons did not go to the theater. Nor did La Bruyère have a selected audience in mind when he wrote that "le peuple écoute avidement, les yeux élevés et la bouche ouverte." As it is said that in the first quarter of the century women of refinement did not go to the theater, we may suppose that it was then frequented by the unrefined, and there is no reason to suppose that the latter gave up the habit after the audience began to include respectable spectators. Nor is the question of expense a serious argument. Even when "quinze sous" represented a day's pay, the man who earned no more than this amount may well have spent it once or twice a year at the theater. Dramatists knew that their plays would be seen by highly mixed audiences at Paris, that they would be carried to the provinces and abroad by strolling actors, and that publication would further increase the number of persons for whom they were writing. The idea that they were working for a chosen few is consequently to be rejected.

If they had been writing for a small circle, they would have been tempted to cultivate the bizarre rather than to introduce into their work such commonplaces as those that can easily be found in Corneille's plays, or to base their witticisms, as Molière often did, on the opinions of the average man. It is not difficult to see that there was a community of interests between authors and their public. Molière did not avoid farce, as Boileau would have had him do. Corneille wrote for both the *doctes* and the *ignorants*. The interest that the century took in good manners, evidenced by the large number of courtesy books then published, is reflected, not only in the behavior in the plays of cultivated characters, but in the general insistence of authors that their main goal was the acquisition of "l'art de plaire." The concessions made to doctrinaire critics were largely due to the fact that such critics formed part of the audience. If they could be won over without offense to others, why not appeal to their tastes? To harmonize a variety of demands was one of the dramatist's chief aims.

Such an appeal might be made in an individual play, or in a day's entertainment that included both a tragedy, or a high comedy, and a farce, or by alternating tragedies and comedies from day to day, or by having different kinds of plays given at different theaters. While the Hôtel de Bourgogne was giving chiefly tragedies, the Palais Royal was specializing in comedy, the Marais in "machine" plays. While the Comédie Française was offering all three kinds, a Parisian could attend a performance of illogical and unrestrained farces at the Théâtre Italien; of opera at the Palais Royal.

The relations between the church and the theater are quite complex. Early in the century Garasse attacked Théophile, cited the text of his *Pyrame* as evidence that he denied the immortality of the soul, and had the play burned along with other works by its author. But this fact shows no antipathy to the theater as an institution and did not keep *Pyrame* out of the repertory of the Hôtel de Bourgogne. The Jesuits themselves gave

Latin school plays, primarily intended to teach morality and Catholic doctrine, but not written to convince young nobles that attendance upon the theater is sinful. Several churchmen, moreover, including Boisrobert, Boyer, Abeille, Genest, and Brueys, wrote plays. Cardinal Richelieu protected drama, as Cardinal Mazarin subsequently favored Italian opera. On the other hand, actors were excommunicated; Molière's body met with clerical difficulties in finding a grave; such eminent performers as la Champmeslé and J.-B. Raisin had to renounce their profession before they were granted at death the services of a priest.

The most celebrated example of interference was set in regard to *Tartuffe*, kept off the stage by the Compagnie du Saint-Sacrement, thanks to its influence with Anne of Austria. Corneille found it necessary to write an apology for drama in publishing *Attila*; Racine, in publishing *Phèdre*. Bossuet denounced Corneille, Molière, Racine, and Quinault for their productions and threatened the abbé Caffaro for defending the theater, but even his influence was not strong enough seriously to interfere with the giving of plays. Though the church delayed the presentation of *Tartuffe*, probably caused *Don Juan* to be withdrawn, and may have prevented Molière from attempting plays on similar subjects, the actors continued to prosper and dramatists were supplied by the church with a new comic type, that of the *abbé galant*.

It has been held that most seventeenth-century plays show no Christian influence. This is true in a sense, but the statement must be qualified. About nine percent of all extant plays that appeared in 1610-1700 are distinctly religious, but most of them were not intended for performance on a popular stage. There were also plays, now lost, the titles of which indicate that they were religious in character and kept up the tradition of the medieval theater. The religious plays known to have been given at Paris constitute two groups: one of tragedies produced about 1639-53 that include Corneille's *Polyecute* and *Théodore*, Rotrou's *Saint Genest*, and Du Ryer's *Saül* and *Esther*; the other of tragedies inspired by the success of Racine's *Esther* at Saint-Cyr and including *Adrien*, *Athalie*, and *Gabinie*. The existence of the first group may be attributed in part to the religious revival in France that formed part of the counter-reformation; of the other, to Mme de Maintenon's educational theories, which included the instruction of girls by the private production of plays, and to Racine's success in applying his genius to themes of this nature. The church is consequently to be credited with the inspiration of several eminent classical tragedies. There are also traces of Christian tradition in a few plays not primarily religious, such as Mairet's *Athénaïs*, d'Aubignac's *Pucelle d'Orléans*, and Tristan's *Mort de Sénèque*. Of course, Christianity played a large part in the ethics of the times, which undoubtedly have to be considered, while the instruction given by the Jesuits may have developed interest in classical Latin plays and have given a taste for the study of motives and for logical composition. It remains, true, however, that most plays of the century show little that can be called Christian except in the sense that they were written in and for a Christian society.

The drama, which, as it requires an audience, is an eminently social form of art, profited by the progress in sociability promoted by improved transportation and postal facilities and by the birth and development of newspapers. The dramatists' love of psychological analysis, their effort to find a form that would suit their subject matter, and their respect for the proprieties doubtless owed something to the salons that developed during the century and to the establishment of academies, especially to that of the French Academy, which from the beginning of its history included several dramatists among its members.

The dominant rôle of Paris in the theater corresponds roughly with the more conscious application of art to drama. To have a center where troupes could play for long periods, which others could visit at Easter, where authors and actors could meet, where the life of France could be studied in that of its metropolis, was probably an essential feature in the development of drama. The influence of Paris was unfortunate in minimizing the value of the country, but this was partially corrected by the facts that many dramatists were not born in Paris and that most actors played in the provinces before establishing themselves in the capital. Molière, Dancourt, and others did not have in this respect the limited interests of Boileau.

As the drama was written for the general public rather than for savants, authors seldom alluded to the latter. Bodin is mentioned in a preface by La Pinelière and in the text of *Sir Politick Would-be*. Montaigne, Charron, and Cureau de la Chambre are referred to in a preface by Gillet de la Tessonerie. Montaigne's style was condemned by Hardy and was said by Palaprat to have promoted his own tendency to digress. Corneille quoted him in publishing *Cinna* and Molière may have taken hints from him in ridiculing physicians. One of the latter, Du Laurens, is mentioned as an authority in a play by the obscure Grouchy. The circulation of the blood, but not its discoverer, is discussed in *Crispin médecin*.

It is hard to establish any considerable influence of Descartes. He and Corneille, when they resemble each other, seem to be drawing on common sources of inspiration. Chappuzeau and Molière alluded to his work, but put their allusions into the mouths of learned women. One of Fatouville's heroines attacked his treatment of animals as machines. Fontenelle made use of Descartes's theory in regard to comets. Molière and Fatouville may have had him in mind when astronomy comes into their work, but they do not mention him in this connection. There is only a passing reference to Descartes in a play by Bordelon.

Pascal's *Provinciales* probably exerted some influence on *Tartuffe* and *Don Juan*, while his invention of the omnibus inspired a play by Chevalier. La Mothe le Vayer, who was a friend of Molière, may have rendered him some slight assistance. La Rochefoucauld is supposed to have inspired the passage on *amour propre* in Corneille's *Tite et Bérénice*. La Bruyère supplied Regnard with the principal source of *le Distrait*. There is little else to show that dramatists were following the thought of French philosophers, scientists, and moralists who wrote in the late sixteenth century or in the seventeenth. They were writing for audiences that took little interest in what M. Paul Hazard calls " la crise de la conscience européenne," or did not think the theater the proper place for the discussion of advanced ideas.

As for the allied arts, their relations to drama vary considerably in importance. Sculpture went almost unnoticed. Architecture is occasionally referred to, notably when the improved appearance of Paris is mentioned. It supplied models for elements of scenery, as did the art of gardening. Both of these arts furnish material for the descriptive passages in *les Visionnaires*, III, 5. Painting was essential to the presentation of plays, but it did not have to be of a high order. Only twice are artists mentioned in this connection. Prat, " qui a la main la plus hardie pour la détrempe," was employed to paint the scenery of de Visé's *Amours du Soleil*. Joachim, an Italian, painted a scene of visitors to a fair for Dancourt's *Foire de Besons*. Poussin gave Scarron a canvas, was mentioned by Bordelon, and was highly praised by Scudéry in the preface to *Andromire*, where his example is cited as an argument for admitting episodes into a play. Brécourt called Le Potre, who illustrated his *Nopce de Village* when it was published, the Callot of his time. Two painters, Ferdinand and Freminet, are mentioned in Mareschal's *Railleur*. Raphael is named in Gilbert's *Courtisan parfait*; Teniers in *Arlequin Homme à bonne fortune*; Carracci in Bordelon's *Lotterie de Scapin*. In Biancolelli's *Fausse Coquette* we read of " les titiens, les pauls-veroneses, les caraches, les michel-anges." A list of seventeen painters, chiefly Italian, is given in Gillet's *Campagnard*. Michelangelo is especially praised. Indeed he and Poussin seem to have been the most admired members of their profession.

Occasionally men are disguised as painters, and pictures form part of the scenery. Durval puts a description of pictures into the text of his *Agarite*. Scarron has a character in his *Gardien de soy-mesme* refer to a

2

painting of Saint George in his village church. Rotrou makes the hero of *Saint Genest* advise a decorator about his art. A picture of Venus constitutes an important element in the plot of Boyer's *Policrite*. An Apollo in the Pantheon is praised in Blessebois's *Eugénie*. It is possible that paintings on the walls of Fontainebleau had some connection with the composition of Durval's *Travaux d'Ulysse*. Corneille admits that painters influenced his mounting Perseus upon Pegasus. Desmaretz declares in the preface of his *Scipion* that he would conceal his art as painters do. Robbe compares his mingling scenes of manners and of farce with the use of " des clairs et des ombres " in painting. Palaprat states that he knew at Paris Vario, an Italian artist who was a friend of actors from his country, but this fact does not indicate that the dramatist was influenced by him.

One may conclude that dramatists were conscious of the pictorial art of their times, but that they were little concerned with criticizing it, that the great artists influenced them little, and that, apart from their use of painters to decorate their scenery, their work would not have been much altered if they had ignored painting altogether.

Music and dancing were introduced into a number of dramatic productions, especially into " machine " plays, *comédies-ballets*, and *comédies-vaudevilles*. A list of musicians had been given by Grouchy as early as 1632 (cf. above, Part I, p. 515). Before Molière's time ballets were occasionally introduced into plays. Subsequently plays sometimes constituted parts of ballets. The ballet was employed by Molière and others in somewhat the way that a chorus had been used by the Greeks. Lully composed the music for several *comédies-ballets*; Charpentier, for *le Malade imaginaire*; Moreau, for the choruses of *Esther*. Grandval and Jacques Raisin composed for Dancourt and other authors of *comédies-vaudevilles*. The establishment in France of opera made it difficult for actors to secure the services of professional musicians, but gave the dramatists new material to introduce into their plays, either as part of their study of manners or as an object of their satire.

But while music, dancing, and painting were of some interest to dramatists, the art that concerned them chiefly was that of putting stories into dramatic form, of analyzing character in order to make it convincing on the stage, of depicting the varying emotions of their fellows, of drawing comic material from their behavior. Their characters belong to all classes and to many professions—those of lawyers, physicians, teachers, merchants, *abbés galants*, etc. The society in which they lived suggested also humbler representatives in peasants, servants, chimney-sweepers, coachmen, porters, cobblers, hawkers, and other members of the lower classes. Various events and customs are portrayed there such as the invention of the omnibus, the visit of Russian ambassadors, the travels of Bernier and Tavernier, the occupation of Madagascar, the activities of la Voisin, the approach of a comet, the effect of war on life at Paris, the introduction of tobacco into good society, and the use of coffee. To amuse their audiences, the dramatists drew upon such sources of entertainment as well as upon various forms of creative literature written in French and in other languages.

Great drama requires primarily writers of genius, but, as it has to express itself through interpreters, it needs a government that is sufficiently stable to give it protection; enough economic prosperity to allow the building of theaters and the proper setting of the stage; actors well trained in their art; spectators that have acquired deep interest in the performance of plays; a literary tradition on which the authors may build. Dramatists must not be oppressed by the feeling that it is useless for them to attempt to rival their predecessors, nor must they forget their art in an effort to astonish or to instruct their audiences. The Middle Ages did not fulfill these conditions in sufficient measure to build up a drama of high value, despite the cleverness of *Patelin* and the quaintness of many medieval plays. The sixteenth century fulfilled some of them, but its men of genius were not dramatists and the Wars of Religion destroyed whatever chances there might have been for the production of great plays. It was under Richelieu that the necessary conditions were found and that the drama of Corneille and his contemporaries was produced. It was when Louis XIV had ended his war with Spain that a second opportunity was given and that Molière was free to build comedy that did not risk competition with earlier productions. Racine had in a sense less encouragement, as Corneille had preceded him, but his special gifts as a poet, the changed interests of French society after the Fronde, and his willingness to concentrate his talents upon a limited portion of Corneille's territory made it possible for him to attain great celebrity.

The circumstances were such that many other dramatists aided these three by suggestion or by rivalry. Some of these minor authors enriched French drama to such an extent that to study only the three leaders gives a decidedly incomplete picture of seventeenth-century dramatic production. Not only incomplete, but misleading, for the three dramatists did not work in isolation, but were part of a busy world of writers, whose numbers were increased most largely around 1630, when Corneille brought out his first play, and around 1660, when Molière had just started on his career as leader of a successful Parisian troupe.

So much for the general conditions under which French drama flourished. I will take up in the next three chapters the question of the dramatists' interpreters, the literary tradition, both foreign and native, on which they built, and their conception of their art.

CHAPTER II

ACTORS AND THEATERS

Throughout the seventeenth century amateur actors gave religious plays in villages of Brittany, the Basque country, the Alps, Burgundy, and other parts of the country, while boys acted Latin dramas in schools under Jesuit instruction. French soldiers in Egypt, the French colony at Constantinople, officers in winter quarters, guests of Mme de Rambouillet, young Jacqueline Pascal and her comrades, noble girls at Saint-Cyr are known to have given private performances. Little is said about the histrionic talents of such persons. Their work shows the popularity of drama, but could not have exerted much influence upon the art of acting. As a rule, the great preferred to hire professionals to act in their homes when they did not attend performances in public theaters.

Such professionals were both foreign and French. None came during the century from the north or north-east, but Spanish actors rented the Hôtel de Bourgogne for the month of April, 1625, and another troupe came in 1660, shortly after Louis XIV married his Spanish queen, played 73 times at court in 1663, and acted occasionally at the Hôtel de Bourgogne until they departed in 1673. These troupes seem to have had little success and to have remained without influence on their French colleagues. Italian actors, on the contrary, were important. They had already come to France in the sixteenth century. They rented the Hôtel de Bourgogne for parts of the years 1599, 1603, 1608, 1613, 1614, and 1621. Scaramouche was living in Paris as a " comédien de la Royne " in 1644. The following year the troupe played before Mazarin. In the second half of the century these actors introduced the *Burlador* with their own spectacular and comic additions, shared the Petit Bourbon and the Palais Royal with Molière, after his death shared the Guénégaud with his troupe, and after August, 1680, until they were suppressed in 1697, took possession of the Hôtel de Bourgogne. The tempo of their plays was never that of those acted by their French colleagues. They had no influence upon tragedy. But they may well have helped develop French farce and have made French actors realize the importance of gesture and of facial expression. When they began to act plays written wholly or partly in French, their productions secured a place in the history of French drama. The popularity they enjoyed at Paris, shown by the fame of Scaramouche, Harlequin, and Colombine, gives evidence that Parisians could be attracted by other qualities than those ordinarily associated with their classical drama.

12

Our principal concern is, however, with French actors. Early in the century they were by no means centered at Paris. Even before it begins, we hear of a well organized troupe at Bordeaux. The fact that Rouen was for a while a more important city for the publication of plays than the capital suggests that dramatic activity there was considerable. After Paris gained the supremacy, it was not there but at Lyons that Molière first prospered and that Chappuzeau and Marc-Antoine Legrand published their first plays, as did Dancourt at Lille and Arras. Actors played in many parts of the kingdom, went frequently to the Low Countries, established themselves in Hannover, Bavaria, Savoy, and even penetrated as far as Copenhagen, Stockholm, and Warsaw. Some are said to have gone to Spain. Some acted on various occasions in England. The increasing success of French drama is shown by the interest it had for foreigners. Traveling troupes became agents for the spread of French culture and an invaluable school for actors who were to enter Parisian companies.

It was inevitable that acting, like most French activities, should have its chief posts at Paris, as it undoubtedly did after the first quarter of the century. Besides a number of *jeux de paume* the capital could offer the hospitality of the Hôtel de Bourgogne, which had come down from the Middle Ages and was still the property of the Confrérie de la Passion, an organization that rented it to various troupes, most frequently to the Comédiens du roi, who took exclusive possession of it in 1629. More highly subsidized by the kings than other French troupes, this company attained the prestige subsequently accorded the Comédie Française and could usually attract actors and actresses from other troupes when it was in need of recruits. In 1680 this troupe was fused with that of the Guénégaud and its hall was turned over to the Italians.

Before 1660 its chief competitors were the actors of the Marais, who came to Paris in 1629 or 1630 and secured for themselves a fairly satisfactory theater by the end of 1634. This troupe became famous for the acting of Montdory, was especially hospitable to early tragedies that were classical in form, was patronized by Corneille, and developed the " machine " play. It lasted until the summer of 1673, when it was broken up and most of its members joined the Guénégaud.

Other troupes visited Paris or were formed there. They played in halls that belonged to the government, at the Hôtel d'Argent, the Hôtel Condé, and in several *jeux de paume*. Molière, the Béjarts, and others tried their fortunes for a few years under the name of the Illustre Théâtre. Subsequently the troupe of Mademoiselle, for which Dorimond wrote plays, appeared at Paris, as did the troupe of children known as the Daufins. None of these efforts was more than sporadic, but Molière, strengthened by his sojourn in the provinces, was granted in 1658 the privilege of sharing with the Italians the hall of the Petit Bourbon, a few years later that of the Palais Royal, which he kept till his death. After this disaster, his troupe, obliged to turn its theater over to Lully, secured the Guénégaud, originally built for opera. Here the troupe with a number of accessions from the Marais in 1673 and combined with the troupe of the Hôtel in 1680, played until 1689, when, forced to move, the actors built a new theater for themselves in the rue des Fossés-Saint-Germain-des-Prés, which remained as the Comédie Française far into the eighteenth century.

These Parisian troupes also acted before the court at Versailles, Fontainebleau, Saint-Germain-en-Laye, even at Chambord. Humbler actors produced farces on the Pont-Neuf and, late in the century, at fairs. These last became the ancestors of the eighteenth-century " théâtre de la foire."

The first French actors to attain celebrity were Valleran, at one time the leader of the Comédiens du roi; Laporte, the first, so far as is known, to write plays; and the latter's wife, Marie Venier, the first Parisian actress whose name is given. Greater fame was won by the three farce actors, Gros Guillaume, Gaultier-Garguille, and Turlupin, who long delighted Parisian audiences. With the growing popularity of pastoral and tragi-comedy there developed much admiration for Bellerose and his equally famous wife. But the greatest of these early actors was Montdory, hailed by Tallemant as the most famous actor since the time of Roscius, a man who studied his rôles with great care and who interpreted those of Massinisse, Herod, and Rodrigue so brilliantly that he seems to have made a large contribution to the establishment of classical tragedy.[1]

In the next generation of actors the most distinguished were Jodelet, whose name appears in the titles of several plays and who passed along the tradition of comic acting from Gros Guillaume to Molière and Poisson; and Floridor, a nobleman who played at the Marais, then at the Hôtel de Bourgogne, where he succeeded Bellerose as leader, who escaped even Molière's criticism, who lived long enough to create the rôles of Nero and Titus in *Britannicus* and *Bérénice.*[2] He was probably the most excellent actor of tragedies between Montdory and Michel Baron.

The leading actor who began to play in the forties was Molière, who lacked the physique required by tragedy, but excelled as did no one else in comedy. He received valuable support from the Béjarts, La Grange, author of his most useful *Registre,* la de Brie, who created the rôle of Agnès, and la Du Parc, who had the unique distinction of being trained by Molière, admired by Corneille, and loved by Racine, for whom she first

---

[1] For these actors and their colleagues cf. above, Part I, pp. 726-52.
[2] For Floridor, Jodelet, and their comrades cf. above, Part II, pp. 21-8, 606-7.

interpreted the rôle of Andromache.[3] Towards the end of his career Molière took into his company Michel Baron, who had belonged as a child to the Daufin troupe and who subsequently became the leading actor of tragedies in France and the author of several comedies. La Beauval, almost as distinguished in comedy, joined the troupe at the same time.

Besides Floridor, the most eminent actors at the Hôtel were, in Molière's day, Raymond Poisson, his chief rival as a comic actor and an author of comedies; the elder Montfleury, second only to Floridor as an actor of tragedy; and la Champmeslé, who created the rôles of Bérénice, Atalide, Monime, Iphigénie, and Phèdre, and is usually considered the leading tragic actress of the century. Her husband was distinguished as actor, author, and in the business affairs of the troupe. The Champmeslés and Poisson, as well as Baron and la Beauval, were most important in establishing the Comédie Française. The most prominent of their colleagues there were Jean-Baptiste Raisin, called "le petit Molière," and his wife, who, in the latter part of the century, began to replace la Champmeslé.[4]

I have referred to several actors as authors. In the first half of the century only three can be named; Laporte, whose works are lost, J.-B. l'Hermite and the elder Montfleury, who composed each only one play. In the fifties the situation was completely altered. Molière wrote the plays most frequently performed by his company. Dorimond supplied a traveling troupe with plays, as did subsequently Du Perche, Nanteuil, Rosidor, Passerat, and Legrand. Actors at the Hôtel who were dramatists included Villiers, Poisson, Hauteroche, Brécourt, La Tuillerie, and Champmeslé. Chevalier and Rosimond wrote for the Marais; Baron, Dancourt, Jacques Raisin, and some of those who had composed for the Hôtel, wrote for the Comédie Française. At times, indeed, more comedies were written by actors than by those who were not.

Nor was the art of acting neglected, a fact that is shown by Montdory's reference to his methods, Scudéry's remarks in his *Comédie des comédiens*, the glimpse that Molière gives of his troupe in *l'Impromptu de Versailles*, and the comments of Tallemant, Tralage, and others. That actors should pay so much attention to their art is the more remarkable if we consider the material difficulties with which both they and their spectators had to contend.

Traveling troupes played in halls placed at their disposal, or in temporary structures to which stages and boxes had to be added. *Jeux de paume* were at times made into theaters. Of a more permanent nature were the

---

[3] For these actors and actresses cf. above, Part III, pp. 20-31 and my *Adventures of a Literary Historian*, Baltimore, Johns Hopkins Press, 1942, pp. 79-96.
[4] For these and their colleagues cf. above, Part IV, pp. 14-29, and my *op. cit.*, pp. 97-114.

old Hôtel de Bourgogne, constructed in 1548 for an almost medieval audience; the Palais Royal, which had formed part of Richelieu's palace; the Guénégaud, built for opera; and the theater opened by the actors of the Comédie Française in 1689, the first to be elliptical in shape. Earlier halls had been rectangular, with rows of boxes along the sides and a stage higher at the back than in the front. There were originally at the Palais Royal only two tiers of boxes, to which a third was added in 1671. Both the Hôtel de Bourgogne, at least in the latter part of its history, and the Comédie Française had three tiers. The theater of 1689 had a ceiling, which protected the spectators from rain and snow, but prevented proper ventilation.

A box ordinarily held eight persons. The parterre was flat and usually had no seats, but stools or chairs might at times be introduced. It accommodated the part of audience that was usually the largest, the most unruly, and the most influential in determining the fate of the play. The amphitheater was a raised platform back of the parterre on which benches were placed. It was often left empty of paying spectators except at performances of "machine" plays. The stage was originally reserved for the exclusive use of actors, but lackeys and pages sometimes slipped up there and guards might be stationed there to keep them off. However, at an early performance of *le Cid* seats for distinguished persons were placed on the stage. By 1649 spectators were allowed there except when spectacular plays were produced. Subsequently even this exception was discarded after the early performances of such "machine" plays as *Psyché* and *Circé*. The final step was taken about 1679, when spectators were admitted to the stage at the first performance, as well as subsequently, of every play. Their numbers may have been decreased by the introduction of *balcons,* first mentioned in July, 1682. They were extensions of the tiers of boxes behind the curtain and above the part of the stage where spectators sat. At times there were few members of the audience on the stage; at others their numbers rose to 150 or 200 persons. In the theater opened in 1689 they were separated from the actors by a balustrade, but, even so, they limited the space in which the actors might move and often disturbed them by their noise. There was some compensation in the facts that the brilliant costumes of the young nobles added, at least for some spectators, to the charm of the stage, and that Molière, as well as some of his contemporaries and successors, made comic material out of the intruders' presence.[5]

Except at court performances, no curtain was used to cover the whole of the stage before 1640 or 1641, when one was introduced into Richelieu's new theater for *Mirame* and probably for d'Aubignac's *Pucelle d'Orléans.*

[5] Cf. above, Part II, p. 18; Part III, pp. 43-4; Part IV, pp. 45-7.

There is evidence that it did not come into general use before the last quarter of the century. Curtains, as well as pieces of movable scenery, were employed, however, throughout the century to cover parts of the setting.

In the first part of the century the system employed for setting the stage was that of the Middle Ages, in accordance with which various localities were displayed simultaneously. About 1633 there were usually five of these, one at the back of the stage, two on either side of it. The action might take place within one of these compartments or in the larger space in front of them. There is every reason to suppose that *le Cid* was given in this manner. Gradually, however, the confusion that resulted from the crowding of the stage with a variety of sets irked the spectators and helped introduce regulations for unifying the tableau. The side compartments shrunk or were removed. The back drop was often eliminated, but reappeared from time to time, especially in comedy, down to the end of the century. One was probably used in a late tragedy, Thomas Corneille's *Essex*, but the most common setting for a tragedy in the last half of the century was merely a "palais à volonté." [6]

This does not mean that Parisian audiences were deprived of varied spectacle, for, as the classical system became more thoroughly established, "machine" plays began to develop alongside of tragedies and tragicomedies. "Machines" had been employed early in the century, especially in pastorals. Partly under the influence of Mazarin, they were used more elaborately in 1648-50, when the most distinguished of them was Corneille's *Andromède*. Partially checked by civil war, the *genre* was revived, flourished especially in 1660-76, but disappeared after 1685, as a result of war and of competition with comedy and with spectacular opera. Its existence, as well as that of ballet and opera, indicates that Frenchmen were not indifferent in the seventeenth century to an appeal to the eye, but that they liked to separate their kinds of entertainment.

It is difficult to determine the number of spectators at a given performance, for we have no record for most theaters and, even when we have them, they do not refer to persons who did not pay admission. As Colombine remarked that five or six hundred persons made a good audience, we may suppose that such numbers filled the Hôtel de Bourgogne fairly well. According to Sauval, there were two halls at the Palais Royal, one holding six hundred persons, the other between three and four thousand. It is probable that Molière used the larger of these, but after changes were made that considerably reduced its capacity. It is reasonable to suppose that the Guénégaud could hold about 1500 persons, though the average

[6] Cf. above, Part I, pp. 717-24; Part II, pp. 17-8.

attendance was about 400; and the theater that opened in 1689, about 2000. At the former the paying spectators never reached 1200; at the latter the largest number recorded for the parterre is 773.[7]

In 1609 admission to the parterre was five sous; to the boxes, ten. Some twenty-five years later these charges were nearly doubled, while in the forties for "machine" plays they were twenty sous in the parterre, sixty in the boxes, or even more. In the second half of the century fifteen sous was the ordinary charge for admission to the parterre, an écu or half a louis for seats on the stage or in a box, but the charges could be raised at the performance of new or "machine" plays. When le Malade imaginaire was given, after the third gallery had been added, the "doubled" charges were: parterre, 30 sous; boxes of the third tier, 2 francs; boxes of the second tier, 3 francs; amphitheater, stage, and lower boxes, half a louis. The usual charges at the Guénégaud were: parterre, 15 sous; third tier, 1 franc; second tier, a franc and a half; amphitheater, 3 francs; stage and lower boxes, 5 francs and a half. When prices were "au double," the three lowest charges were doubled, while five francs and a half were charged in the rest of the house. There were, however, variations. By 1677 the regular charge for the three upper categories had become three francs instead of five and a half, except that the earlier charges were kept when the performance was "au double." Doubling was not employed for one-act plays and was usually limited to the early performances of new full-length plays, given in the winter season, which ran from Nov. 2 to Easter. Boxes sold as units varied from 12 francs to 44. The highest recorded charge for a single seat in any part of the Guénégaud or Comédie Française is 7 francs, 4 sous, in 1696. Certain other variations were caused by taxation or alteration in the value of money.[8]

The Italian actors seem to have charged about the same amounts, but they did not, as a rule, raise their charges for new plays. In the provinces charges were lower, but were raised for new and for "machine" plays. There, as at Paris, the tendency was for the charges to increase with the age of the century. This was partly due to the growing popularity of drama, partly to the depreciation of money. The chief exception is found in the reduction at Paris of upper charges from five francs and a half to three francs, a change that was probably caused by the losses that wealthier patrons incurred as a result of war.

Parisian troupes had other sources of revenue. After they were established at Paris, they occasionally visited the provinces in dull seasons. They played at the homes of the nobility and of wealthy bourgeois. They

---

[7] Cf. above, Part II, p. 20, Part IV, pp. 42-3.
[8] Cf. above, Part I, p. 713, Part III, pp. 39-41, Part IV, pp. 43-5, 983; and my Comédie Française, Baltimore, Johns Hopkins Press, 1941, pp. 15-7.

also acted at court. In the latter case their expenses were defrayed by the government, but, if they were receiving a pension, no other payment was made them. The Italian troupe, that of the Hôtel, and Molière's all entertained the king at Versailles. In the last years of the century the actors of the Comédie Française went to Fontainebleau regularly in September and October, leaving the less distinguished members of the troupe at Paris, where they received a small allowance to make up for the reduction in the size of audiences. In the winter and spring the troupe went to Versailles and to other royal residences. So customary were these visits that one of the decorators was especially charged with staging plays at court.

The troupe of the Hôtel probably received a subsidy soon after it was established at Paris, as the actors were called the king's "officiers." They were certainly receiving 12,000 francs a year by 1641, when the actors of the Marais were paid only half that amount.[9] This is one of the reasons why, despite Montdory and Corneille, the Marais actors remained in a secondary position and why those of the Hôtel were able to win over actors from rival troupes and to pay their leader a share and a half, a usage that did not prevail in other companies. Molière received in 1660-5 considerable sums for playing at court and was himself pensioned as a "bel esprit" at 1000 francs. While he was at Saint-Germain-en-Laye in 1665, the king gave him permission to call his company the Troupe du Roy and promised it an annual subsidy of 6000 francs, putting it on an equality with the Marais. The subsidy was raised to 7000 for the years 1670-1, 1671-2, and 1672-3, but then ceased altogether, probably because of Molière's death. His comrades received no further subsidy until, in 1680, they joined forces with the troupe of the Hôtel.

The subsidy of 12,000 francs was at first paid regularly to the actors of the Comédie Française, but in 1687 it had to be devoted to meeting the expenses of the new theater. The subsidy for 1692 was, probably owing to the war, still unpaid on July 3, 1693. The chance of receiving that of 1695 seemed dubious to the actors, who sold it to a notary for 7400 francs. However, when the war was over, payments were made for 1696 and for the years that followed.[10]

The Italian troupe received a larger sum than the French, 15,000 francs. The size of the sum may be due to the difficulty of persuading such wanderers to settle down in Paris, but it may also help explain their downfall, for in the spring of 1697 Louis's government could ill afford such a bounty.

Troupes made something out of their lemonade booth and the sale of librettos for "machine" plays. The French troupes did not, however,

<hr/>

[9] Cf. above, Part III, pp. 15, 18.   [10] Cf. my *Comédie Française*, p. 18.

receive royalties from published works, as these remained the property of their authors, while the Italians, who seem to have owned their plays, opposed their publication, though not always successfully.[11]

There were many expenses to be met. In 1629 the Hôtel de Bourgogne rented for 2400 francs. In 1658-9 Molière's troupe paid 1500 francs for the privilege of sharing the Petit Bourbon with the Italians. The latter were in turn obliged to pay 1200 francs for the partial use of the Guénégaud. When they took over the Hôtel de Bourgogne in 1680, they paid 2000 francs rent, but they received 800 francs from the Comédie Française to make up the difference. There was apparently no charge for the Petit Bourbon and the Palais Royal, but the actors had to pay for repairs and upkeep. The first renovation of the Palais Royal cost Molière's troupe 4000 francs, half of which sum was paid by the Italians; the second, in 1671, almost as much. It was at this time that a ceiling was substituted for " une grande toile bleue suspendue avec des cordages." [12] The Guénégaud was purchased for 30,000 francs, while the total cost of the theater built in 1689 was about 200,000 francs.

For this last expense it was necessary not only to use the royal subsidy, but to tax the actors for several years. Other taxes had to be paid, contributions were made to charity, and there were many employes: a concierge, decorators, ticket-takers, *ouvreuses*, guards, musicians, *afficheurs*, copyists, prompters, etc.[13]

One important item of expense was the purchase of plays. It is possible that a dramatist like Hardy was paid a salary instead of being remunerated for each production. An actress is said to have complained that Corneille put up the price of plays. The right to act them was probably purchased at that time by a sum agreed on by author and actors. It must have varied with the author's reputation and the special needs of the troupe. Another method was to pay authors a part of the receipts when their plays were first produced. It may have started with authors who were actors, for the first reliable evidence that we have concerns the actors, Dorimond and Molière, each of whom received an extra share as an author.[14] In the summer of 1664 Racine received two shares in the receipts of *la Thébaïde*. According to Chappuzeau, writing in 1673, an author received two shares

[11] Cf. Part IV, pp. 602-3, 607-8.   [12] Cf. La Grange, *Registre*, p. 123.
[13] Cf. above, Part III, pp. 37, 39; Part IV, pp. 33-5; my *Comédie Française*, pp. 14-15. The copyist did the prompting, according to Chappuzeau, but this was not the case at the Comédie Française.
[14] Cf. above, Part III, p. 203, and La Grange, *Registre*, p. 43. The statement of the frères Parfaict (VII, 428-30) that Tristan l'Hermite started the custom of share payments by persuading the actors of the Hôtel to give Quinault one ninth of the receipts from performances of *les Rivales* is supported by no evidence and is obviously inspired by the usage that developed much later, when the troupe of the Comédie Française had over eighteen actors. To have given Quinault one ninth would have been less than double an actor's share at the Hôtel at the time.

in his play whether he was an actor or not. This was doubtless by that time the usual method of paying for five-act plays, but the lump sum of 2000 francs had been paid Corneille for *Attila* and for *Tite et Bérénice,* while 110 francs were paid for a one-act play, *les Usuriers,* as late as 1681.

In 1675, when there were 17 shares in the troupe of the Guénégaud, it was agreed that one seventh, instead of two nineteenths, should go to the author of *Circé.* It was only after the union of the troupes, when the number of shares was over 21, that it was agreed to pay the author of a full-length play one ninth of the profits. A similar system was applied in 1684 to the author of a one-act play, who received one eighteenth of the profits. These amounts were at times increased, but to no great extent.[15] Occasionally the author received nothing, as in the case of *le Bon Soldat,* which was merely an adaptation of an older play, or as in that of *le Retour imprévu,* presented by the actors before another play by Regnard had been withdrawn.

The troupes had to pay for scenery, properties, and exceptional costumes. They were obliged to hire actors, including children, for minor rôles, and musicians to sing or play between the acts. La Grange stated in 1671 that singers had previously been placed in " des loges grillées ou treillissées," but that he and his comrades succeeded in finding some who would sing on the stage, dressed as actors. Soon, however, Lully obtained a monopoly of professional singers, so that the actors were obliged to do without them, to risk a law-suit, as they sometimes did, or to do the singing themselves.

Another source of expense, especially to young actors, was the pension system. This was employed at the Hôtel de Bourgogne as early as 1660, when la Bellerose received a pension. Molière adopted the plan in 1670 for his brother-in-law, Louis Béjart. A full-share actor received at the Comédie Française a retiring allowance of a thousand francs a year, paid him by the actor or actors who succeeded to his share, not by the troupe as a whole. In addition to this Poisson sold his share for 4000 francs, so that, after Easter, 1685, this sum, as well as the pension, had to be paid out of the earnings of new members. The example set by Poisson became the rule whenever an actor retired for some other reason than death.

Troupes were obliged at times to engage in litigation and were put to some expense by having to close their theaters, not only for two or three weeks at Easter, but for other religious festivals, for days of royal mourning, jubilees, etc.[16] Nevertheless, they prospered, as a rule, thanks not only to their histrionic talents, but to the excellence of their organization.

They formed stock companies in both senses of the word. They met to

---

[15] Cf. above, Part IV, pp. 36-8, and my *Comédie Française,* p. 15.
[16] Cf. my *Comédie Française,* pp. 19, 20.

manage their affairs, men and women voting alike. To assure attendance they established in 1683 a system of *jetons de présence*. They adopted financial measures, admitted new actors to membership, selected plays that were to be included in their repertories, and advised authors as to what alterations their productions required. They must have decided, too, how the rôles were to be distributed, except when they were giving the plays of living authors, who had the right to perform this function, and except when a court official intervened.

At first each regular member of a troupe seems to have received a full share, a custom employed by the Italians to the end of their stay in Paris. But Molière gave only half a share to Beauval in 1670, when he and his wife, who received a full share, joined his troupe. In 1672, when La Grange married, his wife was assigned only half a share. The following year Du Croisy's daughter, Angélique, entered the company with only a quarter of a share. It will be noted that, in all three cases, the actor or actress who received a fractional share was closely related to a full-share member of the troupe. A departure from this system was made when Mme Ozillon came over from the Marais and received only three-quarters of a share. This may have been allowed because the husband to whom she was then married was not an actor. It was especially after 1685, when the number of actors in the troupe was fixed at 23, that the fractional system was in vogue and that family relationships were no longer considered. Actors received at times an eighth or three-sixteenths of a share. They usually, however, did not have long to wait before they were more substantially remunerated.[17]

Early in the century plays were probably given by a troupe only twice a week, at two or three o'clock in the afternoon. As the century advanced, performances became more frequent and began at a late hour, sometimes at five. Poor lighting and slim police protection probably explain the preference for the afternoon over the evening. There were probably, as a rule, three public performances a week from about 1629 to 1680. The best days were Sunday, Tuesday, and Friday. The last of these was usually, but not always, the day on which a new play was first acted. After the creation of the Comédie Française, a troupe that had more than twenty

---

[17] For a complete statement about shares at the Comédie Française from August, 1680, to Easter 1700, cf. my *op. cit.*, pp. 9-13. In 1660-73 at the Palais Royal a full-share actor received from about 2200 to 5500 francs a year; at the Guénégaud from about 2200 to 4500; at the new theater in 1689-98, without the royal subsidy, from about 2800 to 5700; in 1698-1701, when the war was over, from about 4500 to 7000. In these last three years the royal subsidy added about 500 francs to the income of each full-share actor, while those who had already completed their payments for the construction of the new theater earned about 1000 francs more. The largest income for such persons rose in 1698-9 to as much as 8720 francs. Cf. La Grange, *Registre*, and my *op. cit.*, p. 19.

members, performances were given every day of the week. When part of the troupe was on a trip, there might be two performances on the same day. The Italians, who, when they shared the Palais Royal or the Guénégaud, gave three or four performances a week, gave five after they took over the Hôtel de Bourgogne.

A single full-length play was often produced alone. This seems to have been the general usage of the Italian troupe. It was also that of the French when "machine" plays were given, or new tragedies, or new comedies in five acts, or new comedies in three acts if they were judged sufficiently long. If, however, the new play was in one act, a longer play preceded it. Again, when a full-length play ceased to be new, its performance was often followed by that of a one-act comedy. On Sept. 29, 1687, even two plays in one act accompanied one in five acts. A new five-act play was usually given at each performance in succession, or at every other performance, until there was evidence that the audiences were falling off, whereupon the charges would be reduced and, if satisfactory results were not obtained in this way, a one-act comedy would be added. In general, the actors tried to vary their offerings, alternating old and new, tragedies and comedies. They sometimes gave plays that would be especially appropriate to the day or the time of the year. They usually produced new five-act plays between November and Easter, when wealthy patrons were in town, there were fewer outdoor distractions, and the admission could be safely raised.[18]

The experience of Parisian troupes gives evidence in regard to the value of competition. The monopoly granted the Confrérie de la Passion probably delayed the development of French drama and the acquisition by Paris of a dominant position in the dramatic world. The competition between two troupes corresponded to the rise of the classical system and the period of Corneille's leading plays. The period when three troupes flourished at Paris is that of French drama's greatest triumph. In 1680-1700 only one theater gave tragedies, a *genre* that then shows deterioration, while comedy suffered less as it still had the competition of the Italians.

Spurred on by a desire to compete with their rivals, actors probably suggested to authors the choice of certain subjects for their plays. There is abundant evidence that they criticized the manuscript the authors read to them and suggested alterations. The Italian actors seem to have altered texts while they were performing. Many French authors of comedies were themselves actors. Others were given free admission to the theater and were in close personal relations with actors. Rôles must often have been composed with a view to their being interpreted by certain actors. Corneille,

[18] For accounts of disorder in the theater cf. above, Part I, pp. 712-3, Part II, p. 19, Part IV, pp. 47-9, and my *Comédie Française*, p. 15.

for instance, probably enlarged the rôle of Jason in *Médée* because of Montdory. He was accused of keeping the Infanta in *le Cid* in order to give a rôle to la Beauchasteau. The different emphasis placed on Antony and on Cleopatra by Mairet and Benserade seems to have been determined by the excellence as actors of Montdory and of la Bellerose. Molière must frequently have taken into account in writing his plays his own peculiar gifts and those of his comrades. Jacques Raisin surely wrote his farces with his brother in mind. Dancourt must have emphasized clever *suivantes* because he knew la Beauval would make them effective. Without la Du Parc, Racine would probably not have conceived Andromache as he did; without la Champmeslé, he could hardly have given such great importance to Bérénice and Monime; without the addition of la Beauval to the troupe of the Hôtel, it is improbable that he could have composed tragedies requiring three important rôles for women, as he did in writing *Iphigénie* and *Phèdre*.

To read a French play of the seventeenth century may give a man of the twentieth an aesthetic experience, but he will not understand how the work came into being unless he takes into consideration the collaboration of various sorts that then existed between the dramatists and their first interpreters.

CHAPTER III

LITERARY INFLUENCES

French drama was undoubtedly influenced to a considerable extent during the seventeenth century by various dramatic and non-dramatic authors,[1] but the extent and importance of such influences have frequently been misunderstood. Students of Spanish drama, of the ancient classics, and of medieval French plays have been especially misleading. One would suppose from reading their observations that French tragedy was a pale reflection of Euripides and Seneca, of Guillén de Castro and Calderon; that French comedy was a repetition of Plautus and Terence, of Lope, Tirso, *Patelin,* and *le Vilain Mire.* But the classical scholar knew little Spanish; the Spanish scholar ignored the classics; and all united in their ignorance of French seventeenth-century drama, supposed to be the chief object of their study. Nor were they careful to distinguish influence on form from influence on material, or to consider what the French did with their borrowings. I will sum up the literary influences, foreign and native, assigning to them whatever importance I have found them to have.

The great majority of plays whose principal sources were foreign were derived, to a greater or less extent, from Greek, Latin, Biblical and hagiographical, Spanish, and Italian writings. The importance of these sources varies in different periods. Before discussing them in detail, I will say a word about minor influences.

A little German and Polish material was dramatized, but it came through other languages. The characters who appealed chiefly to the French were Arminius, Gleichen, and the mythical Queen Vanda. English literature and history had more significance. Before 1610 Sidney's *Arcadia* had furnished Galaut with the plot of a tragedy that was subsequently imitated by La Calprenède. Another episode in the *Arcadia* was dramatized by Mareschal; Greene's *Pandosto,* by Hardy and La Serre; Barclay's *Argenis,* written in Latin, by Du Ryer. Incidents connected with the lives of Henry II, Edward III, Sir Thomas More, Henry VIII, Lady Jane Grey, Mary Queen of Scots, Elizabeth, and Essex were put on the French stage. Racine tells us that he used a translation of Ricaut in composing *Bajazet.* There is no substantial evidence that Shakespeare influenced French drama of the seventeenth century at all. If he did so, it was only sporadically. Of his contemporaries Ben Jonson was alluded to by Saint-Amant but in an uncomplimentary fashion. Plays by later English dramatists, Dryden

---

[1] I do not include among them philosophers, scientific writers, moralists, and critics, whose relations to the dramatists were discussed in Chapter I or will be in Chapter IV.

and the Earl of Orrery, are mentioned by Chappuzeau,[2] but there is no evidence that he imitated them. Saint-Evremond, who refers to plays by Otway, Buckingham, and Jonson,[3] seéms to have been the first French dramatist to imitate an English dramatist, but his *Sir Politick Would-be,* written in England under the influence of *Volpone,* was never played in France and was not published until early in the eighteenth century. The only French play well known in France that was based on an English play was *Manlius Capitolinus* (1698) by La Fosse, who derived half his plot from *Venice Preserved,* a play that has a French source. Less than a score of dramas showed the influence of English history or of books written in English, a very small showing in comparison with the number of English plays that were in debt to France. The barrier of language was no greater for the French than for the English and the irregularity of English plays could have been overlooked, as it was in the case of Spain, but the French were still in the habit of turning to the Mediterranean for their culture, much as we look to Europe rather than to Latin America, a fact that seems enough to explain this neglect of their northern neighbors.

Turkey, though a Mediterranean country, was much more remote than England both geographically and in manners and religion. Its history supplied the French with about a dozen tragedies, of which the most distinguished were Tristan's *Osman* and Racine's *Bajazet.* In these two tragedies and occasionally elsewhere some attempt was made to reproduce Turkish customs. Solyman II, Osman, and several Bajazets were the favorite Turkish princes. Knowledge of the Turks came through persons who had lived in the country, or from historians, or from romantic tales, such as those of Jacques Yver, Mlle de Scudéry, Prospero Bonarelli, and Segrais. Other Mohammedan peoples, earlier Asiatics, Teutonic tribes, etc. appear in various French dramas. As in the case of the Turks, the information about them reached the dramatists chiefly through Latin, Greek, Spanish, Italian, and French sources.

The Greek question is more difficult to answer. Æschylus exerted almost no influence. Aristophanes was imitated only in *les Plaideurs.* The *Antigone* of Sophocles inspired three plays; *Œdipus Rex,* two; *Ajax,* probably one that is lost. Euripides, on the other hand, wrote fourteen or fifteen tragedies that attracted the attention of French dramatists. Of these *Hippolytus* and *Iphigeneia at Aulis* were the most successfully

---

[2] Cf. his *Théâtre françois,* Monval ed., p. 50. He says that he saw two plays acted at London, *la Mort de Montezume, Roy de Mexique* and *Mustapha.* The first, identified by Monval, is Dryden's *Indian Emperour.* The second is Orrery's *Mustapha,* as stated by W. S. Clark, *The Dramatic Works of Roger Boyle,* Cambridge, Harvard University Press, 1937, I, 77.

[3] Cf. *Œuvres,* Planhol ed., I, 210, 215, 233.

imitated. Despite their talk of Aristotle, who would have recommended *Œdipus Rex*, French dramatists preferred the more emotional qualities of Euripides in the time of Rotrou and in that of Racine. The fame of the latter's tragedies has tended, however, to obscure the fact that Euripides supplied plots to relatively few French dramatists.

Of course, the study of Greek tragedies and their Latin imitations must have helped the rise of French classical drama. Greek attention to form, concentration upon a single theme, separation of *genres*, taste, interest in moral conflicts, tendency to generalize rather than to individualize characters must have appealed to many Frenchmen, but there are very decided differences, as the French were writing for men of a different age, made much more of love, gave a larger place to decorum, analyzed their characters more subtly, employed a more exacting technique, usually abolished the chorus, were less lyrical and often less religious. And if Greek plays had only a limited influence upon French tragedy, they had far less upon comedy, tragi-comedy, and pastoral.

So far as direct influence was concerned, that of Greek historians, especially of Plutarch, was greater than that of all other Greek writers combined. From 1610 to 1634, when the late Greek romance was popular, tellers of tales came next in importance to historians, but they subsequently supplied less material than the dramatists. Non-dramatic poets were of small importance. Only a few French authors turned to either the *Iliad* or the *Odyssey*, while only one play was derived from Apollonius Rhodius, only one from Musaeus.

If we leave aside the Vulgate and lives of the saints that were written in Latin, the influence of that language is somewhat similar to the influence of Greek, except for the popularity of Ovid, who, in 1610-34, supplied more plots than all other Latin authors put together, or even than Plutarch. Subsequently he was less influential than Livy and Tacitus, but remained, on the whole, more popular than Seneca. Vergil influenced only a few plays, written chiefly in the first half of the century. Other poets—Horace, Statius, Lucan, and Juvenal—were rarely imitated. Among historians, Livy held first rank, then Tacitus, but many others were utilized, including a number who wrote in Latin after the end of the Roman Empire. The historians were especially important in supplying material to the dramatists that first developed classical French tragedy. After 1634 they constituted by far the most important group of Latin writers, while the second place was held by the dramatists.

Seneca, who may, like the Greeks he imitated, have exerted a general influence on the development of French classical tragedy, was directly imitated chiefly in 1613-4, 1634-7, and 1675-7; Plautus, in 1634-8 and 1668.

Terence influenced only a few plays: La Fontaine's *Eunuque, Scapin, le Muet,* and, perhaps, *l'Ecole des maris* and *Champagne le coiffeur.* It is amusing to find that Terence, in whose steps, rather than Tabarin's, Boileau advised Molière to follow, had to be refined by Brueys and Palaprat before he could be offered to the French public.

Plays of Biblical and hagiographical source have been discussed in Chapter I, where the fact was mentioned that they were written for the Parisian stage chiefly in 1639-53 and again, near the end of the century. Several with Biblical plots are hardly religious at all. Only Racine did justice to Old Testament poetry. The self-sacrifice and moral purity preached by Christianity are echoed in many of the tragedies, sometimes at the expense of dramatic qualities. *Polyeucte* and *Athalie* are, of course, among the leading plays of the century, but, with the exception of five or six others, the rest of the group is inferior in quality to plays whose sources were not religious.

The influence of Italian literature was dominant in the pastoral throughout the career of that *genre.* The *Aminta,* the *Pastor fido,* the *Filli di Sciro,* and the *Pentimento amoroso* were all imitated, some of them translated. They constituted the most important element in the first French movement for the adoption of the unities. After 1634, however, Italian influence diminished with the decay of the pastoral, though in the next thirty years there were various imitations of Italian comedies, while the *commedia dell'arte* was one of the chief ancestors of the French plays written for the Théâtre Italien. Episodes from the *Orlando furioso* were the sources of seven or eight tragedies, the chief of which was Du Ryer's *Alcionée. Jerusalem Delivered* was less often imitated. Boccaccio, Bandello, Cinthio, Marino, and a few other writers were occasionally drawn upon. Italian influence was more important than Spanish in the first fourth of the period under consideration, thanks to the pastoral, and in the last fourth, thanks to the Théâtre Italien, but less so in the rest of it. It dominated, as I have said, the pastoral, supplied tragedy and tragi-comedy with a certain number of plots, was of considerable importance in the history of comedy, not so much in regard to plot, as in spectacle, horseplay, gesture, and music. Its influence upon opera affected a number of French dramatists in the last part of the century.

There is no reason to believe that Spanish drama exerted any influence upon French before 1629. The *Diana* of Montemayor supplied a few pastoral themes, of less consequence than those that came from Italy. There is a curious echo, but not more than that, of *Don Quixote* in *l'Heureux Désespéré* of 1613. Hardy drew the plots of five extant tragicomedies from the *Diana* and from *novelas* by Cervantes and Diego de

Agreda as well as the plot of a tragedy from a novel by Lope de Vega, and probably the plots of two lost plays from *Guzmán de Alfarache* and Diego de Agreda. In 1628 the first plot was derived from *Don Quixote,* that of Pichou's *Folies de Cardénio.* In 1629 appeared the first French adaptation of a Spanish play, Rotrou's *Bague de l'Oubly.*

Pichou's second play was based on a tale by Céspedes y Meneses. La Croix's *Inconstance punie* seems connected with the legend of Don Juan. The *Amadis* supplied the plot of an obscure play; a novel by Salas Barbadillo, that of another. Lope's *Peregrino,* already utilized by Hardy, gave Beys the subject of his *Hôpital des fous,* while three of his plays besides the *Sortija del Olvido* had, before 1635, been adapted to the French stage by Rotrou. Out of some 280 plays that have survived from 1610-34, seventeen owed their plots to Spanish authors, only four to a Spanish dramatist. Moreover, the leading plays of the period—*Pyrame, les Bergeries, Sylvie,* Corneille's early comedies, *Hercule mourant,* and *Sophonisbe*—show no Spanish influence. As, moreover, Hardy and Pichou died before 1634, the only prominent author left to propagate Spanish influence was Rotrou.

In 1635-51 the situation changed, as to both the number and the importance of the imitations. The *Amadis* and Mariana each furnished material for a French play. Cervantes's *novelas* inspired four; his *Don Quixote,* four others. French authors began to turn to other dramatists than Lope, borrowing from Tirso de Molina for *la Comédie des Tuilleries* and from Guillén de Castro for *le Cid.* Despite the great success of the latter play, it was really with d'Ouville, about 1638, that the great vogue of Spanish drama began. He, Scarron, and Thomas Corneille derived most of their comedies from that source, while Rotrou continued to adapt Spanish plays and was followed by Corneille in *le Menteur,* its *Suite,* to a certain extent in *Don Sanche,* and by Boisrobert, Desfontaines, and the elder Brosse. Nearly thirty plays were written under the influence of the *comedia,* but this influence was felt very little in tragedy and to no great extent in tragi-comedy. Even in comedy, where it was predominant, very considerable alterations were often made by French dramatists, who now borrowed from Calderon, Rojas, Alarcón, and many other dramatists besides Lope.

In 1652-72 the attitude of French dramatists was again altered. The only borrowing from Cervantes is found in one act of Quinault's *Comédie sans comédie.* Montfleury borrowed a plot from a tale by Castillo Solórzano; Chappuzeau, part of another. Brécourt tells us that the source of his *Jaloux invisible* was a Spanish work that has not been identified. There are only minor traces of Pérez de Hita and Gil Polo. On the other hand,

Spanish plays influenced about as many French comedies as in the earlier period, though the proportion influenced is much smaller, as the number of French comedies had greatly increased. Moreover, about three-fifths of the plays written under Spanish influence were composed by three older authors, Boisrobert, Scarron, and Thomas Corneille. Authors who began to write after 1651 turned chiefly to other sources. When Molière was accused of abandoning " la belle comédie," it was because his comic devices were not characteristic of the *comedia*. He showed, indeed, little Spanish influence except in *la Princesse d'Elide*, half of *l'Ecole des maris, Don Juan*, which goes back, through French and Italian plays, to the *Burlador,* what he derived for *l'Ecole des femmes* from María de Zayas by way of Scarron, and minor details in *Tartuffe* and *Psyché*. Calderon was in this period the most popular Spanish dramatist, while, after Boisrobert's *Folle Gageure*, Lope was abandoned.

As the century drew to a close, Spanish influence declined sharply. Apart from that exerted by dramatists, it was almost nil, for I find only slight suggestions derived from Pérez de Hita and little besides Dufresny's lost *Sancho Pança* from the non-dramatic work of Cervantes. Montfleury and Thomas Corneille derived two comedies from Tirso and Moreto; Hauteroche, two from Calderon and Hurtado de Mendoza; Poisson, part of one from an *entremés* by Cervantes. After 1684 no new French play acted at Paris had a source in the *comedia,* for the two adaptations of Rojas and Lope, made at the end of the century, were never acted.

Spanish influence was largely confined to French plays that appeared between 1629 and 1670. It was felt by few tragedies and tragi-comedies, but was at one time of great importance in comedy. Without Spain France would not have had *le Cid, le Menteur, Saint Genest, Venceslas, l'Ecole des maris, l'Ecole des femmes,* and *Don Juan*. But what Spain supplied to other French plays was largely limited to plot, to the use of magic, to comic situations, to such characters as comic valets and queer country squires. The emphasis put in many of the *comedias* upon complex themes and physical action may have diminished the popularity before Molière of a simpler type of play, may have held back the development of French classical comedy, which appeared later than classical tragedy. Spanish influence must be considered in any history of French seventeenth-century drama, but, if its importance is exaggerated, the reader will have little idea of its very decided limitations. It is such exaggeration, accompanied by a large number of conclusions that had nothing but similarity of titles to support them, that has rendered ridiculous the work of Puibusque and von Schack, and has made it necessary to revise in very large measure that of M. Martinenche.

There remains to be considered the influence upon French dramatists of earlier writers in their own language. Farce probably has a continuous history from the late Middle Ages and the sixteenth century to the end of the seventeenth. Collections of older farces were published in the latter century and we know that a farce was often acted immediately after a longer play. As, however, there have survived only a few titles and almost no texts of farces acted in the first half of the century, it is difficult to draw conclusions that will carry much weight. About all the evidence we have of direct influence lies in the survival of *le Vilain Mire* in *le Médecin malgré lui* and in the use by Poisson and some contemporaries of eight-syllable verse. But we may well suppose, with Lanson, that the existence of farce, descended from the Middle Ages, helped Molière and others break away from complications of plot and put their emphasis upon character and manners. Yet to see only farce in Molière is almost as great a mistake as to deny its influence upon him.

Other medieval forms were forgotten except among provincial amateurs, though the method of setting the stage in the first third of the century and the division of a few plays into *journées* were doubtless medieval survivals. Nor can much more be said about sixteenth-century comedies and tragedies. The evidence of borrowing from Larivey is either unconvincing or unimportant. Jodelle and Jacques de la Taille gave Hardy a few suggestions. Garnier inspired verses in several writers, but nothing of much importance. Hardy regarded him as a model, but followed him little. The abandonment of the chorus, the conception of drama as moral action rather than lamentation, and decided changes in the language made such imitation difficult. More important were the non-dramatic writers, Rabelais and Jacques Yver. The former exerted some influence upon the *Comédie sans comédie, le Mariage forcé,* and *les Plaideurs.* His five books were the principal inspiration of Montauban's *Panurge.* Yver gave plots to Mainfray and Desfontaines. To these may be added Belleforest, chief source of Montfleury's *Trasibule,* and Marguerite, one of whose tales descended to *les Carrosses d'Orléans.* The record is slight in comparison with that made by more modern material.

In 1610-34 French dramatists turned to their contemporaries rather than to their predecessors, not to historians and non-dramatic poets, but to novelists and fellow dramatists. Earlier pastoral plays furnished themes to Hardy, Mairet, and others for their pastorals. Borée imitated Hardy; Mairet and La Serre, Théophile's *Pyrame.* Corneille repeated material from one of his comedies to another. The debt to novelists is larger. Rosset, Nervèze, Gombauld, Audiguier, and Sorel supplied each the source of at least one play. Boisrobert dramatized a novel of his own. Far more important is the *Astrée*, episodes from which gave the principal intrigue of no less than seventeen plays, the subordinate intrigue of another, and may have given hints to still others. D'Urfé was in this period a more important source than Plutarch, Ovid, or any other author, despite the fact that none of his episodes was completed till the third part of the *Astrée* had appeared and most of them only in 1627. This fact is good evidence that the dramatists wished to give their spectators the kind of material they were reading. The emphasis placed on love in the *Astrée*, on heroic deeds, on adventure, the limpid, but prolix style, and the occasional affectations are reflected in its imitations. The plays it inspired attracted audiences that could learn to appreciate later productions that would pay more attention to the analysis of motive and to the form of its expression.

In 1635-51 the *Astrée* was the source of only two plays, but other novels took its place, furnishing material for twenty plays, chiefly tragi-comedies. The most popular of them were Desmaretz's *Ariane*, La Calprenède's *Cassandre*, and Mlle de Scudéry's *Grand Cyrus*. Authors of tragedy, however, usually avoided novels or derived from them only minor incidents. They preferred to follow Plutarch, Livy, or other ancient historians. They did not, however, forget their countrymen, who left their mark upon eighteen tragedies. Father Caussin was the most frequently utilized, but information was gathered also from Coeffeteau, Matthieu, Du Haillan, Baudier, and others.

In this period, however, as French plays gained in distinction, they became a more important source for other plays than either novelists or historians. Prose plays were put into verse. When actors induced dramatists to write plays on subjects that were being dramatized for another troupe, an author sometimes borrowed from his rival. The habit of writing sequels to popular plays like *le Cid, Mariane*, and *la Mort de César* came into vogue. Dramatists imitated one another for other reasons. The result was that, though only one non-dramatic poet supplied a dramatist with a plot, the most frequently utilized source of plays in this period was French literature of the century as written by dramatists, historians, and novelists. Though it surpassed Latin literature little as source material, it was distinctly ahead of Greek or Spanish writings and far exceeded Italian.

The situation was much the same in 1652-72, with a slight decrease in material from foreign sources. French literature is still more dominant in 1673-1700, when Italian source material is rarely used except in the Théâtre Italien, where themes of the *commedia dell'arte* probably persisted, and when Spanish, especially after 1684, becomes of little importance. Greek and Latin historians and dramatists continued in both periods to supply material for tragedy, but the fact that far more comedies were produced than tragedies prevented either from equalling French in this respect.

If, now, we examine the sources both native and foreign by *genres*, rather than by languages,[4] we find that, in 1610-34, when the majority of French plays were tragi-comedies and pastorals, the most popular sources were novels and tales; next, plays and the work of non-dramatic poets, of whom Ovid was the most largely utilized,—two groups of about equal importance; while, despite the popularity of Plutarch, historians lag far behind. With the recrudescence of tragedy and the disappearance of pastorals, the period 1635-51 shows historians in the lead, followed, in this order, by dramatists, authors of narrative literature, and non-dramatic poets. In the last half of the century this relationship is maintained, except that the dramatists take first place; the historians second.

The relative importance of these sources changes, if we consider their influence upon different French dramatic *genres*. Authors of pastorals turned primarily to Italian pastoral plays; next, to earlier French pastoral plays and French and Spanish pastoral novels. Authors of tragi-comedies at first drew mainly upon tales and novels, especially the *Astrée*, though poets and historians were not excluded. This state of affairs continued in 1635-51, but with an increase of subjects taken from historians or from plays. After the middle of the century, when the *genre* was declining in popularity and was approaching tragedy in form and temper, the principal source of tragi-comedies was other plays; the next, historical works; and finally, novels and tales.

Throughout the century the main source of tragedy was ancient history. In 1610-34 Greek historians, especially Plutarch, and Greek themes were more popular than Roman. Tragedies were also inspired by Ovid, Seneca, and Italian poets. In 1635-51, on the other hand, Roman history became for the French about as important as all other histories of ancient peoples combined. Of much less consequence were histories of the Teutonic tribes, Spanish, Italian, and French history, ancient plays, Ovid, Lope, and the *Astrée*. It was near the end of this period that Corneille wrote the first fully developed "machine" play. It had, like most of those that were to follow, a mythological subject. In 1652-72 Roman was still the most important history, but mythology inspired *Ariane, Bellérophon, la Thébaïde, Andromaque,* and eight "machine" plays, which in this respect as in some others were forerunners of opera. Of minor importance were novels, plays, and histories of the Teutonic tribes, of France, the Turks, and medieval Italy. In 1673-1700 Roman history, though still important,

---

[4] In this paragraph and the next I leave out of consideration the influence of Biblical and hagiographical literature.

was less so than that of ancient peoples who were not Romans. Ancient dramatists came next to historians. Of less influence, though not negligible, were ancient non-dramatic poets; English, Turkish, Moorish, and French history, French romance, and Ariosto.

It is surprising that so little use was made of French history, but it is a mistake to suppose that it was never dramatized. Early in the century the *intermèdes* of Chrétien des Croix's *Amantes* were drawn from this source. Subsequently d'Aubignac composed a prose *Pucelle d'Orléans*, of which a form in verse was made. Mareschal wrote a tragedy on Charles the Bold. Magnon proposed to write a play derived from French history, but apparently failed to carry out his intention. Boyer's *Clotilde* has to do with the Franks, who are referred to in Corneille's *Attila*. A few plays that may not have been performed were also concerned with French history. Finally, Ferrier wrote *Anne de Bretagne*, in which Louis XII appears and Charles VIII plays an important, though absent rôle. The fact that none of these plays met with great success may explain why so rich and convenient a field was infrequently utilized.

The history of comedy is different from that of the other *genres* in that frequently the authors had no definite literary source. This was the case with the very few comedies written before 1629. In 1629-37 about a third of them had sources, of which six are Latin, three are Spanish, one is Italian, and one Greek. It is in 1638-58 that the influence of Spain is dominant. Out of 88 comedies 33 have sources in Spanish plays, six or seven in Spanish novels or tales. Italian and Latin influences combined are only about half as extensive. Strangely enough, the period is one in which France and Spain were at war. When peace came and Molière returned to Paris, Spanish triumphs in comedy ended. Thereafter, while the plots of French comedies occasionally came from Latin, Italian, and Spanish plays, as well as from novels, tales, non-dramatic poems and even from writers like La Bruyère and Callières, the chief sources were other French plays and the life the authors knew at first hand. The latter supplied them with operas, tragedies, and fairy tales to be parodied, with law-suits to be dramatized, with *faits divers*, with manners, customs, and incidents of many kinds.

French seventeenth-century drama is not an offshoot of any other. The wandering troupes that first kept alive the theater needed new plays, as those of the Middle Ages and of the sixteenth century were, with the possible exception of farce, unsatisfactory. Their demand for plays was greater than were similar demands at the beginning of the centuries that have followed, when there were plenty of old plays to be acted. Nor were the dramatists hampered by fixed ideas. They turned to the French works and the translations of foreign productions that were most readily accessible. A few were scholarly enough to address themselves to Seneca, but most of them preferred such good tellers of stories as Plutarch, Ovid, and d'Urfé. It was not until the sixteen-thirties that they began to worry about their art and to make any considerable borrowings from Seneca, Plautus, and Spanish dramatists. The theoretical conclusions that they reached affected in turn their choice of material, but it never restricted it to any one field. History, drama, and romance from many other lands, as well as from France herself, went to make up much of the raw material out of which writers that showed varying degrees of talent and culture produced their plays. In the next chapter I will endeavor to show what ideals they followed in adapting this material for the entertainment of their audiences.

CHAPTER IV

THE DRAMATISTS' CONCEPTIONS OF THEIR ART

If we could question French dramatists of 1610-29 in regard to their art, we should, perhaps, get as great a variety of answers as from English or Spanish dramatists of the same period. The French authors doubtless believed that a play was a composition destined to be acted before an audience, with a plot that progressed, by means of conversation, monologues, and physical action, to a fairly definite ending and with qualities that would justify its classification as a tragedy, a tragi-comedy, a pastoral, a comedy, or a farce. If it was to be acted, it could not be very long. Racan's *Bergeries,* which runs to about 3000 lines, is exceptional. Most of the plays are not much over half that length. One could, however, produce, as in the Middle Ages, a play divided into *journées,* of which there are eight in Hardy's *Théagène et Cariclée,* two in *les Heureuses Infortunes.* The plays were usually subdivided into five acts, but at least eleven contain only four, while farces rarely had more than a single act. Scenes were also employed, but often were not all marked, and even Hardy could be guilty of having only one scene to an act.

While the idea of *genre* existed, limits were ill defined. Tragedy and tragi-comedy at times approached each other so closely that a play was given both classifications. There were *tragi-comédies pastorales* and *comédies pastorales* that combined the characteristics of the *genres* represented in such designations. There were so-called comedies that resembled pastorals or farces. Occasionally an author might prefer to use none of these terms and call his play a " poème héroïque " or a " poème sentencieux."

All tragedies of 1610-29 and most plays classified as belonging to other *genres* are written in verse, but prose is the principal medium of several farces, three pastorals, a comedy, a tragi-comedy, and of Baro's *Célinde.* Prose is also found in plays that are chiefly in verse; verse, in plays mainly written in prose. The alexandrine has become the prevailing meter, a position it had secured in drama before the end of the sixteenth century, but many pastorals are written in ten-syllable verse, while one or two plays have preserved the eight-syllable lines of medieval farces. There is, moreover, very considerable variety in verse, as is shown by the development of the lyric monologue, subsequently called *stances,* such dialogues in couplets as that found in *Sylvie,* d'Urfé's excursion into rimeless verse, and the retention in certain cases of the chorus.

It is difficult to discuss choruses, since, as Hardy declared that it was too much trouble to prepare them for publication, they may have appeared in plays without being preserved in printed form; and, on the other hand, they may still appear, without having been spoken or sung when the play was acted, a custom that was quite general, according to Boissin de Gallardon. They occur, placed at the ends of all acts except the last, in two tragedies by Hardy, in Prévost's tragédies, in plays of 1619-24 written in Belgium, so far as I have been able to examine them, in a few pastorals whose authors paid special attention to style—*les Bergeries*, d'Urfé's *Sylvanire, la Princesse, Palemon,*—and in one or two other productions. They indicate in tragedy a conservative tendency; in pastoral, probably an effort to follow the example of Tasso's *Aminta*. Elsewhere a single chorus is occasionally introduced and may lose its lyric character.

The authors seem to have selected almost any subject that came to hand. They bring in the gods, ghosts, and satyrs, but usually concern themselves with human beings. The leading characters in most plays are aristocrats, but there may be exceptions, notably in Hardy's tragedy, *Scédase*, where the persons with whom we sympathize belong to the middle class. Children appear in three or four plays; a priest in *Gillette*. There is little realism in the modern sense, but one can at least get a glimpse of manners and find occasional references to folklore. The inner struggle that was subsequently to be of great importance occurs in Hardy's *Didon* and *Mariamne* and is fairly frequent in 1628-9, but it is by no means regarded as an essential. There are a few spectacular plays, some scenes of horror. Tragedies end in death, but at times those in whom we are interested escape, while most tragi-comedies and pastorals end in happiness. No obvious effort is made to follow the Aristotelian doctrine in regard to the tragic subject. Only in a few plays are the authors concerned with the fate of empires.

Restrictions on time and place are accidental, for certain plays represent a period of many years (*Heureuses Infortunes*), or move their character from one continent to another (*Elmire*). Episodes are freely admitted. Passages are allowed that would have struck the next generation as coarse or trivial. Style may vary from that of Hardy, pretentious and obscure, to that of Racan, with Malherbe's clarity, harmony, correctness, and love of the obvious, or that of Théophile, a genuine if minor poet, who at times introduces *concetti* that were to thrive with the help of Marino. There was as yet little interest in psychological analysis, small concern with verisimilitude, form was often neglected, and departures from good taste were freely admitted.

The liberty enjoyed by the dramatists failed to bring distinction. Hardy was well known, not for the quality of his work, but because he composed an extraordinarily large number of plays. Théophile and Racan were regarded chiefly as non-dramatic poets, d'Urfé as a novelist. French dramatists were not known abroad.

Then came a new generation with higher ambitions. After composing two successful plays that reflected the work of his older contemporaries and showed considerable skill in versification, Jean Mairet felt that he might go farther. Advised to look to Italy for guidance, he perceived that Tasso's *Aminta* had won more fame than Hardy's hundreds of plays. He found there attention to form that contrasted sharply with the increase in tragi-comedy that was taking place in France and with the popularity of the play in two *journées*. He may have been aided in his effort to establish rules for drama by the example of Richelieu in politics, of Mme de Rambouillet in social usage, and of the authors who were to form the French Academy in the art of writing.[1]

There had been some reference to the unities in France earlier in the century. Chapelain had asked for the unity of time in 1623. By 1628 there were persons who had demanded strict regulation, but of whom we know only through the reports of those who disagreed with them. Mairet was the first to apply the rules, while telling us that he was doing so, as he did in *Silvanire* (1630) and its preface (1631). His example was quickly followed by two other authors of pastorals. By 1632 the great majority of successful pastorals respected the unities; by 1634 the greater number of the better comedies, including an imitation of Plautus. Only about a fourth of the tragi-comedies showed the effect of regulation. Corneille, Rotrou, and Du Ryer experimented, varying between regular and irregular plays. The three tragedies of 1634—two of them adaptations of Seneca, the third Mairet's *Sophonisbe*—won over this *genre* to regularity.

In these five years the unities meant that the time represented was not over twenty-four hours, that the places were those that might be found in a city or a small island, and that episodes that did not influence the main intrigue should be sparingly employed. The plays that did not keep the unity of place occasioned, when the stage was set, a somewhat confused tableau—a fact that may have helped the demand for regularity. While the rules were less exacting than they were subsequently to become, not only did many dramatists refuse to accept them, but there are other evidences of variations in taste. It is true that imitations of Seneca and Plautus helped Mairet's reform, but the *genres* in which they were imitated, tragedy

---

[1] He says that he adopted Italian rules for structure and the " bienseance des choses et des paroles." He adds that Italian rules were those of the ancients, but, from the emphasis he places on Tasso and Guarini and the fact that he first applied his rules in a modern dramatic *genre*, the pastoral, we may conclude that his guides were these Italians rather than their Greek and Roman predecessors.

and comedy, were still far less patronized by dramatists than tragi-comedy and pastoral. The chorus had disappeared from most plays, but it is still found in five pastorals. Prose is the principal medium in one of these and in two tragedies, though verse prevails elsewhere. About half the tragi-comedies admit *stances*; about half avoid them. They mingle tones and social classes, though tragedy seeks unity in these respects. While Corneille was eliminating from comedy tragi-comic, farcical, and pastoral elements, he was aided by Mairet and Rotrou, but others sought quite different effects, among them the authors of the *Comédie des proverbes* and of the two plays that show actors at work, each called *la Comédie des comédiens*.

Mairet's *Sophonisbe*, however, had greater influence than his *Silvanire*. It is more genuinely classical than the earlier play, for not only are the three unities observed, but its subject comes from ancient Roman history, preparation and suspense are effectively employed, love is emphasized, there are inner struggles, there is little spectacle, no chorus, a style of which Malherbe would have approved, and, except for a few comic passages, general unity of tone. In the two years that followed its first performance late in 1634, a tragedy was produced by every distinguished author. These tragedies followed in the main Mairet's usage. Roman history became the most popular field, the unities of time and action were preserved, the place represented seldom exceeded the limits of a city, and a psychological problem was often discussed. In some tragedies, as in *Sophonisbe*, there are a few comic passages. Others are less thoroughly classical, introducing a larger amount of spectacle, or allowing rape as a theme. Scudéry, as he tells us, wrote one tragedy in which the new rules are observed, one in which they are not. Corneille introduced *stances* into tragedy after employing them elsewhere. Subject matter is varied by the facts that Mairet himself employed a Turkish theme; Dalibray, a Gothic; Tristan, in the most striking tragedy of the group, a Jewish. On the other hand, Du Ryer went a step farther than Mairet by linking all the scenes in each act of his *Lucrèce*.

Other *genres* were less affected by the classical movement than tragedy. Over half the tragi-comedies violated the unity of time; two cities are represented in one play, two countries in another; three plays are close to comedy; and there is little effort in any of them at analysis of motive. Pastoral was practically extinct. Comedy showed its independence of unity in Corneille's *Illusion comique,* with its double frame, and in the *Comédie des Tuilleries,* which, composed at Richelieu's command by five authors, lacked the unity of the dramatist.

This was the situation when Corneille, early in January, 1637, produced *le Cid,* the first dramatic masterpiece of modern France. By making it a tragi-comedy with variety of tone and form, the excitement of battle and duels, the prospect of happiness at the end he won the applause of the people, while his observance of the unity of time, his representation of localities not far apart, his emphasis upon psychological struggles won over ultimately the learned. The play's tremendous success showed that it was quite possible to combine the new rules of art with popular appeal, but narrow critics and jealous rivals pointed out that Corneille had violated the unity of action, had crowded too much material into twenty-four hours, and especially that his heroine did not show proper respect for her father's memory, thus insisting upon three cardinal tenets of French classicism: unity, verisimilitude, *bienséance*. The large number of pamphlets that were published for and against le Cid, Richelieu's interest in the affair, and the participiation of the Academy emphasized the importance of dramatic criticism, encouraged the production of such treatises as those of La Mesnardière and d'Aubignac, and made Corneille reflect more deeply upon his art.

Such results were not obvious in 1637-9. In the wake of *le Cid* the number of tragi-comedies increased and far exceeded that of tragedies. Mairet and Scudéry, who had been among Corneille's chief opponents in the quarrel, sought to rival him by writing tragi-comedies. Though there is an increased tendency to observe rules for unity and propriety, to introduce historical characters, and to diminish comic elements, it is still possible for a tragi-comedy to represent places both within and outside of a country and to make great use of music and spectacle. Tragedy shows less unity than in 1635-6, while there is considerable spectacle in several tragedies, an attempt to reproduce Senecan horror in Monléon's *Thyeste*. It may be said, however, that Du Ryer gave in *Alcionée* a more perfect model of unity in form and tone than had previously been seen in France. Comedies of the period constitute a more important group than those of 1635-6 and one that is more nearly classical in technique. They include *les Visionnaires* with its marked emphasis on the characters rather than on the plot and with a discussion of the unities in its text. It pointed the way for the development of French classical comedy, but its influence remained slight, for not long after it appeared the Spanish vogue turned many French authors in a different direction. Neither this play, nor *Alcionée* can be shown to have owed their classical characteristics to *le Cid*, though both derived from it certain suggestions.

In the meanwhile Corneille continued to meditate. By producing *Horace,* early in 1640, he threw the weight of his influence in favor of the kind of tragedy that Mairet, Tristan, and Du Ryer had already attempted. When this play was followed by *Cinna* and *Polyeucte,* tragedy was definitely established as the leading *genre* in France and the classical type as the kind that was to be preferred. This influence is indicated by the facts that in 1643-8 more tragedies were written than tragi-comedies and that the latter *genre* came to be more and more like the former. Corneille was doubtless aided by his contemporaries of 1640-2, who composed twenty-two tragedies, most of which show similar characteristics to his except Baro's *Saint Eustache*, a quite irregular play, and seven tragedies that were written in prose.

A tragedy, according to Corneille's usage in 1640-8 and that of most of his contemporaries is a play concerned with the circumstances, largely psychological, that bring about a deed of historical or legendary importance. Corneille did not feel free to invent his subjects, though in *Héraclius* he came near doing so, for he feared that, without a legendary or historical guarantee, they might be regarded as unreal. He and his contemporaries sought subjects that would give them an opportunity to create persons torn by an inner conflict, or several persons whose wills are opposed to one another. They tried to preserve unity of tone, excluding physical violence, the comic, the trivial, and persons of the middle and lower classes. Their events usually take place within twenty-four hours and in a single room. Subordinate interests are allowed if they influence the main outcome. The exposition, telling who the characters are, their relations to one another, their purposes, and the means at their disposal, is completed in the first act. The action, which may begin there, too, becomes more intense as the play progresses, and brings about the main event, placed at the end except for a few lines devoted to "unfinished business." There must be careful preparation, so that, though an event may surprise, it will not seem inexplicable when it occurs. There must be suspense, fluctuation in fortune, danger of death. The tragedies are written in alexandrine couplets that may be varied by *stances* or responses of oracles in other measures. There are five acts, subdivided into scenes, the number of which is not fixed and which are usually linked throughout an act by the presence of one or more of the characters.

These principles were not always strictly respected, but they were in the main. An author was free to stress various emotions, to separate intense scenes by those designed to inform the spectators or to allow him repose. Corneille regarded love as essential, but did not consider it stern enough to be dominant. He excluded neither altogether good, nor altogether evil characters. He allowed the *merveilleux*, but made sparing use of it except in his religious tragedies. He usually preferred that his characters should make their decisions with full knowledge of what the results were likely to be. His leading contemporaries, Rotrou, Du Ryer, and Tristan, had many of the same ideals, but at times they gave a larger rôle to love and

4

were less successful in analyzing situations and in wringing out of them, as Corneille usually did, all the arguments that are to be found in them.

Tragi-comedies were also influenced by the classical movement, but they retained the happy ending. It is true that five were written in prose and that two were each composed of five plots unrelated except by a frame, but Du Ryer wrote several that in form and in the insistence upon psychological analysis rather than upon physical action were close to tragedy. While most of them have less unity of tone and structure than tragedy, they resemble more closely the latter *genre* than do tragi-comedies of earlier years.

Authors of comedy kept up an appearance of classical structure, but, for the study of characters and manners that one would expect to find, is often substituted a primary interest in a complicated intrigue. This fact seems due in large measure to imitation of Spanish and Italian comedies and a consequent turning away from Plautus and from the methods employed in comedies like *les Visionnaires*. *Le Menteur*, though derived from a Spanish play, is an exception, but *l'Intrigue des filous* and *les Songes des hommes esveillez*, in which studies of manners abound, support this view, as they are free from foreign influence. This inconsistency in comedy between emphasis upon intrigue and classical aims does not seem to have disturbed the critics of the time, perhaps because they were primarily interested in tragedy. D'Aubignac declared that the principles of dramatic art were so well known to dramatists that his *Pratique* was intended, not for them, but for the public.

The main point to notice is that the classical rules for tragedy were well established in France before the middle of the century and that they were applied to a certain extent in other *genres*. Then the Fronde overthrew the predominance of tragedy, gave tragi-comedy a prolongation of its life, and brought about the triumph of comedy. It was especially in this last *genre* that new developments were to take place. Farce had continued to lead a somewhat obscure existence at Paris, thanks especially to the exertions of Jodelet at the Marais. One composed by Boisrobert was published in 1655, owing probably to its having been played as part of an elaborate ballet. In the provinces farces had probably remained much more popular and had doubtless attracted the attention of Molière. Chappuzeau had published one in 1656 at Lyons in which were sketched the manners of *arrivistes* and of learned women. When Molière returned to Paris, he won his first great success with the *Précieuses*, which combines qualities of the farce with those of a comedy of manners. It is with this play that he abandons complications of plot and returns to the simple type of comedy that had been illustrated by *les Visionnaires* before the influence of Spain was seriously felt. Molière took suggestions from many sources, but it is especially *les Précieuses, Sganarelle,* and *l'Ecole des maris* that lead up to *l'Ecole des femmes,* which occupies in the history of French comedy the position that *Horace* had acquired in the history of French tragedy over twenty years before.

Comedy, as exemplified in *l'Ecole des femmes* and in a number of plays that followed it, is primarily concerned with drawing comic material from character, using manners as an accessory, presenting a delightful dialogue, and minimizing plot. The unities of time and place are usually respected, the notions of preparation and suspense are those of tragedy, but episodes that do not influence the main plot are admitted, unity may be obtained through character rather than through structure, comedies may be in one act, or in three acts, as well as in five, prose is often employed instead of verse, and the vocabulary is larger and less abstract than in tragedy. Kings and princes are excluded, but aristocrats may appear, although most of the characters belong to the middle or lower classes. Danger of death is removed and there is little sentimentality, but there may be variety in tone, for both dialogues of considerable elegance and those that descend to the vulgarity of farce are admitted. The test is not whether the main events have the support of history or legend, but whether they seem, from our knowledge of life, to be likely to have happened and to be significant.

Molière's leading characters are persons warped by egotism, avarice, hypocondria, or some such cause of maladjustment that makes them the source of comic material. They are at their best in his high comedies, but sometimes appear elsewhere, for he also wrote farces, *comédies-ballets,* or imaginative and spectacular productions like *Amphitryon* and *Psyché.* When critics, wedded to the intrigue type of comedy, attacked him, he created in reply a one-act play devoted to dramatic criticism. His opponents retorted with similar productions. The publication of one-act plays became popular. Many actors followed his example and composed comedies, a phenomenon that is in marked contrast with the usage of the first half of the century. Some of them, like Poisson and Chevalier, employed at times eight-syllable verse and came nearer than Molière to preserving the characteristics of early farces. Comedy, as conceived by Molière and his contemporaries, combines characteristics of such farces with suggestions for plot and situations from the more complex comedies they replaced, and for form and analysis of motive from classical tragedy. Out of varied sources plays were written that renewed comedy, as tragedy had been renewed by the preceding generation, with such success that comedy remained the leading *genre* through almost all the rest of the century.

Meanwhile Corneille had returned to dramatic composition, and, in a series of tragedies, helped to restore interest in that *genre*. His general principles remained the same as they had been before. He made them clear in 1660 by publishing three treatises on his art. He sought variety by the form of the verse he employed in *Agésilas* and by drawing the portrait of a barbarian in *Attila*, but, as in *Pompée*, he tended to scatter the interest over too many characters and, except in *Suréna*, his treatment of love had become frigid, so that these later tragedies did not rival his earlier ones or those that Racine was writing in and after 1667.

Thomas Corneille, Quinault, Boyer and others also wrote tragedies, some with complex plots, others quite simple in structure, but none of them altered the general classical concepts. Nor did Racine, though he imparted new life to tragedy by emphasizing love more than his predecessors and contemporaries, by giving it a genuinely tragic quality, by a more careful analysis of his characters, by his personal skill at making the latter live, and by his gift of poetic expression. His conception of drama was narrower than Corneille's. With the exception of *Bérénice*, his tragedies do not have simpler subjects than some written by his contemporaries. But, reaching maturity after classical principles had been established, he adapted himself to them more readily than older dramatists, he was unwilling to sacrifice the *vraisemblable* to the *vrai*, and the emphasis he placed on psychological analysis rather than upon heroic devotion to certain principles made him more acceptable than Corneille to a generation that had known the disappointments of the Fronde. Racine's tragedies are the best justification for the classical system. The rules do not account for his genius, but without them he would not have written as he did. Unfortunately his example gave less gifted persons the impression that, merely by keeping the rules, they could equal his achievements.

Since neither Racine's tragedies, nor comedies like *Tartuffe* and *le Misanthrope* satisfied the craving of Parisian spectators for spectacle, two other types of plays flourished in their time. In *les Fâcheux* Molière made ballets integral parts of the comedy, a custom that he and others continued in a number of plays, the most successful of which were *le Bourgeois Gentilhomme* and *le Malade imaginaire*. In *Amphitryon* and *Psyché* he contributed to the "machine" play, a type that had come into existence long before, but which was cultivated especially in the time of Molière and Racine.

Such plays have their roots early in the century, when Hardy composed his *Proserpine* and *Gigantomachie*; Monléon, his *Amphytrite*; Durval, his *Travaux d'Ulysse*; and when pastorals occasionally introduced divinities in "machines." The first of these plays, in altered form, was presented to the public by Claveret about 1638. Not long afterwards appeared Chapoton's *Orphée* and Sallebray's *Jugement de Paris*. A decade later the presence of Torelli and of mechanisms brought from Italy enabled Corneille to compose *Andromède*, the most elaborate play of the kind composed up to that time. Boyer's *Ulysse* and a play derived from Rotrou's *Sosies* were contemporary with it. As thus definitely established, the type was characterized by a mythological subject, elaborate and varied spectacle, including flights in the air, and the subordination to the spectacular of plot, characters, and other elements of tragedy.

The Fronde checked the immediate development of the type, but in the fifties it acquired more modest representatives in Montauban's *Félicie*, the last act of Quinault's *Comédie sans comédie,* Gilbert's *Endimion* and that of Françoise Pascal, and a revival of Sallebray's production. When the war was over, its ending and the marriage of Louis XIV were celebrated by Corneille's *Toison d'or*, as spectacular as *Andromède*. Chapoton's work was revived. Boyer composed *Jupiter et Sémélé*, one of the most striking " machine " plays of the century. Molière was hampered by the limitations of his theater in producing *Amphitryon*, but, once his stage was enlarged, he was able to bring out *Psyché*. The vogue continued after Molière's death with several " machine " plays by de Visé and with Thomas Corneille's *Circé*. A less expensive type, without the mythological subject, was exemplified by *l'Inconnu, la Devineresse, le Triomphe des dames*, and *la Pierre philosophale*. There were also revivals of several earlier " machine " plays. After 1685, however, the cost of these productions, the growth of opera, whose spectacular qualities they had probably helped to inspire, and the popularity of the comedy of manners made it inadvisable to continue them. Their history shows how incomplete is one's idea of seventeenth-century tastes if one studies only the leading tragedies and comedies of the period and how classical regulations could be laid aside to follow the still more important " art de plaire."

The existence of *comédies-ballets* and of " machine " plays may have combined with that of tragedy and comedy to put an end to the popularity previously enjoyed by tragi-comedies. In 1659-66 a number of them were written that showed classical tendencies, but, after the latter date, the term is applied only to Rosimond's *Nouveau Festin de Pierre* and to two provincial productions. It is true that five others were composed in 1670-2, but it was found advisable to disguise them under the term, *comédie héroïque*. There was, indeed, little need for tragi-comedies after they had been deprived by the classical system of their chief characteristics and after they had come closely to resemble tragedies.

Attempts were made in 1652-5, in 1660-72, and occasionally at later periods to revive pastorals. Some of them were written for courtly festivities. Some were written by amateurs who were out of touch with the drama of Paris. None of them ever attained more than brief success. The *genre* is, indeed, after 1634, largely negligible.

In the seventies Molière died, Corneille wrote his last play, and Racine withdrew from dramatic composition in order to be one of the royal historiographers. It was now more difficult for young authors to show originality, as they had to contend with the prestige acquired by the work of the three major dramatists. The critics had, indeed, supplied them with recipes for concocting plays, but they had also furnished the spectators with reasons for attacking them. In tragedy Campistron sought novelty by the use of the disguised subject and by reviving the theme of incest, a few authors dramatized modern, even national subjects, and Racine, returning briefly to the drama, composed two biblical tragedies in which he treated larger themes than he had formerly done, introduced choruses, and made greater use of spectacle and lyricism. None of these efforts was followed, however, to any great extent. While a number of interesting tragedies were produced by these and by more conventional methods, most tragedies of the last two decades of the century merely continue the work of earlier authors.

Comedy, on the other hand, was not only more flourishing than tragedy, but developed various new tendencies. By stressing manners, it was able to offer much material that has little or no resemblance to the work of Molière. While the comedy of character was revived, the prevailing form was that of the one-act play, especially associated with Dancourt. More comedies were written in prose than in verse. While the unity of time had become a law and the unity of place was rarely violated, the unity of action and the rules for linking scenes were often disregarded. Music and dancing were more frequently introduced than formerly. The plays often lacked the significance of Molière's, but several dramatists acquired mastery in composing comic dialogue. At the same time the Théâtre Italien supplied many scenes written in French that respected none of the classical rules, differed in tempo from the work of the Comédie Française, and showed that Paris could appreciate comic devices that had almost no relation to Molière. With such farces, as well as with the development of the *comédie-vaudeville*, went the danger that the art of amusing an audience had been so generally acquired that clever improvisation was threatening the existence of the long art on which Horace had insisted.

The art of the dramatist differed in various periods of the century. At first there was a time of freedom that brought little distinction. Then regulation was introduced, was experimented with, and was accepted in tragedy because it seemed to produce better results than composition without the revision occasioned by the rules. Authors were made to reflect upon their art. Their achievement justifies their acceptance of rule, though what was good for them was not necessarily desirable at other periods and in other lands. The principles of classical tragedy were well established in the thirties and forties. Those of classical comedy, delayed by the influence of Spanish and Italian comedy, triumphed in 1659-72 with Molière. French classical drama, most thoroughly exemplified in tragedy by Racine and Corneille, in comedy by Molière, became the model for many Frenchmen and for many Europeans outside of France. If anyone thinks, however, that these three writers represent the whole of French production, he should study the history of tragi-comedy, of "machine" plays, of the Théâtre Italien, of the comedy of manners as it was written by Dancourt and his contemporaries. The variety of French dramatic art in the seventeenth century is remarkable. The universal acceptance of fixed standards by the authors is a fiction created in the eighteenth century and still cherished by those who prefer to judge by samples of their own selection rather than by an extensive examination of extant plays.

CHAPTER V

DRAMATISTS WHO BEGAN TO WRITE BEFORE CORNEILLE

The first French seventeenth-century dramatist of note is Alexandre Hardy, to whom I have already devoted a chapter (II, Part I). I showed there that Rigal's estimate of him has had to be revised. He was, it is true, the most prolific dramatist of the century, but the quality of his work does not give him similar distinction. The plays that have survived are tragedies, pastorals, and tragi-comedies or "poèmes dramatiques." He looked upon himself as a disciple of Garnier and Ronsard, but he had to meet the demands of the actors for whom he wrote. His tragedies show, like Garnier's, opening monologues recited by ghosts, long tirades, occasional choruses and stichomythias, and are primarily concerned with the pathetic fate of distinguished individuals, but it is hard to discover in them the application of any consistent aesthetic theory. He may dramatize larger issues than the fate of individuals, give his main characters struggles in their souls, introduce an Aristotelian hero, or compose a *tragédie bourgeoise*. One feels that such characteristics are due to the sources he happened to select rather than to his seeking material that would illustrate his theories. His tragedies represent a compromise between the kind that Garnier had inherited from Seneca and the irregular variety that is closely related to tragi-comedy. The relative importance given to men may be due in part to the scarcity of actresses.

His five pastorals were written under Italian influence, with highly conventionalized characters and themes, with the intervention of gods and satyrs, and in verses of ten syllables. He deserves credit for humanizing certain characters, for his use of preparation, and for his reduction in length of discussions and tirades, but his work seems to have added little to the importance of the *genre*. Later authors of pastorals preferred alexandrines and a number of them have left us choruses, as he failed to do.

Much more important is his contribution to tragi-comedy, which without him might not have acquired its special characteristics, for few of those, other than his, written in 1595-1625 possess them. He threw his influence into making the typical tragi-comedy a play with a romantic plot derived from a work of fiction, showing preparation, suspense, and progress towards a definite dénouement, while admitting episodes that do not affect the main outcome, stressing incident rather than character, allowing representatives of various classes to appear, not excluding the comic, and ending in happiness. It was probably his example that induced the next generation to make so much of tragi-comedy, which became the popular *genre* while classical tragedy was developing.

Hardy's work shows serious structural defects, an antiquated vocabulary, a ponderous and unattractive style. He is tasteless and obscure. Auvray's reference to the "suitte confuse de ses paroles mal arrangées" is not too severe. Most of his plays had probably ceased to be acted a few years after his death, while those that had a longer appeal had to be rewritten. He was a typical hack-writer, pressed for time, unwilling to adapt his verses to the requirements of a changing vocabulary, living long enough to see his work largely replaced and bitterly to resent it. He has, however, historical importance owing to the mass of his work, to the fact that certain of his characteristics were subsequently to be developed, and to the example he set of one who believed that dramatic composition might fill a man's life instead of being merely an occasional avocation.

Among his contemporaries of 1610-19 the two who seem most worthy of mention are the Normans, Mainfray and Troterel. The former drew inspiration from Ronsard and showed the general characteristics exhibited by Hardy, except that he wrote only a few plays and had a less turgid style. Five of his productions are derived from the Bible, Seneca, Petronius, other ancient writers, and a French sixteenth-century novelist, while the sixth is an allegorical pastoral written in praise of Louis XIII. He handled his material with great freedom and improved his style as he proceeded. In *l'Ephésienne*, which is probably his, he showed very considerable humor and psychological discernment. His independence is indicated by the freedom with which he altered Seneca, by his covering some twenty years in his *Cyrus triomphant*, and by the fact that two of his plays have each only four acts. *La Chasse royalle* is a curious mixture of allegorical, mythological, and realistic elements. His work had elements of promise, but he did not concentrate sufficiently on any one of his interests to make him long remembered.

Troterel was more productive, composing ten plays of various *genres*. He is chiefly known for his *Sainte Agnès*, which has characteristics of later religious tragedies: the Christian saint, the milder Christian, the pagan who appreciates Christianity, and the pagan who persecutes. Pastoral and comic elements are introduced and there is a curious picture of the modern underworld, despite the religious atmosphere of the play. *L'Amour triomphant*, written in prose, refers to a number of customs of the day. *Les Corrivaux*, one of the few comedies of the period, resembles a Renaissance comedy, while *Gillette*, both in its eight-syllable verse and in its style, recalls the Old French farce. The last pastorals, *Aristène* and *Philistée,* are noteworthy for a trial scene in the former and the portrayal of peasant life in the latter. Troterel's gifts were essentially those of an author of comedies, but the tastes of his day turned him to pastorals and to religious plays, so that the best part of his work is submerged in material that he was ill equipped to dramatize effectively.

It is in 1620-21 that we first find genuine poets interesting themselves in composing plays that have survived. Racan's *Bergeries*, while awkwardly constructed and filled with conventional elements, is remarkable for its unity of tone, the correctness of its prosody and style, and its appealing treatment of young love and of rural life. It is in this pastoral that Malherbe's reforms begin to influence dramatists. Racan showed feeling for nature as it appeared in the neighborhood of early seventeenth-century Paris, he employed various concrete terms, and he wrote with considerable charm. He did not, however, repeat his experiment and his one play was not well enough adapted to the requirements of a popular stage for it to exert any considerable influence upon those that followed.

Théophile's *Pyrame* was better known among dramatists. It remained for some time in the Parisian repertory. Though carelessly constructed and notorious for its *concetti*, it still appeals by the haunting quality of the verse, the emphasis on love and death, the portrayal of lovers struggling against Fate. Though it was soon criticized for its affectations, it remained popular until Boileau and his disciples, oblivious of its fine qualities, condemned it in the name of reason.

Like Racan and Théophile, d'Urfé, whose *Astrée* was to become a mine of dramatic material, left but a single play, remarkable chiefly for the author's attempt to introduce rimeless verses. Bazire d'Amblainville is noteworthy for the stylistic alterations made in successive versions of a pastoral under the influence of Bertaut and Malherbe. There was still need for an author who could perfect dramatic technique, employ the prosody of Malherbe, and compose enough plays to bring about dramatic reforms.

The man who was young enough to make the attempt was Jean Mairet of Besançon, who studied at Paris, was protected by the duc de Montmorency, and took part in the war against the Protestants. He began his career by imitating the leading French authors of the day. *Chryséide* is derived from the *Astrée*, owes much to *Pyrame*, and is the kind of tragicomedy that Hardy favored. There are lyrical passages, a *récit* of military adventures, comic dialogues, changes of fortune, psychological struggles, a spectacular final act, with the solution of the problem in the last few lines of the play. There is concentration of interest, though as yet no formal attempt to follow rules. The play introduced Mairet to Parisian audiences and encouraged him to write his still more popular *Sylvie*, a pastoral with elements of tragi-comedy. A dialogue contained in it was, according to Fontenelle, often recited " par nos pères et mères à la bavette." It attracted audiences to whom both pastorals and tragi-comedies appealed. After composing it, Mairet was prepared to become a reformer.

Desiring to rival the reputation of Tasso, he embodied the new rules of unity in his *Silvanire*, a reworking of d'Urfé's play. He reduced its length, employed alexandrines instead of blank verse, eliminated vulgarity and affectations, and, in imitation of Tasso, gave it choruses and greater unity than it had had. Less original than his earlier works, the play met with little success, but it prompted the publication of a preface that rallied dramatists to the new rules, somewhat as they were, two centuries later, to be urged by Victor Hugo, in *la Préface de Cromwell*, to abandon them.

Mairet, however, did not apply his rules in his next play, a gay, immoral, though not indecent comedy, *les Galanteries du duc d'Ossonne*, Neapolitan in setting, with references to manners and a lively dialogue. It was followed by *Virginie*, a tragi-comedy that has about the unity of *Silvanire* and seems to have attracted attention by its highly developed intrigue. Mairet then turned for the first time to the fourth *genre*, tragedy, and brought out, late in 1634, his most distinguished production, *Sophonisbe*.

I have referred in the last chapter to the classical qualities of this play, in which the mingling of war and love and the fact that the manners are those of the seventeenth century must have attracted partisans of tragi-comedy who would not have been interested in the new method employed. Winning both radicals and conservatives, Mairet accomplished much both in making tragedy again popular and in causing the partial acceptance of the classical system. He was now the leading French dramatist, but, to keep that title, he had to compose other tragedies, as he did in writing *Marc-Antoine* and *Solyman*. In the first he again put on the stage an African princess in conflict with Romans and supplied an important rôle for the actor, Montdory, who had distinguished himself in *Sophonisbe*. The play was well received, but did not increase the author's fame. *Solyman*, an adaptation of an Italian tragedy, was not acted till the winter of 1637-8, after Mairet had got himself involved in the quarrel over *le Cid*.

Resenting Corneille's claims to originality and fearing that *Sophonisbe* might be forgotten, he attributed most of *le Cid* to Guillén de Castro, overlooking the fact that his own *Solyman* owed quite as much to an Italian dramatist. Corneille replied with an insulting reference to Mairet's comedy. Further argument occasioned the latter's absurd production of his family tree. His part in the controversy was not to his credit and seems to have made him limit himself to tragi-comedies in the vain hope of rivaling *le Cid*. The four that he wrote are feeble productions, chiefly remarkable for the fact that two of them violate his own rules and that one of these, *Athénaïs*, contains a Christian element. Instead of seeking to develop this last novelty, he devoted himself, after the fourth of these tragi-comedies, to diplomacy, was forced by Mazarin to return to Besançon, and there lived out a long life, which ended in 1686, watching from a distance the evolution of French classical tragedy, which he had fathered, but to which, after Corneille's influence became dominant, he had made no contribution. He remains primarily the author of *Chryséide, Sylvie,* the preface to *Silvanire,* and *Sophonisbe,* works that were important when they first appeared. He was a reformer, but he was obliged to leave many elements of the reform to abler hands.

Mairet had begun his career in 1625. About three years later he was joined by several young men who helped him swell the Parisian repertory. Pichou composed four plays, of which one derived from the *Astrée* is lost. The other three came from Spain or Italy: the first French dramatization of an episode in *Don Quixote,* a tragi-comedy based on a tale by Céspedes y Meneses, and an adaptation of Bonarelli's pastoral, *Filli di Sciro.* Pichou wrote verse with considerable skill, employed *stances,* as only a few had done before him, emphasized psychological struggles, turned *récits* into action, and added spectacular effects. He might have had an important career if, in 1630 or early in 1631, he had not been assassinated. Auvray, who dramatized two episodes of the *Astrée,* indulged in many verbal conceipts. He had attacked Hardy and preferred a clearer style than his, but substituted more modern affectations for those of the old dramatist.

A third young author was d'Urfé's secretary, Baro, who, after completing the *Astrée,* derived dramatic material from it, first in his *Célinde,* a " poème heroïque " mainly in prose that has the distinction of being the first French dramatic work to contain an inner play, the first in which a dramatist writing for the popular stage drew material from the Bible, and one of the first to make considerable use of contemporary manners. His prose, which is often prolix, probably prevented his play from making a greater impression. He next composed a pastoral, derived from the *Astrée* and conforming to Mairet's rules, and two lost plays, one of which appears to have been a comedy of manners. About 1639 he wrote a most irregular *Saint Eustache,* the first of a group of plays composed for the Parisian stage and derived from lives of saints. After this he accepted the classical system, composing a tragedy and four tragi-comedies that he called " poèmes dramatiques " or left without indication of *genre.* Despite his membership in the French Academy, he remained an independent dramatist, as is shown especially in *Célinde, Saint Eustache,* the element of horror in *Rosemonde,* and his clinging to romantic subjects towards the end of his career, when most of his contemporaries were turning away from them.

Much more important than these three writers was Pierre Du Ryer, son of a minor poet and dramatist, who must have given him a sound classical education. He was, like Corneille, a lawyer and ultimately a translator, but, like him, preferred during most of his career the drama. His early work shows tendencies similar to those of his friend Auvray, with whom he attacked and was attacked by Hardy, but he also utilized his knowledge of ancient tongues, drawing his first three plays from Plutarch, a late Greek romance, and Barclay's Latin novel, *Argenis*. They are all tragi-comedies, of which the last is in two *journées*. He next dramatized a French novel, adapted an Italian pastoral, based a tragi-comedy, *Alcimédon*, on another late Greek romance, composed a comedy with pastoral elements, and derived a tragi-comedy from the *Astrée*. Like Mairet, he had by this time written plays in three *genres* and avoided tragedy, but he had laid greater stress on tragi-comedy with thrilling events, considerable use of spectacle, and occasional *concetti*. He had, however, preserved the unity of time in his pastoral and had achieved considerable concentration in *Alcimédon*, which has a small cast, observes the unities as understood at the time, and is the first play to keep " liaison de présence " for the scenes of each act. But he was merely experimenting, for he did not respect the unities in the last two of these five plays.

These were his comedy, *les Vendanges de Suresne*, and his *Cléomédon*. The comedy is written in an agreeable style, is located down the river from Paris, and has various references to manners. The farce-player, Gros Guillaume, has a rôle in it, as he had had in two earlier plays by Du Ryer. While the latter continued the tradition of tragi-comedy in *Cléomédon*, he had improved his art so decidedly that d'Aubignac cited it as an example of a play with a " belle intrigue." Not long after it appeared, Mairet brought out his *Sophonisbe* and Du Ryer, like many of his contemporaries, turned for the first time to tragedy.

Like Mairet he selected a subject from Roman history and constructed his play in accordance with the unities. *Lucrèce* is remarkable for preserving the proprieties despite the difficulty of the subject, for the psychological preparation displayed in it, and for the author's making of it, except for the rank of the villain, a *tragédie bourgeoise*. It is the first tragedy in which the scenes are linked throughout each act. It must have encouraged Du Ryer in his effort at compression, as he chose for his next tragedy, *Alcionée*, the smallest amount of material that any French author had selected or was to select before Racine's *Bérénice*. Limiting his cast to three characters and their attendants, he made of his play a purely psychological tragedy, in which a series of discussions and monologues leads to the hero's suicide. The play suffers, however, from this lack of material. Speeches are unduly lengthened and there is insufficient variety in the scenes. The heroine suppresses so completely evidence of her love that there is no resemblance to the interviews between Rodrigue and Chimène.

The effect is somewhat that of a *tour de force*, but the tragedy was quite successful, owing, perhaps, to the portrayal of the weak and scheming king and to the pity aroused by the hero. D'Aubignac reported that, though there had never been a tragedy " moins intriguée," few had had a " plus favorable succez."

In Du Ryer's third tragedy, *Saül*, he produced the first biblical play of the century written for the Parisian stage. The hero is one of the most striking creations of the classical theater in his hopeless struggle against the fate to which he knows he has been condemned. His patriotism and his paternal devotion develop his character admirably and in a manner that the unity of time rarely allowed. The surroundings of the witch and the interview with Samuel's ghost add a considerable element of spectacle. The play is also unusual in that sexual love is reduced to a minimum. Unfortunately the minor characters do not compare in interest with the protagonist, a fact that may explain why it did not have greater success.

It may have been the realization of this weakness in the tragedy that made Du Ryer produce a different type of play in *Esther*, which, though also derived from the Bible, is not religious in spirit, but a tragedy of court intrigue with a happy ending for the heroine. No character compares with Saul, but Esther, Vashti, Ahasuerus, and Haman have more dramatic qualities than the minor characters in the earlier tragedy. The play has, of course, been overshadowed by Racine's less dramatic, but much more poetic treatment of the same subject. One may, however, credit Du Ryer with treating, long before Racine did, a larger subject than that of an individual's fortunes, and with a plea for religious tolerance.

The same desire to supply a number of good rôles was shown in his next and most successful tragedy, *Scévole*, which has a patriotic hero and heroine, the magnanimous king who is their enemy, and his *protégé*, the embittered and skeptical " roi en exil." The startling vision of murder and hand-burning is, of course, kept behind the scenes, but the characters are brought together in a manner that lacks neither variety nor power. It was probably influenced by *Cinna* and is the most Cornelian of Du Ryer's plays, except for the fact that we sympathize with the Roman republic, as we are not supposed to do when we read Corneille. It remained in the repertory of the Comédie Française till 1747, longer than any other tragedy written in the first half of the seventeenth century except *Venceslas* and plays by Corneille.

A patriotic theme was again attempted by Du Ryer in *Thémistocle*, which deals with the conversion of an internationalist to the religion of the *patria,* a theme that is fresh enough today, but much of the work is devoted to petty and uninteresting court intrigue that deprived the play of the success that its original conception deserved. It had at least the mérit of influencing Campistron's *Alcibiade,* which was acted almost as late as *Scévole.*

One is struck, in reading these tragedies, by the variety of Du Ryer's sources, which include Greek and Roman history, the Bible, and Ariosto, and by the liberality of his point of view, which brought him to express sympathy for Saul, though condemned by Jehovah, to make a plea for religious tolerance, and to uphold the Roman republic, despite the fact that his tragedies were written in the midst of monarchical and clerical rule. He showed decided ability at drawing character, at handling moral problems, and at creating situations, but he often failed in attention to details and he lacked the style necessary to make his tragedies rank with those of Corneille.

His conversion to the classical point of view made him an innovator in regard to *liaison des scènes* and in an attempt to dramatize a very small amount of material. It also led him to create classical tragi-comedy. This he did in *Clarigène* (1637-8), where the romantic machinery of the tale is shoved into the background and the emphasis is placed on a series of moral struggles, presented in a play that is as well unified as are his tragedies. He renewed the attempt a few years later in *Bérénice*, written in laborious and antithetical prose, with too much information reserved for the last act, and in *Nitocris*, which, influenced by *Cinna*, closely approaches a tragedy with a happy ending. His *Dynamis* contains a larger amount of material and possesses less unity, but in *Anaxandre* he returned to the methods employed in the composition of *Clarigène* and *Nitocris*. If we compare *Anaxandre* with *Cléomédon*, which it resembles, we can see how different Du Ryer's attitude had become in the score of years that separate the two plays. He completed his last play at the end of the Fronde and may have been discouraged by the public's lack of interest at that time in serious plays. Instead of continuing as a dramatist, he devoted himself to translation and, as he died in 1658, could not, like Corneille, return to his earlier art. He did more to establish French classical tragedy than any other dramatist except Mairet and Corneille. Among authors of tragedy in the first half of the century the merit of his work was surpassed only by Corneille and, perhaps, by Rotrou.

The latter probably had a position similar to Hardy's as a provider for the troupe of the Hôtel de Bourgogne. He consequently turned out a large number of plays, many of which are lost, but he differed from Hardy in the care with which he wrote and in the fact that a great deal of his material is derived from plays written in Spanish, Italian, Latin, and Greek. In the first ten years of his career he produced forty-two plays, of which eighteen are lost. Many of them suffered from hasty composition. He employed much romantic machinery, presented his characters superficially, and often lacked structural skill, yet there are in these early productions many things of interest, such as the psychiatric device by which a character in *l'Hypo-condriaque* is convinced, by fear of death, that he is alive; the fanciful use of magic in *la Bague de l'Oubly* and *l'Innocente Infidélité*; the portrayal of jealousy in the latter production; of young love in *Filandre* and *Laure persécutée*; the references to poetry and the drama in *la Pèlerine amoureuse, Célimène,* and *l'Heureux Naufrage*; and poetic passages elsewhere.[1] He was the first to adapt Spanish plays to the French stage and one of the first to adapt Plautus and Seneca. While he owed much to his models, he often rendered them more dramatic and more in accordance with the taste of his audience. His *Hercule mourant,* which preceded *Sophonisbe,* is, except for its spectacular features, almost as thoroughly classical. His *Sosies* served as an intermediary between Plautus and Molière. His *Céliane, Célimène,* and *Deux Pucelles* were rewritten, after his death, by other dramatists. His *Antigone,* held to be one of the best tragedies of its decade, was not without influence on Racine. This last play, *Hercule mourant, la Bague de l'Oubly, l'Innocente Infidélité, les Deux Pucelles,* and *Laure persécutée* still possess much that is genuinely tragic, charming, or comic.

After 1637 he seems to have been allowed to compose more slowly, with the result that only eleven plays were produced in twelve years. Imitation of other dramatists continues. Though some of his productions are not superior to those he had written before 1638, others are undoubtedly his masterpieces. His *Iphigénie* was closely imitated by Le Clerc in an effort to compete with the *Iphigénie* of Racine. His *Bélissaire* passed on to the latter suggestions, first made in a play by Mira de Amescua, for a scene in *Britannicus.* The "Turkish" scenes of his *Sœur* served as a link between Della Porta and *le Bourgeois Gentilhomme.* He is at his best in *Saint Genest, Venceslas,* and *Cosroès.* The first of these, while lacking action, combines Christian inspiration with picturesque and dramatic references to the stage. The second presents the striking characters of old King Venceslas, torn between his sense of justice and paternal affection, and that of his son, one of the most violent characters to appear on the classical stage. The scene in which the latter learns that he has killed his brother is especially effective, more so than in the Spanish original. It remained in the repertory of the Comédie Française until 1857 and had by that time been acted there more frequently than any other tragedy written in the first half of the seventeenth century except six by Corneille. *Cosroès* is also an effective tragedy, forcefully written and with irony that recalls that of *Nicomède.*

Rotrou showed throughout his work considerable ability as a stylist, a

---

[1] Cf. above, the quotations on pp. 492, 558-9, 640, 643 of Part I, and on p. 215 of Part II.

respect in which he is superior to Du Ryer, though his extensive borrowings from other dramatists marked him as less original. Both authors avoided participation in the quarrel over *le Cid* and worked with Mairet and Corneille to establish the classical system. In one respect Rotrou antici- pated Racine more than they did, for he showed, while the latter was a boy, the tragic nature of love, which Ladislas called "cet amour, non amour, mais ennemi des hommes!"

Inferior to Rotrou and Du Ryer, yet warmly welcomed by them when he published his first play, is Mareschal, in whose nine dramas can be clearly traced the conversion of a romantic author to classical regularity. He began with a tragi-comedy in two *journées*, confused in plot, superficial in psychology, with much variety in setting, in tone, and in the social classes introduced. When he published this play, he underscored in the preface his oppositon to the three unities. His next work, *les Inconstances d'Hylas*, derived amusing material from the *Astrée* and gave it unity only through the personality of Hylas. This fact entitles it to be called the first French comedy of character. *La Sœur valeureuse* violates rules both of unity and of propriety. Though *le Railleur*, the first play that he wrote after *Sophonisbe* had appeared, respects the unities superficially, its value lies, not in its form or in its analysis of character, but in its sketches of comic types, including those of a poet, a financier, and a courtesan. He followed this with a modernized adaptation of Plautus, a play derived from Sidney's *Arcadia*, a spectacular tragi-comedy with an ancient theme, and a tragedy that puts Charles the Bold on the stage. Finally, in *Papyre* he produced a thoroughly classical tragedy, with a Roman subject, few characters, unity of structure, and a dominant moral struggle, but by 1646, when it appeared, these qualities were far from being new. He showed originality by centering action around character, by his use of incest, by certain types that he portrayed, and by his turning to English literature and to what he took to be French history for themes, but he was unable to develop his ideas effectively, so that he was obliged to resign himself to accepting the leadership of a school he had once strongly opposed.

A word should be said about Rayssiguier, three of whose six plays were derived from the *Astrée*. He was the first to dramatize the leading story of that novel and showed in his *Célidée* that a moral theme could be extracted from it. He made an adaptation of Tasso's *Aminta*, composed two tragi-comedies that emphasize localities near Paris, and paid some attention to manners. Limiting himself to tragi-comedy and *tragi-comédie pastorale*, he did not continue writing long enough to attempt tragedy and is to be classified with Auvray rather than with Du Ryer and Rotrou. There were other dramatists who wrote less than he. Among them

Schelandre may be remembered for rewriting as a tragi-comedy in two *journées* his tragedy of 1608. Frénicle, for his limipd style: La Croix, for producing a play connected with the legend of Don Juan and composing it in varied meters; Monléon for his operatic *Amphytrite* and his attempt to reproduce Senecan horror in his *Thyeste*.

In short, the principal French authors to whom Corneille may have looked for guidance were Hardy, Racan, Théophile, Mairet, Du Ryer, and Rotrou. Hardy had led the way by regarding a play as primarily a composition that was to be acted and by his fixing the special characteristics of tragi-comedy. Racan and Théophile had modernized dramatic style and the latter had shown how emotion could be expressed. Mairet had begun the movement towards classical regulation. He, Du Ryer, and Rotrou were developing classical ideas while Corneille was bringing out his early plays. These authors had, however, paid little attention to comedy, tragi-comedy held too important a place in the public mind, and there was still a good deal to be done in giving meaning to the new rules and in writing plays that would have a long life at home and considerable influence abroad. Let us see what Corneille was able to accomplish.

CHAPTER VI

PIERRE CORNEILLE

A Norman student of the classics and of law, who may have heard his Jesuit instructors discuss " cas de conscience," was inspired by a love-affair, according to a family tradition, to begin writing plays. His models, as he tells us, were the productions of Hardy and of a few younger authors, probably Mairet, Du Ryer, and Rotrou, if no more than these. He was not at first influenced by ancient or by Spanish dramatists, nor was he then aware of classical rules. He experimented, first with comedy, then with tragi-comedy, and finding the former more rewarding, wrote in succession four other comedies. This was, indeed, to be his general method. He would try two or more *genres*, then concentrate for a while upon one of them.

Although he began to write when pastorals and tragi-comedies were popular, he wrote none of the former and, after trying the latter once, preferred to devote himself to comedy, as few of his contemporaries were doing to any great extent. In *Mélite* he sought to reproduce the talk of " honnêtes gens " and avoided stock characters, indecency, and pastoral settings. He showed little originality in themes and characters and did not banish affectations, but he made an approach to comedy of manners and presented his work in a pleasing and graceful style, with a suggestion of the irony for which he was subsequently famed. It was obviously superior to *Clitandre*, a tragi-comedy of violence and horror, crudely constructed, though unified in time and place.

The four comedies that followed resemble *Mélite* and reproduce certain themes in that play or imitate one another with slight variations. Corneille improved his style in writing them, added to his study of manners, deepened his concept of character. The scenes of the merchants in the *Galerie*, the location of that play and the *Place royale* in definite places in Paris, the wistful character of the *suivante* in the comedy that bears her name, the willful Alidor of the *Place royale*, the introduction of literary criticism into the text of a play, the reference in one comedy to another are elements worth recalling. After toying with the unities in *Clitandre* Corneille rejected them in *la Veuve* and *la Galerie*, applied them strictly in *la Suivante*, but less so in *la Place royale*. He also experimented in style, in drawing character, in the study of love. He must have felt that he had done more than anyone else to restore comedy to favor and that he was ready to try other fields.

Rotrou and Mairet had brought tragedy to the attention of the public, the former by adapting Seneca. Corneille followed their example by now composing a tragedy, *Médée*; more especially Rotrou's, as he also made an adaptation of Seneca. Like him, too, he eliminated the chorus, made considerable use of spectacle, and altered his source freely. He greatly enlarged the rôle of Jason, probably because he knew that Montdory would play it. He gave his heroine great strength of will, preserved the unities about as Mairet had done in *Sophonisbe*, and introduced for the first time *stances* into a tragedy. The play gave him an opportunity to illustrate principles he was subsequently to enunciate, that tragedy should admit love, but not as its chief passion, and that, if a subject is taken from a well-known historical or legendary source, the author need not fear that its lack of verisimilitude will interfere with its acceptability.

His next play was a comedy very different both from his earlier work in that *genre* and from *Médée*. *L'Illusion comique* is a " play within a play within a play " and resembles a moving-picture. The novel form left little room for psychological analysis. The creation of a *miles gloriosus* violated a principle of which he had boasted. But the play is attractive in its curious form and the variety of its effects, as well as in certain passages, one of which is worthy of a picaresque novel, while another makes an eloquent defense of the theater. As his experimental mood was still upon him, he decided, after this tragedy and comedy, to make a new attempt to produce a tragi-comedy.

He had already turned to a foreign dramatist, Seneca, while Rotrou, who had pointed the way, had also imitated a Spanish dramatist. Corneille again followed his example, selecting a play by Guillén de Castro for imitation, and produced *le Cid*, first acted early in January, 1637. Availing himself of the hybrid *genre*'s popularity, he gave his audience a tale of love, of war, and of duels, a violent scene in which an old man is slapped, the vision of a sword shown to the heroine by her lover while wet with her father's blood, touches of comedy, variety in setting, and a happy ending. For the sake of those who were troubled about classical principles, he crowded the events into twenty-four hours, represented places in one city only, and put the battles and the duels behind the scenes. Of greater importance is the fact that he carved away much of the material offered by his source, emphasized the struggle in the hearts of Rodrigue and Chimène more than anything else, and arranged his material in such a way that *amour-devoir* and the law of the vendetta struggle against *amour-passion* first in the soul of the hero, then in that of the heroine. In presenting this conflict he was able to use all the resources he had acquired in scenes of preparation, suspense, and repose, a monologue of despair, *stances*, the narration of a battle, a debate before a king, scenes of analysis and argument between lovers who oppose each other and at the same time rouse each other to emulation.

Not only Rodrigue and Chimène, but noble and mortally offended Diègue, the overbearing Count, the somewhat superfluous Infanta, and Don Sanche are well characterized, but their parts are so skillfully arranged that minor interests do not cause us to forget our principal concern. The style furnishes examples both of *préciosité* and of precise and striking maxims. *Le Cid* was not so well written as some of Corneille's later productions, but it has a youthful ardor that he never recaptured and that has made many consider it his finest work.

This was not universally admitted at the start. Corneille was criticized for crowding his action, for failing to mention the Moors early in the play, for the ineffectiveness of the Infanta, and especially for the heroine's apparent willingness to marry her father's slayer, but these criticisms were soon forgotten in the great success of the tragi-comedy. Corneille's ninth play gave modern French drama its first masterpiece and showed what was to be the soul of classical French tragedy, a moral struggle, effectively presented.

The *Cid* quarrel neither seriously discouraged Corneille, nor converted him to the ideals of Chapelain, but it made him take thought and resolve to win the approbation of both " doctes et ignorants." Had he not gone through this experience, he might have continued to write tragi-comedies, for *le Cid* was more successful than *Médée* or *l'Illusion comique,* but he must have believed that tragedy, backed by the prestige of the Greeks and Romans, would be more likely to appeal to the learned than tragi-comedy, he was sure of the general public in any case, and his chief dramatic opponents in the quarrel, Mairet and Scudéry, whom it would be well to defeat with their own weapons, had won their chief laurels in tragedy. The result was that in three years he brought out four plays that made tragedy the most popular *genre* in France and definitely established its main principles for the classical period.

Unlike Rotrou's first tragedy, but like Mairet's *Sophonisbe* and Scudéry's *Mort de César,* all four of Corneille's plays were concerned with ancient Romans, but all four avoided the period of the Republic. *Horace* is essentially a war play, the tragedy of a hero who allows his patriotism to stifle his humanity, of a woman whose love overcomes her patriotism, of her lover who regretfully puts his patriotism above family ties, of the fate that war brings us whatever we may do. Here love plays an important, but secondary rôle, there are no startling violations of the ancient story, the characters analyze in detail their motives, and the whole is presented in stricter accord with the unities, especially that of place, than earlier French tragedies.

The *merveilleux,* of which Corneille had made much use in *Médée,* is reduced to the consultation of the oracle and its effect upon Camille. There is unity of tone, careful preparation, frequent clashing of wills, though no such internal conflicts as in *le Cid.* The criticism of the heroine in the latter play by the Academy affected Corneille so little that, though he had been reproved for not having her refuse to marry the man who had killed her father, he now allowed a brother to murder his sister.

Cinna is primarily concerned with government, a hymn to benevolent autocracy. The strong, wise, and somewhat weary emperor contrasts with the futile republican, Maxime, the hesitant conspirator, Cinna, and violent Emilie, whose conversion points to the wisdom of accepting imperial rule. The plot is simpler than that of *Horace* and quite as unified except that there is a single break in *liaison.* *Stances* and the *merveilleux* are excluded. The second act is a model of dramatic deliberation on affairs of state. The happy ending enlarged the choice of subject-matter for tragedy, while the play made admiration as worthy a goal for the tragic dramatist as pity or awe.

Though the supernatural element plays an essential rôle in *Polyeucte,* as deeply concerned with religion as had been *Horace* with war, or *Cinna* with government, the tragedy is full of human interest. Polyeucte, Sévère, Félix, and Pauline are drawn with a masterly hand. The spiritual progress of both Polyeucte and Pauline is carefully indicated. The ending, with the opportune conversion of the wily politician, may be defended as a final tribute to the power of Grace. The play is written in a simple unaffected style, with varied scenes, careful analysis of motives, perfect unity of structure and harmony of tone. It became the model religious play, the only one of its group to figure permanently in the Parisian repertory. Late in the century it was often given as the last performance before the Easter recess, as if to prepare spectators for this religious festival and to remind them that there is no essential conflict between drama and religion.

It is difficult for a modern reader to put *Pompée* on a level with these three tragedies, though there is evidence that Corneille's contemporaries did so. In Lucan's wake, he employed a more pompous style than he had done before and he introduced too many distinguished persons to do them all justice. The studies of Ptolemy's weakness, of Cornelia's magnanimity, and of Cleopatra's politics are interestingly presented, but do not compensate for the grandiloquence of the speeches or the faulty structure.

Corneille seems to have thought that he had, for the time being, contributed sufficiently to tragedy. He returned to comedy and, as in *le Cid,* imitated a Spanish play. *Le Menteur* has more comic force than his earlier comedies, is gayer and less moralistic than the model. The scene is transferred to Paris, the growth of the city is described, and the manners of those who would pass as military heroes are ridiculed. The protagonist is presented as an artist in lying who is left unpunished at the end of the play. The work may be called a comedy of character, though it is less profound than Molière's plays of that kind. It furnished pleasing comic relief after the four tragedies and met with such success that the author gave it a sequel, derived from Lope. This *Suite* is quite inferior to *le Menteur*, despite interesting allusions to the latter play, the dramatic criticism contained in it, and appealing verses on the nature of love, for the hero's character is not satisfactorily presented and the comic effects are weak in comparison with those of the older play. It was probably its lack of success that induced Corneille permanently to abandon comedy and to return to tragedy.

He was not satisfied, however, to repeat the methods that had brought him fame. Each of the new tragedies differed materially from those he had previously written, though, with the exception of *Andromède*, they show similar regularity of structure. In *Rodogune* he impressed his audience chiefly by the character of the principal person, ambitious and heartless Cleopatra, by the manner in which the action progresses, and by the exciting and spectacular conclusion, but the exposition is unsatisfactory, the twins are too much alike, and Rodogune wins little sympathy. The melodramatic quality of the play brought it much popularity, till it paled in contrast with tragedies of the Romantic period. In *Théodore* Corneille sought to outdo the heroism of *Polyeucte* and displayed great technical skill, but the statuesque characters of the heroine and her Christian friend were far from showing the human qualities of Pauline and Polyeucte, while the talk of prostitution was not well received. In *Héraclius* Corneille devised a plot that is scarcely historical except in the names of four Greek emperors. Its chief fault lies in the fact that the plot depends upon a complicated series of relationships. It is a mistake to suppose that the tragedy was derived from Calderon, or that its complications are Spanish, for, when Corneille has once indicated them in a skillfull exposition, the plot is easy to follow and consists largely of psychological situations that have nothing Spanish about them. That the play did not win more than moderate success is probably due to the effort of memory it requires and to the fact that a secondary character is essential in bringing about the dénouement. Finally, in *Andromède*, Corneille wrote a tragedy that was the first important "machine" play of the century, one in which spectacle is the primary consideration, rather than character, ideas, structure, or verses. The play showed his versatility, but did not add to his reputation. In short, these four plays are remarkable for their author's technical skill and three of them were well received, but they did not possess the permanently satisfying qualities of *le Cid* and the three tragedies that were the first to follow it.

While Corneille was waiting to see a performance of *Andromède*, delayed by the Fronde, he brought out a " comédie héroïque," which he might have called a tragi-comedy, *Don Sanche*, a romantic production with use of surprise and recognition, then returned to tragedy and produced what is probably his greatest play among those that followed *Polyeucte*. *Nicomède* is celebrated for the irony of the protagonist, the intense struggle between the Romans and the Asiatics they seek to oppress, the finely developing character of Attale, feeble and scheming Prusias, and his dominating queen, who more than meets her match in the hero. If the Germans were to allow the play to be given in Paris today, they would be shocked to see how strikingly it fits the present situation, when a distinguished Frenchman and his unscrupulous followers are, like Prusias and his queen, ready to compromise their country's future; when other Frenchmen are as eager to resist as was Nicomède; when there are Germans in Paris acting as did Flaminius in Asia Minor; and when the youth of France is waiting, like Attale, to be won over to active service in their country's cause. In moments of national disaster Frenchmen cannot afford to forget Corneille.

Though the Fronde continued, the dramatist made another attempt to supply the stage with a tragedy and produced *Pertharite* late in 1651. The first part of it resembles *Andromaque*, but is much less appealing, for Rodelinde, though meant to be a *personnage sympathique*, shocks us by calmly proposing that her son be put to death, her husband has an inglorious rôle, there is an unfortunate shift of interest in the middle of the play, and the ending is melodramatic. After its failure, Corneille ceased for seven years to write plays, probably because he realized that it was difficult for tragedies to be properly presented during or shortly after a civil war.

When the conflict with Spain was over, he composed ten more plays and part of an eleventh. That none of them had either the merit or the success of *le Cid* or *Polyeucte* is obvious, but it is a mistake to regard them as if they were made out of one piece. Boileau's remark that

Tout son mérite . . . se réduit à huit ou neuf pièces de théâtre qu'on admire, et qui sont, s'il faut ainsi parler, comme le midi de sa poesie, dont l'orient et l'occident n'ont rien valu,[1]

is true only in a general sense, for some of his later works are quite as good as some written when he was at the height of his powers, and there are important distinctions to be made among them.

They appeared when their author was between the ages of fifty-two and sixty-eight, while he felt convinced that his methods were still the proper ones, though his public had become considerably altered. He continued to experiment, as had been his custom, and he retained his technical skill, but

---

[1] *Réflexions sur Longin*, VII.

he could not regain his youth or the freshness of inspiration he had once displayed. *Œdipe, Sophonisbe,* and *Tite et Bérénice* suffered by comparison with tragedies on the same subject by Sophocles, Mairet, and Racine. Corneille's search for what is generally true prevented his availing himself of picturesque elements he could have found in the sources of *Sertorius, Agésilas, Attila,* and *Suréna.* He divided the interest of his audiences in *Œdipe, Sophonisbe,* and *Tite et Bérénice,* as he had done in *Pompée.* He continued to regard love as essential to tragedy, but as secondary to sterner emotions. This fact would not necessarily have marred his plays, but in all of them except *Psyché* and *Suréna* love is treated in unconvincing fashion. It serves political ambition in *Sertorius, Sophonisbe, Agésilas,* and *Tite et Bérénice.* In this last play Corneille introduces a passage about love that is cynical enough to have been penned by La Rochefoucauld. *Pulchérie* ends in a " mariage blanc." Even in *Suréna,* where the women are genuine lovers, there are lines that point out the futility of a desire for children. Such an attitude towards love was especially unfortunate while Racine was writing *Andromaque, Bérénice,* and *Bajazet.*

The ten plays are classical in structure, except that occasionally the unity of action is slightly violated, or a mildly comic situation or observation is allowed. In *Attila* there is a reference to blood, seen by persons on the stage, of which Racine would probably not have approved. Hampered at times in his efforts to preserve the unity of place, Corneille proposed that the stage should be supposed to represent a kind of room that could not have existed in a seventeenth-century palace, one in which any of the characters might discuss their intimate affairs, however improbable it might be that such affairs would be discussed there, and into which a superior might go to meet an inferior. He did not often avail himself of this privilege, but his proposing it shows a certain loss of contact with reality that may help to explain why his later plays were not more effective than they were.

However, *Œdipe* was successful at a time when Sophocles's tragedy would have been considered horrible and not sufficiently logical. *La Toison d'or,* which has the merits and shortcomings of a " machine " play, is as satisfactory as *Andromède. Sertorius,* despite its treatment of love, presents striking studies of the hero and Pompey, brought together in a remarkable third act. It had special interest in the period after the French civil war, as it has today in its portrayal of those who resist dictators and of those who trust merely that time will dispose of them. This play is worthy to rank with *Rodogune* and *Pompée,* as is *Attila,* with its study of a wily, ruthless, and ironical barbarian, who dominates the play till his anger brings on his fatal physical affliction. The fact that this shows itself by his bleeding from his nose diminishes for us the tragic effect that may have been attained when the play was first produced. *Othon*, too, has very considerable interest, with its portrayal of court intrigue round an aging monarch. There are many admirable verses in *Psyché*, but Corneille neither planned the play, nor wrote the whole of it.

On the other hand, *Sophonisbe* failed, not only because Corneille sought in it to avoid the elements that had brought Mairet success, but because neither the haughty heroine, nor her unnecessary rival wins our interest, and because Syphax, the only person with whom we sympathize, disappears from the play too soon. *Agésilas* was condemned for its characters and its plot as well as for the use of " vers libres " that do not fit their form to the sentiments they express, as do those of *Psyché* and *Amphitryon*. In *Tite et Bérénice*, which was by no means a failure, the emperor's weakness and the women's lack of charm made it incapable of competing long with Racine's *Bérénice*. *Pulchérie* is quite superior to it, with its striking portrait of the capable Byzantine princess who suppresses her love in the interests of state and its suggestion that Corneille, like his heroine, was not yet ready to yield the dramatic throne to a younger rival, though he realized that some day he would have to do so. These qualities, however, were probably not appreciated by an audience that preferred the portrayal of more exciting emotions. *Suréna*, his last play, has in its treatment of the two women's love the same warmth he had put into *Polyeucte*, but he did not sufficiently develop his suspicious and jealous king, or avail himself of all the possibilities that lay in his hero's character.

Corneille composed thirty-two plays, most of the verses in *Psyché*, and an act in each of the two plays by the " Five Authors." He brought out his first work in 1630, before the classical system had been developed in France; his last, after Molière had died and less than three years before Racine was to sacrifice dramatic composition to service of Louis XIV. His active life stretches across the century as did that of no other dramatist except greatly inferior Boyer. He was hailed as the greatest of his profession and his successors owed him much.

He had a broader conception of drama than either Racine or Molière. He composed *le Cid*, chief of French tragi-comedies. He established tragedy as the leading type of drama, lifted comedy to a position of importance, and contributed spectacular " machine " plays that were to be among the forerunners of opera. While his comedies are inferior to Molière's and his tragedies are not, on the whole, as appealing as the best of Racine's, he showed greater variety in his tragedies than the latter and contributed to the success of his rivals.

Corneille's view of life is a stimulating one. His creation of strong-willed characters has often been stressed, but he could also portray the weak, as he did in such figures as Félix, Valens, Prusias, and Orode. He was a classicist in seeking important and typical traits of character and in neglecting what he considered less significant, but this does not mean that his characters fail to make a distinct impression. He was a convinced monarchist, as he shows in *Cinna* and in his avoidance of rousing sympathy for Roman republicans. He exalted the prevailing beliefs of his day in strong government, an aristocratic society, patriotism, Christianity, national unity, and clemency.

He was an artist in his use of preparation, his creation of dramatic situations, the keenness of his psychological analysis, the contrasts he employed in characters and scenes, his methods of whetting the appetite of his audience and then satisfying it. In his effort to create situations and to wring out of them all that they contain, he forgets at times reality. His persons may argue and analyze too much. His earlier work shows certain affectations. His constant effort at experimentation was not always restrained by logic or taste, as when he gives each act of *la Suivante* exactly the same number of lines, or attempts highflown speech in *Pompée*, or ventures in *Agésilas* upon "vers libres" without fitting them to his thought. While he wrote many striking phrases, he is at times confused and laborious, does not always avoid the commonplace in thought and rime, and lacks the vocabulary of subtle expression. This is only to say, however, that he sometimes nods and that he left for others room to perfect French drama or to extend its domain. His devotion to his art, which he did not abandon like Racine, his sense of moral values, his ability to create characters, situations, and phrases that have been often repeated, his mastery of technique overshadow the faults one may easily find in many of his productions.

Corneille was the first of the great French classicists, the first French dramatist to acquire extensive appreciation in his own country and outside of it. Following Mairet and others, he experimented with his art, came to definite conclusions about it, and contributed more than anyone else to embodying it in plays that established the classical system. He always allowed himself a certain freedom in the application of his principles and may well have thought that it was not desirable to insist too much upon regulation. For the narrow channel into which some of his followers guided the movement, they were more responsible than he. It can be said of him more truly than of anyone else that the whole course of French drama might have been materially altered if he had never written.

CHAPTER VII

CORNEILLE'S CONTEMPORARIES WHO BEGAN TO WRITE
IN 1630-48

The older dramatists of this period began to write under the same conditions as Corneille, while those who first produced their plays in 1640 or subsequently had a larger number of French models to follow and had taken part neither in the first introduction of the unities nor in the quarrel over *le Cid*. About 1630 the most prominent writers after Hardy, then nearly on his deathbed, Corneille, Mairet, Du Ryer, and Rotrou, were Scudéry and Boisrobert, one of whom is especially remembered for his literary association with his sister and his activities during the *Cid* quarrel, the other for amusing Richelieu and helping to found the Academy.

Scudéry's extraordinarily high opinion of his talents as a dramatist contrasts comically with reality. He was essentially an author of tragi-comedies, the *genre* to which twelve of his sixteen plays belong, and a dramatizer of modern fiction, which supplied him with three-fourths of his known sources. He was one of the first French authors to turn often for dramatic material to French seventeenth-century novels. He was interested in exciting situations, spectacle, violent language, sentimental endings. At first he noisily refused to be hampered by classical restrictions, but the success of *Sophonisbe* seems to have made him experiment with them. He applied them in *la Mort de César* and *l'Amant libéral*, but not in *Didon*. The attack he made upon Corneille won him over to the unities and caused him to imitate the man he had criticized. His *Amour tyrannique* shows how he and Chapelain would have treated a subject like that of *le Cid*. His subsequent plays, which are all, like *le Cid*, tragi-comedies, show various imitations of Corneille.

But Scudéry never understood the meaning of classical regulations. This is obvious in his *Mort de César*, which has only one dramatic act, and in his general inability to develop a psychological problem. His talents, such as they were, were those of an author of melodrama. His most interesting and least pretentious play is *la Comédie des comédiens*, in which the manners of a troupe and ideals of good acting are set forth. *Le Fils supposé* has a few passages that show a turn for comedy. *Didon* unexpectedly introduces a "libertin." One can follow with pleasure the adventures described in *le Prince déguisé* and *Ibrahim*, but none of his plays was long successful or prevents our smiles over his praise of them. In 1643 he ceased to write plays in order to applaud less experienced dramatists, "pour les exciter à la gloire" and to show them "le Prix qui les attend." Some twenty years later, when Boileau attacked " bienheureux Scudéry," the latter's plays were sufficiently forgotten for the satirist to make no specific mention of them.

Boisrobert was slow in coming to the drama. Except for a lost translation of *le Pastor fido*, his first play was *Pyrandre*, produced when he was nearly forty. It is a dramatization of episodes in a novel he had composed and shows him as chiefly interested in surprise, violence, and scenic effects, but with some regard for the unities and some liking for the comic. He wrote two acts in the productions of the " Five Authors," then, in 1637-41, four tragi-comedies, the best of which is *le Couronnement de Darie,* and a tragedy derived from Justin and Vergil, which presents Dido as chaste and maligned and has a personal element in suggesting that, banished from the court, he was suffering a similar fate. In composing two of these plays he is said to have received suggestions from d'Aubignac. After the last of them, he relapsed into silence, but after seven years he turned, as his brother had done, to Spain for inspiration and began the most active portion of his career as a dramatist.

Between 1649 and 1657 he produced twelve plays, of which seven are derived from *comedias* by Tirso, Lope, Villegas, Rojas, and Calderon, one is taken from a Spanish tale and an Italian play, and one from a French tragi-comedy. Some of them are little more than adaptations, but he occasionally improves the plot, adds comic touches, or enlivens the style. One should note especially the gaiety of *la Jalouse d'elle-même* and the reference to manners in this play, in the early portion of *la Folle Gageure,* in *les Trois Orontes,* and in *la Belle Plaideuse*; the spectacle and mystery achieved in *la Belle Invisible*. The *Belle Plaideuse* is his best play, a comedy of manners with excellent comic scenes. It became an important source of *l'Avare*. Lines from it were repeated in his *Amant ridicule,* the first one-act play of the period to be published.

Boisrobert's reputation suffered from the fact that several times he adapted plays that had already been, or were soon to be adapted by others, but he acquired considerable mastery of technique and the ability to compose at times sparkling verse. Except for *la Belle Plaideuse,* however, his plays seldom rise above mediocrity.

Several other authors who were writing in 1630-3 deserve at least a brief mention. Claveret, like Corneille, applied himself first to comedy. *L'Esprit fort* has various references to manners and two entertaining characters, one of them a forerunner of the " petits-maîtres " that were to become popular late in the century, but the author relied too much upon description to show his characters in action. Three or four plays that followed may have furnished suggestions to Corneille, but unfortunately are lost. A spectacular adaptation of a play by Hardy has attracted some attention, thanks to the author's effort to explain how he could lay his scenes in Heaven, on earth, and in Hades without violating the unity of place. Finally, after a long residence away from Paris, he brought out a comedy of provincial manners, *l'Ecuyer*, that was in 1665 less a novelty than it would have been when he first began to write. In short, his career was not sufficiently distinguished to make one forget Corneille's slurring reference to him in the *Cid* quarrel, though he made some contribution to both the comedy of manners and spectacular productions.

His plays are more interesting than those of La Serre, who composed in 1631-43 six tragedies and a tragi-comedy, all in prose that is monotonous, antithetical, and artificial. He is chiefly to be remembered for this unfortunate experiment and for putting Sir Thomas More on the French stage. He is far less original, except for his form, than Durval, an opponent of the unities, who struggled against them for a while, but finally, in disgust over his failure in this contest, ceased to write plays. Those that have survived are largely series of tableaux that show fondness for spectacle and the *macabre*. The best of them is *Agarite*, a romantic tragi-comedy with a ballet incorporated into the intrigue, touches of realism, and a situation that recalls *Winter's Tale*. It is unfortunate that he saw merely restraint in the new rules, for, if he had properly understood them, they might have aided his imagination to produce plays of considerable value.

Dalibray was a link between Italy and France, an adapter of four Italian plays. Though, long before Boileau, he attacked the affectations of *Pyrame*, he was far from equalling Théophile's ability as a poet. Gombauld was but occasionally a dramatist. His *Amaranthe* may have helped Mairet introduce the unities, but it has merely the merits of a conventional pastoral. Some fourteen years later, when tragedy had become the leading *genre*, he wrote *les Danaïdes*, composed according to the most thoroughly classical prescriptions and possessing little originality except in an effective passage that describes a horrible situation. His only other play is lost. Gougenot, who derived a tragi-comedy from an episode in the *Amadis*, is chiefly known as the first French author to dramatize the affairs of a troupe. Beys, after attempting tragi-comedy in a play that is a typical imbroglio, composed one called *le Jaloux sans sujet*, which recalls in its ironical style passages in Corneille's early comedies, and another, *l'Hôpital des fous*, derived from a novel by Lope, but emphasizing more distinctly a series of comic types. Nearly a score of years later he rewrote this tragi-comedy as a comedy called *les Illustres Fous*, an amusing production, with references to the art of the dramatist and to that of the actor, as well as to other professions, represented by inmates of an asylum, who are guarded by a philosophic concierge. Its references to manners, its satirical spirit, and its style make this one of the most important comedies that appeared near the middle of the century.

Guérin de Bouscal, whose first play was published in 1634, attempted all four *genres* and wrote eleven plays. The first three are of little note except that his *Mort de Brute,* a sequel to Scudéry's *Mort de César,* contains, before *Cinna,* a discussion as to the relative merits of republican and dictatorial governments, but the eight that he brought out in 1638-44 are all of distinct interest. He was the first French dramatist to understand *Don Quixote,* from which he derived three clever plays. His *Cléomène* and *Mort d'Agis* are appealing tragedies, the first distinguished by its patriotic spirit and by the inclusion of a merchant in its cast; the second by the question of private property, discussed at some length, but not properly connected with the action. He also composed three tragi-comedies, one satirizing contemporary novels, the others devoted to somewhat unusual historical fields, Italy in the time of Theodoric and Constantinople during the Fourth Crusade. Patriotic, idealistic, endowed with a sense of humor and a gift for verse composition, he profited by his contemporaries' technical improvements and was ever ready to attempt new themes. His best work is his Cervantine trilogy, but there are also many interesting passages in his tragedies and tragi-comedies.

Though far better known, Benserade made less valuable contributions to drama. Except in *Gustaphe,* he dramatized familiar classical themes and, though he sought to keep the unities, added a sort of epilogue to his *Mort d'Achille.* He was fond of spectacular effects and quite artificial in his language. His most successful play was probably his *Cléopâtre,* though his *Méléagre,* the best dramatization of Ovid's tale made during the century, is superior to it in suspense and in unity of effect. Despite his fame as an author of ballets, he must have received little encouragement from the reception accorded his plays, for he wrote no more after 1639, unless it was he, rather than La Mesnardière, who put into verse d'Aubignac's *Pucelle d'Orléans.*

Chevreau and Desfontaines were mediocre dramatists. The former sought to rival or improve upon Hardy in his *Coriolan* and *Deux Amis;* upon Corneille in *le Mariage du Cid;* upon Du Ryer in his *Lucresse romaine;* and possibly upon Rotrou in *les Frères rivaux,* but in most cases he was singularly unsuccessful. A more original work is *l'Advocat duppé,* which has some interesting passages on the administration of justice and on poets. His reputation is due chiefly to his non-dramatic work and to the effort of his biographer to lend him distinction. Desfontaines has not had the latter advantage. He was quite prolific, leaving eight tragi-comedies and five tragedies, but they are constructed with little care, often violating the unity of action. His *Saint Eustache,* though brought out as late of 1642, has an action that covers some ten years and takes place both in Italy and on an island near Persia. He turned frequently to novelists for inspiration, wrote sequels to *le Cid* and to Scudéry's *Ibrahim,* and was attracted to such peculiar subjects as those represented by the legends of Saint Alexis and Valentine and Orson, and by the less familiar tale he dramatized in *Alcidiane.* His best production is *l'Illustre Comédien,* which has some of the charm found in works on the same subject by Lope and Rotrou. His other productions recall the fact that he was probably an actor in a provincial troupe, too busy to give much time to plays written for his comrades.

In contrast with these two dramatists, two others possessed genuine talent, La Calprenède and Tristan l'Hermite. The former composed in 1635-41 six tragedies and three tragi-comedies. Though his plays are largely classical in form, he never lays his scene in Rome. The countries of his preference are England and Spain. To write four plays dealing with English sovereigns or indirectly derived from Sidney's *Arcadia,* and to be the first person to give at length the story of Elizabeth, Essex, and the ring should attract readers of English blood. There is considerable pathos in *Jeanne d'Angleterre, les Enfans d'Hérodes,* and *Herménigilde.* La Calprenède portrays excellently elderly men like Mithridates, Northumberland, and Warwick. His study of Elizabeth is remarkable. He sometimes suggests larger interests than those of his characters: the triumph of Rome over minor states, the establishment of strong rule in England, the victory of Catholicism in Spain. Many of his situations are thoroughly dramatic. His classical form is surprising in one who was to write two longwinded novels and half of a third. Both the popularity of *Cassandre, Cléopâtre,* and *Faramond,* and the reaction against them have obscured his merits as a dramatist.

Tristan l'Hermite, though he wrote fewer plays, attained greater fame by his contributions to drama. He began by selecting two subjects that Hardy had treated. Instead of following Josephus step by step in the first of these, as Hardy had done, he rearranged the material so as to bring out the thoroughly passionate and dramatic character of Herod, with whom contrast the proud and gracious heroine, her cowardly mother, and vindictive Salome. These rôles and the excellence of the style made *Mariane* the most effective tragedy that preceded *Horace.* The second play, *Panthée,* suffered from the fact that Montdory, who was to take the part of Araspe in it, was stricken with paralysis of the tongue before he could act in it. He was consequently unable to compensate Tristan for the alteration he had made in his material. The tragedy was followed by its author's two most original plays, *la Folie du sage,* a tragi-comedy weak in plot, but with striking passages on medicine, death, and the nature of man; and *la Mort de Sénèque*, a tragedy distinguished by the characters of Seneca, Nero, Sabina Poppaea, the poet Lucan, and especially Epicaris, who expresses herself crudely, but with extraordinary force. *La Mort de Chrispe* is of much less value, despite a slight resemblance to *Phèdre*, but *Osman* is noteworthy as the first Turkish play to make extensive use of Turkish manners.

Tristan subsequently wrote two plays, a comedy derived from an Italian imitation of Plautus and a pastoral that is little more than a new edition of Rotrou's *Célimène*. The great success with which the latter met was brief. The comedy was played as late as 1683, thanks to certain clever passages, but offered little that was new in characters or plot. Tristan's fame rests, not on these, but on *Mariane, la Mort de Sénèque*, and certain scenes in *la Folie du sage* and *Osman* that show genuine dramatic gifts of a high order.

While these two authors were devoting themselves primarily to tragedy, others seemed more gifted in writing comedy. Discret composed *Alizon,* an amusing presentation of lower middle-class life, and *les Noces de Vaugirard,* which combines curiously realistic scenes with others that recall the pastoral. Saint-Evremond was probably the principal author of a clever attack in dramatic form on the French Academy, *la Comédie des Académistes.* Claude de l'Estoile, one of the "Five Authors," composed a tragi-comedy concerned with the romantic adventures of captives in Algeria, a lost and probably realistic *Secrétaire de Saint-Innocent,* and *l'Intrigue des Filous,* a comedy that deals with the world of thieves and their associates and is mainly written, with many popular expressions, in a lively manner, but strikes a darker note when the fate of robbers is described. Desmaretz, induced by Richelieu to write seven plays, one of them for the opening of his new theater, one to defend his political conduct, one a highly romanticized account of Scipio in Spain, made his chief contribution to drama with *les Visionnaires,* the simple plot of which is subordinated to the presentation of "plusieurs sortes d'esprits chimériques ou visionnaires": a braggart, a poet who affects the style of the sixteenth century, the lover of an ideal woman, a man who imagines that he is soon to be wealthy, and three women who are infatuated, respectively, with the theater, Alexander the Great, and her own charms. Despite the absence of rapid dialogue and the exaggeration of the characters' idiosyncracies, the comedy is often witty, avoids the complications of its predecessors, and prepares the way for Molière.

The influence of *les Visionnaires* was checked for some years by the popularity of comedies that emphasized plot rather than character or manners. One of the men largely responsible for this tendency was Bois-

6

robert's brother, d'Ouville, who had lived in Spain before he wrote comedies. His first play is a tragi-comedy that contains an interesting satire on life at court and may have influenced *Tartuffe*. After this he brought out, in 1638-49, nine plays, of which five are derived from *comedias* by Calderon, Lope, and Montalván, while one may have been inspired by Remon. When he imitated Spanish plays, he shifted the scene to Paris, sometimes simplified the plot, and added comic traits of his own, but in the main he followed his models closely, stressing the intrigue at the expense of nearly everything else. Thanks to his activities and to those of Scarron, supported by Pierre Corneille in two comedies and by Brosse in one, half the French comedies of 1640-8 were derived from Spanish plays, a vogue which was established for the first time. With it largely disappeared the predominance of manners that we have seen in a few plays and which Molière was to restore.

Other authors who began writing in the late thirties sought different effects. Chapoton left two plays: *Coriolan*, chiefly remarkable for its setting, and *Orphée*, an early example of the "machine" play that was to be revived after Corneille's more spectacular *Andromède* had appeared. Sallebray contributed to the latter type of drama his *Jugement de Paris;* wrote a sequel that makes less appeal to the eye, *la Troade*; then drew from a French novel *l'Amante ennemie*, which, like *le Jugement de Paris*, introduces music; and finally derived from a *novela* of Cervantes *la Belle Egyptienne*, which contains not only songs, but a ballet. The better of La Caze's two plays, *l'Inceste supposé*, has dramatic situations and romantic charm. Le Vert wrote a comedy, *le Docteur amoureux*, that introduces amusing speeches by a pedant, his valet, and an old maid; a tragedy, *Aristotime*, that puts a boy on the stage; and a tragi-comedy, *Aricidie*, that is the first French play to introduce the Emperor Titus and combines tragic scenes with others that would not be out of place in a comedy of manners. Regnault, who seems to have been primarily interested in the fate of French princesses abroad, composed a tragedy on the death of Mary Queen of Scots, distinguished by its partisan spirit and its pretentious style, and a tragi-comedy on the misfortunes of Blanche de Bourbon, married to Peter the Cruel, persecuted, and finally triumphant. The latter play is the more interesting, with its use of magic and the struggle in the soul of the king.

All of these authors have some claim to attention, but none of them produced more than four plays. Gillet de la Tessonerie wrote nine: five tragi-comedies, three comedies, and a tragedy. The last of these, derived from the *Astrée*, is noteworthy chiefly for introducing a heroine who dies on the stage as a victim of her emotions. The best of his tragi-comedies is *Sigismond*, a classically constructed play dealing with the false accusations brought against the hero and ending in his complete vindication. Two others, original in form, consist each of five different tales enclosed in a frame. The tales dramatized are derived chiefly from Plutarch and other ancient historians and are purely didactic in purpose, warning against love, jealousy, ambition, and desire for admiration, or recommending justice, clemency, magnanimity, continence, and liberality. The second of them, *l'Art de régner*, was intended for the moral instruction of the youthful Louis XIV, as *Télémaque* was subsequently to be for that of his grandson. Unless the reader is seeking moral instruction, he will take greater pleasure in Gillet's three comedies, *Francion, le Desniaisé,* and *le Campagnard,* all written in an agreeable style and introducing many references to customs of the day, though only the last of them, with its portrayal of a country nobleman out of his element in Paris, is a comedy of manners. Gillet employs geographical and astronomical references, allusions to alchemy and painting. As he was not influenced by Spanish dramatists, he might, had he concentrated more decidedly upon comedy, have proved an important influence in oppositon to d'Ouville and Scarron.

There were ten authors of some importance who began to bring out plays in 1640-8, a much smaller number than in the nine years that had preceded, when there was probably less competition from predecessors. Most of these new authors were interested chiefly in tragedy and in tragi-comedy and most of them accepted classical regulation as a matter of course.

D'Aubignac had shown his interest in the theater by criticizing Tristan's *Panthée* and by undertaking *la Pratique du théâtre.* Not satisfied with theory alone, he wrote three prose tragedies that attracted enough attention to be turned into verse by other dramatists. They concern the fortunes of Zenobia, Joan of Arc, and an imaginary heroine, Cyminde. The emphasis upon women may be due to d'Aubignac's familiarity with salons of the day. *La Pucelle* is exceptional in its national subject and in the emphasis upon spectacle that is also found in *Cyminde.* All three plays are written, as the author boasts in regard to *la Pucelle,* according to " les rigueurs du Theatre." They demonstrate the fact that rules alone are not enough, for the author lacked the psychological insight and the stylistic gifts required to make his prose appealing. That he realized his limitations is shown by the fact that after 1641 he confined his dramatic activities to advising dramatists and spectators.

The work of Gabriel Gilbert was composed in two periods of his life, separated by his soujourn in Italy and his employment by Queen Christina of Sweden. In 1640-6 he wrote three tragi-comedies and two tragedies, all with ancient themes except the first, derived from English history. *Rhodogune* suffers by comparison with Corneille's tragedy of that name, which influenced it considerably; *Hypolite,* by comparison with Racine's

Phèdre, which owes it a few suggestions. *Marguerite* is creditable as a first work, while *Téléphonte,* subsequently imitated by La Chapelle, and *Sémiramis* show decided ability at creating effective situations. The second period indicates greater originality. *Diane et Endimion* is one of the first "machine" plays to appear after the Fronde; *Chresphonte,* a play with a limited cast in which he joined Du Ryer in his effort to produce classical tragi-comedies; *Arie et Pétus,* a tragedy of court intrigue with interesting portraits of Nero, Petronius, and the heroine, Arie.

After composing these plays, he began to write comedy, contributing to the group of plays inspired by *les Précieuses ridicules* a *Vraye et Fausse Prétieuse* that is unfortunately lost and, three years later, *les Intrigues amoureuses,* chiefly noteworthy for containing the first description in the century of a fashionable woman's day—" My day " as an eminent lady now calls it—and for a passage in which the inhabitants of various parts of France are characterized. Comic material is also found in Gilbert's so-called pastoral, *les Amours d'Ovide,* which introduces Ovid in person, and in a tragi-comedy, *le Courtisan parfait,* which contains an inner play, puts Aretino on the stage, and gives a glimpse of amusements enjoyed at a small Italian court. His remaining plays are a negligible *Angélique et Médor* and four that are lost. He was the author of seventeen contributions to drama, the first of which appeared shortly after *Horace,* the last just before *Andromaque.* He sought to follow classical regulations, but his ability at structure did not allow him always to keep the unity of action. He often stressed women's rôles, though his contemporaries considered him cold. His interest in tragi-comedy lingered late in his career. His best work is found in one of them, *le Courtisan parfait,* and in a tragedy, *Arie et Pétus.* Though there is considerable interest in his work for a student of the period in which he wrote, he produced nothing of lasting importance.

In 1643-9 the brothers Brosse composed six plays. Only one of these was written by the younger author. Based on Cervantes's tale of the *Curioso impertinente,* it is chiefly remarkable for the fact that its author was only thirteen when he composed it. His brother wrote a tragi-comedy containing a sentimental version of the story of Seleucus and Antiochus, a comedy that is little more than a faithful adaptation of Calderon, and a tragedy derived from the *Æneid, Turne,* in which a curtain is dropped just in time to prevent the audience from accusing him of wishing to " ensanglanter la Scéne, et imiter hors de temps les rudes spectacles des Colleges." Much more interesting are his two comedies. *Les Songes des Hommes esveillez* consists of a series of entertainments devised to cheer a man who thinks he has lost his sweetheart. They bring in a genuine peasant, references to the war that was then going on, to cards, to the *Gazette,* and to the contemporary stage. An inner play recalls the fact that the hero and heroine had once participated in a performance of Scudéry's *Ibrahim*. Plot is in this comedy subordinated to manners as it is in *les Visionnaires*. The other comedy, *l'Aveugle clairvoyant*, though it has a well developed plot, does not forget manners and is distinguished by the fact that the principal character is an elderly man who, far from being the traditional father of Latin comedy, has a somewhat complex personality and completely dominates the action. These two comedies make one regret that their author did not continue to work in this field.

So far as can be determined, Michel Le Clerc, who became a member of the French Academy, had little talent for drama. Of six plays attributed to him,[1] only two have survived, a *Virginie Romaine* that shows he had mastered technical rules of structure and prosody, but possessed no more substantial qualities, and an *Iphigénie,* written to compete with Racine's and devised on a simpler plan, but owing so much to Rotrou's *Iphigénie* that it is hardly more than a new edition of that tragedy. Nor can much more be said for Le Royer de Prade, who produced three tragedies: *la Victime d'estat*, which dramatizes the death of a contemporary of Tiberius; *Annibal,* which puts a great historical figure on the French stage, but fails to do him justice; and *Arsace*, a Parthian play with at least one dramatic situation, for the invention of which the author claimed priority over Thomas Corneille and Quinault. None of the three plays obtained or deserved any considerable success.

Jean Magnon began his career by dramatizing for Molière's Illustre Théâtre an ancient Persian theme, already put on the stage by Boisrobert. He subsequently turned into verse the prose of d'Aubignac's *Zénobie*. In his other plays he selected varied themes, writing tragedies from Roman, Turkish, and fifteenth-century Italian history, tragi-comedies derived from Roman history, from a novel by La Calprenède, and from a Buddhist legend. He wished to lead the way in putting French history on the stage of his own country, but he seems never to have carried out his plan. Unfortunately he did not show corresponding originality in structure, characterization, or style. His form is classical. The chief novelty in the ideas he brings into his plays lies in the fact that both in *Artaxerce* and in *Jeanne de Naples* he has persons discuss the relative merits of hereditary and elective monarchical systems. His most striking characters are those of women: Livie in *Séjanus*, Roxane in *Oroondate*, Bérénice in *Tite*. To these could be added that of the plebeian Catanoise in *Jeanne* if he had given her a more considerable rôle. His chief title to fame is the fact that he was the first Frenchman to dramatize the love of Titus and Berenice.

[1] Cf. above, Part II, p. 605, Part III, p. 167, Part IV, pp. 217-8.

Boyer made a much greater impression on his public. His life as a dramatist extends over a longer period than that of any other man who wrote for the French stage in the seventeenth century. His first play apppeared in 1645, shortly after Corneille had become recognized as the master of classical tragedy; his last play that was acted, in 1695, when Corneille was dead and Racine had ceased to write. Though he gave up dramatic composition for ten years, 1649-58, he had acquired such fame by 1662 that Chapelain then considered him second only to Corneille, but some of his later plays were not successful enough to be published and he was attacked by Racine and Boileau. He struggled on, however, was rewarded by the triumph of *Agamemnon* in 1680, and, when he was seventy-seven, by that of *Judith*. He is even said to have read a revised play to the actors the following year. Such persistence contrasts admirably with the attitude of Mairet, Scudéry, and Racine.

He wrote no comedies and gave almost no evidence of possessing a comic gift. He had little success when he sought in 1669-71 to revive the pastoral. He occasionally wrote tragi-comedies, was a leader among authors of "machine" plays, but devoted most of his efforts to tragedy. His first plays show that he could make careful use of classical technique, but without escaping certain affectations of the time. In *Porus* he dramatized a subject that was subsequently to tempt Racine. *Aristodème* shows marked improvement in his ability to devise striking situations; *Tyridate* is one of a group of plays that employ danger of incest to create pathos; *Ulysse*, acted before *Andromède*, may be considered a "machine" play. After the Fronde he composed *Clotilde* and *Démétrius*, which stress the emotions in a manner that was to be Racine's, though they lack his style. It would be interesting to know why his lost *Tigrane* was suppressed by censorship after the first performance. His *Policrite* is a romantic tragi-comedy derived from *le Grand Cyrus* and tending towards the picturesque; his *Oropaste*, the tragedy of a usurper, ennobled by his position as king, despite the means he has employed to obtain it; his *Jupiter et Sémélé*, a "machine" play that combines elaborate spectacle, music, dancing, and, in the prologue, dramatic criticism.

As Racine's star rose, Boyer's began to be obscured. His next "machine" play was less effective than *Jupiter et Sémélé*; his *Jeune Marius* and *Policrate* are not distinguished productions; his *Fils supposé* is a reworking of *Tyridate* with a milder ending; his *Atalante* and *Démarate* are lost; in his *Conte d'Essex* he followed La Calprenède's old play and was unable to compete with Thomas Corneille's on the same subject. At last he composed *Agamemnon*, which, to avoid criticism, he presented as if it had been written by Pader d'Assézan. The play owes much to Seneca and Racine, but Boyer was able to profit by his imitations and to produce a simple and moving tragedy. Nor is his *Artaxerce* without merit, though the attempt to praise Louis XIV in its text did not silence Boyer's critics. He again ceased to write, but, after eight years, brought out two religious tragedies, *Jephté* and *Judith*, biblical plays altered to suit Catholic customs and lacking Racine's feeling for Hebraic literature. *Judith* must have brightened his last days, though it did not deserve the success it won. Boyer seems to have written a *Zénobie* in 1693 and to have altered it as late as 1696, but, as the play is lost, its qualities cannot be determined.

He had the merits of a careful craftsman who was able to adapt himself to varying tastes in other fields than that of comedy. He rid himself of his early affectations, learned to write spectacular plays, tragedies of passion, religious tragedies, but he was unable to dramatize clashing political theories, or to show noteworthy psychological discernment, or to develop a style that might have charmed his audience. His best work is found in *Oropaste, Agamemnon*, and, if we take into consideration the requirements of its *genre, Jupiter et Sémélé*. So many of his plays are, however, distinctly inferior to these that one can understand the neglect into which he has fallen.

The two remaining dramatists are much better known. One of them, Cyrano de Bergerac, owes his fame, however, to his astronomical fiction and to Rostand's play rather than to the comedy or the tragedy that he wrote himself. *Le Pédant joué* is a prose comedy with stock characters and with a dialogue that shows little knowledge of the stage. It deserves notice chiefly for introducing the first French peasant of the century who talks patois and for supplying Molière with the phrase, " Que diable allait-il faire dans cette galère? " Nor is his tragedy, *la Mort d'Agrippine*, more skillfully constructed, nor keener in characterization, except for the portrait of Sejanus, who is assigned striking lines on the impotence of the gods and the mortality of the soul. Cyrano had an interesting personality, but he was a mediocre dramatist, who occasionally redeemed his work by flashes of comic or tragic inspiration.

Scarron, on the other hand, made as great a reputation by his plays as he did by his other writings, his *Roman comique* and burlesque verse. He owed even more than d'Ouville to the *comedia*, which is the source of eight out of his nine full-length plays and of at least one of the three fragments that he left. He was the first French dramatist to imitate Rojas. He usually located his action in Spanish cities, but he added at times references to French manners. He is not, however, a realistic dramatist, but one who escaped from physical suffering by turning to burlesque or to romance. Only the former element appears in his one-act *Matamore*; only the latter in his tragi-comedy, *le Prince Corsaire*. In most of his plays the two elements are mingled and he sometimes uses one to poke fun at the other. He is especially clever in ridiculing the country squire, the valet, usually called by the stage-names of the actors Jodelet and Filipin, the racy maid, ordinarily known as Béatris, and the old man, whose Spanish sense of honor is amusingly contrasted with his mental and physical limitations. Unity and order he may have, but never at the cost of comic situations. He has great verbal dexterity, inventing comic words, juggling with sounds, satirizing the *stances* of tragedy or the eloquence of romantic characters. He descends to indecent observations, to practical jokes, to plays on words, and is never profound, but his *verve* was so irresistible that at least two of his comedies, *Jodelet maître* and *Dom Japhet* were played, respectively, until 1806 and 1893. To understand what Molière achieved, it is well to begin by reading Scarron, whom he occasionally imitated, but whose conception of comedy he opposed and finally overthrew.

From what has gone before it can be seen that Corneille was a much larger dramatic figure than any other Frenchman who wrote before the Fronde. In tragedy and tragi-comedy his chief rivals were Rotrou, Du Ryer, Mairet, Tristan l'Hermite, and La Calprenède; in comedy, Desmaretz and Scarron. When the war was over, most of these and of their contemporaries had ceased to write plays, but a few continued to do so, or, after a season of silence, had begun again to compose. There were also authors who made their début during the difficult days of civil war. Their work will be estimated in the next chapter.

CHAPTER VIII

THOMAS CORNEILLE, MONTAUBAN, QUINAULT;
WOMEN DRAMATISTS

The leading authors who began to produce plays during the Fronde were Thomas Corneille, Montauban, and Quinault. The first of these brought out even more plays than his brother. The thirty-eight that he composed either alone or in collaboration fall into four chronological groups, in the first of which comedy dominates; in the second, tragedy; in the third, comedy and tragedy; in the fourth, " machine " plays.

At first, like Scarron, he drew eight of his nine plays from Spanish *comedias*. These eight are comedies of intrigue. In *Dom Bertran* the comic element is supplied mainly by a country squire; in the other seven, primarily by the valets, among whom Jodelet of the *Geôlier de soi-même* is the most amusing. The plays show considerable structural skill, some verbal invention and satire of romantic ideas, not a little buffoonery. Comic effects are more subtle in *l'Amour à la mode* and *le Charme de la voix* than in the more successful *Dom Bertran*. The one play that is not derived from a *comedia*, *le Berger extravagant*, is a somewhat pale dramatization of Sorel's novel, but with entertaining additions concerned with French pastoral plays. Written during or shortly after the Fronde, the nine productions profited from the drift of public interest towards comedy and established the author's reputation to such an extent that he was able to devote himself to the revival of tragedy.

He began with *Timocrate*, which is derived from a novel by La Calprenède and is characterized by surprising changes of fortune and the double rôle of the irresistible hero. Though the claim that it was the greatest dramatic success of the century has not been established, the play must have been well received, so well that its author was encouraged to continue to write tragedies. *La Mort de l'empereur Commode* has a much simpler theme than *Timocrate*, an interesting study of a tyrant, and resemblances to *Andromaque*, though the presentation of love in it seems perfunctory. In the tragedies that followed Thomas Corneille varied his usage between simple and complex plots, those of *Bérénice* and *Pyrrhus* contrasting sharply with those of *Stilicon* and *Camma*, which are quite as simple as those of *Andromaque* and *Britannicus*. The most effective of these early tragedies is *Stilicon*, a play that presents the tragic theme of a statesman who sacrifices his principles in order to make an emperor of his son, only to find that his schemes have brought about the latter's death. Most of these plays have to do with court intrigue, but do not show Pierre Corneille's ability at dramatizing political problems. Some of them, like the one comedy that Thomas wrote in this period, can be praised only for the technical dexterity they display, but *Commode, Stilicon,* and *Camma* prepare the way for Racine.

In the third period he composed five tragedies, three comedies, and a tragi-comedy, besides helping Montfleury with *le Comédien poète.* The tragi-comedy has a clever and fairly simple plot that makes it rank among the best plays of its *genre,* which was about to disappear. The three comedies are taken from Spanish *comedias* and lay the same emphasis upon intrigue and upon clever valets that his earlier comedies had shown. The tragedies are more ambitious. *Laodice* recalls *Rodogune,* as *la Mort d'Annibal* recalls *Nicomède,* for the heroine of the first is an impressive, if inhuman character, while Hannibal and his daughter have some of the irony for which Pierre Corneille was distinguished. Little can be said in favor of *Théodat* and *la Mort d'Achille,* but *Ariane* is the most effective of its author's plays. The heroine's rôle, created by la Champmeslé, is admirable in its pathos and in the fact that Ariadne's efforts to meet the difficulties of her situation only make things worse. Her appealing character and the simplicity of the plot have made some critics suppose that the tragedy was written in imitation of Racine, but there is no proof that this was the case.

The use of mechanism in the *Comédien poète,* or the example his brother had set, may have attracted Thomas to " machine " plays. In *Circé* he gave one of the most elaborate specimens of the *genre.* It is written in *vers libres,* introduces music, and employs many aerial flights and changes of scene. The *Inconnu,* which followed, was composed in collaboration with de Visé. It showed a reduction in the spectacular and an increase in the comic element. It is the first " machine " play that does not have a mythological subject, a characteristic that it shares with the three that followed: *le Triomphe des dames,* written by Thomas alone, *la Devineresse* and *la Pierre philosophale,* in which de Visé collaborated. The first and last of these have survived only in librettos that show the plays to have been series of tableaux, some of which are strikingly romantic. *La Devineresse* is of much greater interest, concerned, as it is, with the contemporary affairs of la Voisin, who appears as la Jobin, the principal character. She is not represented as the sinister figure that the murderess was, rather as a clever charlatan, but the numerous consultations and mystifications that the authors devised are highly entertaining. This play and *le Triomphe* were well received, but the failure of *la Pierre philosophale* may well explain why Thomas Corneille subsequently abandoned this type of play.

Before doing so, he had turned the prose of Molière's *Don Juan* into verse, with certain alterations that made it less open to criticism on religious or structural grounds. His changes appealed so much to the public that it was in this form that Molière's play was acted down to the middle of the nineteenth century. He had also composed *Essex*, a tragedy that rivaled *Ariane* in its success, though the choice of so recent a subject as Elizabeth's execution of Essex was unusual and though the tragedy has no character so effective as Ariadne. After this play of 1678 and the *Devineresse* of the following year, the author's fortunes waned, for the *Baron des Fondrières* failed even more quickly than *la Pierre philosophale,* while *Bradamante,* a mediocre tragedy, written about 1682, was not acted until 1695. What may have been a more interesting production, *l'Usurier,* written with de Visé, concerned with banking, and introducing a real or pretended abbé, is unfortunately lost.

Thomas Corneille was a most active dramatist, well skilled in constructing plays, not altogether submissive to rule, as his change of place in *Dom Bertran* and *Essex* shows, but lacking the qualities that made eminent his brother, Racine, and Molière. He was unable to bring out, as Pierre did, the deeper aspects of the themes he treated, nor did he often write striking lines. He could abandon romantic complications for a simple presentation of psychological problems, but, except in *Ariane,* he could not, like Racine, portray the tragic nature of love, nor could he express himself in haunting verses. In comedy he remained largely an adapter of Spanish plays, made too much of the intrigue, and trusted for comic effect to clever valets and to several grotesques. His " machine " plays could not long keep his memory fresh. He won great applause with *Timocrate, Circé, Ariane,* and *Essex.* The last two and *Stilicon* are among the dozen best tragedies by minor authors of the century, while *Dom Bertran, le Geôlier,* and *la Devineresse* have much that is still amusing, but his work as a whole was not marked by enough originality to make him live as much more than the younger brother of a great dramatist.

Jacques Pousset de Montauban was primarily a lawyer. The Fronde gave him enough leisure to become a playwright, so that, on Sept. 22, 1653, he obtained permission to publish two tragedies, two tragi-comedies, and a pastoral. He was the first French author to dramatize the story of Zenobia and Rhadamistes, which Tacitus had related and Crébillon was to render famous. He seems to have imitated Corneille in depicting Zenobia as a strong-willed heroine with an important secret of which she makes effective use. In his other tragedy, *Indégonde,* he turned La Calprenède's prose *Herménégilde* into verse, producing a play that is more heroic and more classical in form than his predecessor's, but less religious and less pathetic. *Le Comte de Hollande,* a tragi-comedy, resembles *Héraclius* in that it derives interesting situations from complex material. It is superior to *Séleucus,* a dull and artificially constructed play. *Les Charmes de Félicie* is written in a lighter vein. It owes much to earlier French plays and to Spanish pastoral novels and is chiefly distinguished by its use of music and of mechanical devices that caused it to be revived in 1681.

After the civil war Montauban's practice must have taken up most of his time, as he did not produce another play until 1674, when his country was again at war. His long silence was, however, beneficial to his art. *Panurge,* his masterpiece, is the first play that owes most of its material to Rabelais. While the plot is original, it is built up so as to bring in as large a number of characters and situations from Rabelais as possible. Women, of course, have a larger share in the play than in its source, as Montauban was writing for actresses as well as for actors, and many male characters are suppressed, but the flavor of the original is often recaptured. It is a pleasure to meet again Panurge, Frère (become Maître) Jean, Rondibilis, Bridoye, and others and to hear echoes of the old master's exuberance and humor. This play is Montauban's chief title to our remembrance of him, for most of his work is not that of a professional dramatist, but rather the product of a lawyer's leisure moments, allowed him while his fellow citizens were too busy with war to require his professional services.

Quinault, on the other hand, was primarily a dramatist and a librettist. His plays were violently attacked by Boileau; the librettos he wrote for the budding opera, greatly admired both in his own and in the eighteenth century. He deserved neither such sweeping condemnation, nor such high praise. Under the tutelage of Tristan l'Hermite he began his career when about eighteen by rewriting Rotrou's *Deux Pucelles* as a comedy with a larger comic element, a simpler and more nearly unified plot. He next composed *la Généreuse Ingratitude,* which combines the violence and surprise of tragi-comedy with pastoral elements, but he returned to comedy in *l'Amant indiscret,* which has the same source as *l'Etourdi,* the same comic element arising from the lover's tendency to spoil his chance for happiness by his blundering. It is more realistic than Molière's play, but the dialogue is far less brilliant. A third comedy, *la Comédie sans comédie,* is remarkable for its form, its praise of the stage, its variety of tone. Gougenot and Scudéry had introduced actors who, under their own stage-names, discussed their profession. Gillet de la Tessonerie had written two plays in which a frame is employed and each act tells a different story. Quinault combined the two methods by having actors of the Marais, in order to defend their art, perform in succession a pastoral, a farce derived from Cervantes and Rabelais, a tragedy, and a tragi-comedy with " machines."

In these four plays Quinault had shown more talent for comedy than for tragi-comedy, yet it was the latter *genre* to which he next devoted his chief attention. He brought out in five years seven plays, of which five are tragi-comedies, one is a tragedy, and one an allegorical pastoral that is lost. He seems to have been asked to give form to a play partly written by others in order that actors might compete with their rivals, who were putting on one derived by Boisrobert from a *comedia*. His *Coups de l'amour et de la fortune* imitates both Calderon and Boisrobert, improving upon the latter chiefly in structure. This and the play that followed, which is also derived from Calderon, are his only borrowings from the *comedia*, a fact that is important in showing the drift away from Spain of his generation. He did not on that account, however, come closer to reality, for his next four plays are filled with romantic and improbable incidents, covered with a thin historical veneer. Especially in *la Mort de Cyrus* does he portray the dapper and love-lorn hero for whom he was ridiculed by Boileau; in *Stratonice*, the young lovers who express their emotions with excessive refinement.

The five plays composed in 1662-71 contain his chief successes before he gave himself up to opera. *Agrippa*, which probably owes much to Boyer's *Oropaste*, has the improbability of his earlier tragi-comedies, but it possesses at least one important character who is not moved by sexual love and it has a skillfully devised plot, filled with surprises and changes of fortune. *Astrate*, his best-known tragedy, has as its leading character a murderous princess redeemed by love and was noted in the seventeenth century for its introduction of a ring. It has dramatic qualities that a reader of Boileau would not suspect. *La Mère coquette*, Quinault's cleverest comedy, owed much to de Visé's play of the same name, but is superior to it in style and situations. The mother who struggles against advancing years and is her daughter's rival, the brilliant valet, and the pretended marquis are well-drawn comic figures. In his last two plays Quinault came nearer to Racine. *Pausanias* resembles *Andromaque*, while *Bellérophon* is a simple and unified tragedy with a dominant heroine whose passion leads to her suicide, somewhat in the manner that Racine was subsequently to illustrate in *Phèdre*.

Quinault was a master of dramatic construction, but he had little regard for reality. Disguise, misunderstandings, chance occurrences are his stock in trade. He has become especially famous for his young lovers, for the scenes in which their *aveu* is made, for their timid approach to life. Love is his chief theme, but, except in the characters of Elise and Sténobée, it is not the kind of passion that Racine describes. It is usually the languorous emotion that was subsequently to distinguish Quinault as an author of operas. He made extensive use of his contemporaries and immediate predecessors, always without acknowledgment, but he was impervious to the criticism he received for such borrowings and for his unheroic portraits of historical warriors. He went serenely on his way, winning abundant success, although much of his writing was done while Racine and Molière were producing masterpieces. *La Comédie sans comédie, Agrippa, Astrate, la Mère coquette,* and *Bellérophon* are probably the plays by which his friends would have preferred to have him judged. They would show that he possessed ingenuity, delicacy, and wit, but their good qualities did not conceal the fact that he was essentially a librettist, a fact that became generally obvious as soon as the introduction of opera made it possible for him to write for musicians.

The first plays of the century that were written by women and were promising enough to be published appeared during the Fronde. Previously Jacqueline Pascal at the age of eleven had composed with two other girls a lost play in five acts that they twice performed, and the Duchess of Croy had left a manuscript, dated 1637, that contained a tragi-comedy called *Cinnatus et Camma,* in three acts, with a song at the end of each and rôles assigned to Hymen, Morpheus, and the devil. In 1650 Mme de Saint-Balmon and Marthe Cosnard each published a religious play that shows some knowledge of Corneille, but little talent for dramatic composition. After the Fronde we hear of two actresses who helped prepare plays for the stage. La Beauchasteau is said to have " dressé le sujet " of one that became in Quinault's hands *les Coups de l'amour et de la fortune,* while Madeleine Béjart altered for Molière's troupe Guérin de Bouscal's dramatization of *Don Quixote.*

None of these six women concerned herself with more than a single play. The first woman to go farther was Françoise Pascal of Lyons, who composed about 1655-64 three tragi-comedies and three farces. The tragi-comedies, derived from French seventeenth-century novels, suggest the nature of the author's reading. One is religious, one makes a moderate use of " machines," and the third, *Sésostris,* is superior to the others, especially in the portrait of the repentant king. Her first two farces present each a grotesque central character, an old maid, or a poet, possibly conceived under the influence of *les Visionnaires.* The *Vieillard amoureux,* written in verses of eight syllables, is superior to these and portrays to a certain extent the life of Lyons and the character of a miser. Her work as a whole possesses little originality and distinction, but at least extended the domain of an old maid's occupations.

The ablest woman dramatist of the century was Mlle Desjardins, who received advice from d'Aubignac for her first production, *Manlius.* While this tragi-comedy is imitative and possesses a sentimental ending that violates Livy's account, it is superior both in its dramatic qualities and its prosody to the work of Françoise Pascal and the women who had published during the Fronde. It was followed by a tragedy derived from Herodotus that suffers from its decorum, a peculiar failing on the part of one who was so far from illustrating that quality in her life. Her third and most interesting play is *le Favori*, derived from Tirso de Molina, but presented in such a way as to make effective use of suspense and to introduce a compliment to Louis XIV. The plot is simple and unified, the protagonist is well drawn, and the style is pleasing. The play was acted in the gardens at Versailles by Molière's troupe, an occasion described by the author herself. Unlike Mme de Saint-Balmon and Mlles Cosnard and Pascal, she did not make use of novels or of lives of saints in writing her plays and she succeeded in having them acted by Parisian companies.

In the next generation Mme Deshoulières produced a tragedy that was in the repertory of the Hôtel de Bourgogne, *Genséric*, derived from the *Astrée* and a play by Georges de Scudéry. In composing it, she seems to have been torn between imitations of Corneille and Racine. Though too many characters are introduced for her to do them justice, she shows some ability at depicting the decay of Rome and the contest between a victorious barbarian and a captive empress. Her other play, *Jule Antoine*, has survived only in a fragment.

Catherine Bernard was more successful. She wrote two tragedies that were acted at Paris, *Laodamie* and *Brutus*. In the first she described the rivalry of two sisters and produced certain dramatic effects, but she failed to give her characters sufficient relief and was hampered by her prosaic style. *Brutus* is a more effective play, though its style suffers similarly. The chief characters are the two sons, one of whom, before the play begins, has abandoned his patriotic principles in the hope of becoming a Quisling, while the other, despite his fine qualities, is induced during the tragedy to betray his city. Unfortunately Catherine lacked the qualities of her relative, Pierre Corneille, required to embody in these men the political principles that might readily have been suggested by their conduct.

The only other woman who sought during the century to become a dramatist was Mme Ulrich. She claimed to be the author of *la Folle Enchère* when it was published, though Dancourt's comrades seem to have believed that the play was mainly his and though it was subsequently brought out in his collected plays. She probably devised the plot, which is no great title to fame, while he probably wrote most of the dialogue and made the production acceptable to the actors of the Comédie Française.

While many actresses were having distinguished careers, their sisters who composed plays were merely helping to undermine the wall that barred them from full participation in the life of the times. These eleven authors achieved little in comparison with the work of Mme de La Fayette and Mlle de Scudéry in the novel, or of Mme de Sévigné in letter writing, but they at least showed by their persistence that they could write plays and even have them acted with temporary, if not with lasting success.

CHAPTER IX

RACINE AND OTHER AUTHORS OF TRAGEDY, 1664-1700

In 1664-72, when Racine was establishing his reputation, he was, so far as can be determined, the only new author whose tragedies were being acted at Paris. So great had become the popularity of comedy that the younger authors preferred that *genre*, with the result that Racine's rivals in tragedy were the brothers Corneille, Boyer, and Quinault, men who had had their first plays acted from eleven to thirty-four years before Racine. As these men had grown up in an older tradition, the new dramatist, while imitating certain of his predecessors, had a clear field for creating his own variety of classical tragedy.

He had had excellent training in Greek and Latin, had practised the art of writing verses, and must have experienced in his own surroundings a dramatic conflict between the teachings of his pious Jansenist relatives and teachers on the one hand, and those of the persons he met at court and in the circle of the duc de Chevreuse on the other.

His first attempts were unsuccessful: a play called *Amasie*, one on the love-affairs of Ovid and Julia, and, if we can trust the statement of his son Louis, one derived from Heliodorus. None of these has survived, but his fourth play, *la Thébaïde*, was acted by Molière's troupe with moderate success. He combined in it imitation of Euripides and of Rotrou. He depicted the deadly struggle between shifty Eteocles and overbearing Polyneices, the efforts of Jocasta and Antigone in their behalf, and the machinations of Creon, who is given a quite unnecessary love for Antigone. Racine showed in this play his liking for a Greek theme, his mastery of classical technique, and his interest in love, but not the psychological subtlety or the poetic charm that are associated with his name. Nor are they found in his next tragedy, *Alexandre*, in which he treated, in Quinault's manner rather than in Corneille's, a subject previously dramatized by Boyer. He skillfully distributed a small amount of material over five acts and made effective use of Porus's famous reply to Alexander, but he represented both the latter and Porus as sighing lovers, though he did more justice to the Indian, introduced two women that move us little, and failed to take advantage of picturesque elements that his sources offered. The play was, however, well received and was important in Racine's life, as it occasioned his break with Molière, under circumstances that were not to Racine's credit, and induced him to have the rest of his secular tragedies acted at the Hôtel de Bourgogne. His *liaison* with la Du Parc, who left Molière to join his rivals, may also have been partly the result of this affair.

When he had learned from her the ways of passion, he produced *Andromaque*, his first great play, in the composition of which his own experiences may well have had a greater part than Euripides, Vergil, or French dramatists. He made love dominant, but he showed that it could be as tragic as other emotions. He created four unforgettable characters, a model of dramatic structure, with an action that oscillates around the decisions of a central person. He achieved a poetic evocation of the past and developed for the play a style that is close to the talk of ordinary life, almost comic at times, yet retains its tragic intensity. The play is open to criticism chiefly for a few affected phrases and for the shifting of interest from Andromache to Hermione, but these characteristics did not prevent the public from receiving it with great admiration. It lifted Racine to equality with Corneille.

Encouraged, Racine invaded Corneille's special territory, that of Roman history, and produced *Britannicus,* which has a larger number of good rôles than *Andromaque* and is written in a style that shows no lapses into affectation. The play is especially famous for the portraits of Nero, beginning his career of crime, of Agrippina, who feels her power slipping from her hands, and of Narcisse, the French Iago. Nor are the young lovers, pathetic victims of more experienced persons, and Burrhus, whose virtue has become slightly tarnished by his residence at court, lacking in interest. Nero occupies the central position that Andromache had held in the structure of the earlier play. Various psychological scenes are justly celebrated. The background of Roman court intrigue is given in a manner worthy of Tacitus, but the politics described are purely personal, not mixed with theory, as in *Cinna.*

Then, as if he wished to show his structural skill, he dramatized a subject on which he probably knew that Corneille was already at work, that of Titus and his Jewish princess. With only three important characters and a theme of parting lovers he produced *Bérénice,* in which he held his audience during five acts " par une action simple, soutenue de la violence des passions, de la beauté des sentiments et de l'élégance de l'expression," despite its frequently conversational tone. He could scarcely have ventured to produce this play, if he had not had la Champmeslé as his interpreter. While Titus is the central character, in whose mind the obligations of power struggle with those of love, we are especially interested in the heroine, whom we see eagerly expecting to be married, seeking to explain the emperor's apparent coldness, warning him of what separation means, taunting him desperately, and finally resigning herself to an inevitable situation that she has come to understand. It is the simplest of his tragedies and the only one in which there is no violence, perhaps the one that comes closest to ordinary experience. It is quite superior in human interest and in the charm of the verses, which express deep emotion with very little ornamentation, to the rival play that Corneille had composed. After writing it, Racine may have felt that he had risked a dangerous experiment, one that he did not attempt to repeat.

His next play is not only far less simple in plot, but keeps the thought of death constantly before us and ends, as Mme de Sévigné put it, in a " grande tuerie." The subject of *Bajazet* was probably suggested by a novel of Segrais. It is more nearly akin to Tristan's *Osman* than to other plays, but in dramatizing it Racine seems to have been influenced by Corneille's *Othon* and by his own *Britannicus*. Just as the characters in *Bérénice* have relations with one another that resemble those of Pyrrhus, Hermione, and Orestes in *Andromaque*, so the characters of *Bajazet* resemble, except for the change of sex, four important persons in *Britannicus*. The central character, Roxane, corresponds to Nero; Acomat to Agrippina; Bajazet and Atalide to Junie and Britannicus. While the young lovers are well presented, they are overshadowed by Roxane, inspired by a strong physical desire for Bajazet, whom she sends to his death when she finds that she cannot have him, and by Acomat, the experienced Oriental politician, ever calm, but capable of swift action when the occasion calls for it, looking upon love as a weakness in others that may put them in his power and further his political aims. Nor should we forget the Sultan, who remains behind the scenes, but whose power is felt throughout the tragedy, like that of fate.

Mithridate is the last of his secular tragedies for which he did not have a dramatic model to follow, since La Calprenède's *Mort de Mithridate* could have done little more than suggest to him the subject. He used, however, a number of devices he had formerly employed. There are four main characters as in *Andromaque* and *Bajazet;* only one of them is a woman, as in *Bérénice*; there are hostile brothers as in *la Thébaïde*; the leading person is a distinguished warrior as in *Alexandre*; there is a long passage giving a background to the political side of the play as in *Britannicus*. At the same time there are novelties: the fact that the three men love the same woman, the scene of the *aveu*, employed previously by Quinault, but not by Racine, and the somewhat sentimental ending. The double plot, partly concerned with the old king's struggle against Rome, partly with the rivalry of the three men, is skillfully unified. Special emphasis is laid on Mithridates, selfish and cruel, yet admirable in his military prowess and his tireless patriotism, and on Monime, gracious, tactful, and charming, one of Racine's finest heroines. The play was especially adapted to spectators whose country was at war, but who retained their interest in the analysis of emotion, expressed in effective verse.

Racine now returned to the Greeks, as Thomas Corneille and Quinault had recently done. He selected a play of Euripides in which war has an essential part and dramatized, like the Greek dramatist, the conflict between public demands and private affections. In *Iphigénie* Agamemnon is less a patriot than in Euripides, but equally ambitious and diplomatic, a complex figure with an intense moral struggle. Iphigeneia, older than in the Greek play, is now in love. Clytemnestra is more queenly than in the latter, but is still primarily a mother. Eriphile, for whom Euripides offered no equivalent, is a striking creation, an illegitimate child who has been embittered by social injustice, one whose jealousy of Iphigeneia is as strong as her love for Achilles. The supernatural data that the source offered are retained, but minimized sufficiently to allow the human element to make the chief impression. This use of *le merveilleux*, the more complex plot, and a descriptive tendency distinguish the play from the five that had preceded it.

Similar characteristics are found in *Phèdre*, though, as is true of *Iphigénie*, there is no weakening in psychological discernment. Often considered his masterpiece, *Phèdre* is especially famed for the title-rôle, that of a woman intensely passionate, yet constantly moved by her repugnance to the gratification of her emotion. Theseus, Hippolytus, and Aricie, though they make no such impression, are ably conceived, while even the usually conventional rôles of nurse and messenger take on life in the characters of Œnone and Théramène. Nowhere did Racine show more completely his ability to make his action progress through varied scenes, clothed in a style that produced many memorable lines. If he had surpassed Corneille in *Bérénice*, he showed in *Phèdre* that he could surpass Euripides.

He then planned an *Iphigénie en Tauride*, but did not complete the play, as Louis XIV had named him one of his historiographers. Abandoning his art to serve the king, he returned to it only when Mme de Maintenon asked him to write a play for her girls at St.-Cyr. He was obliged to select a moral theme, to avoid love, and to provide many short rôles for amateur performers. In composing *Esther* he managed both to meet these requirements and to pay a compliment to the Esther of Versailles, who had also married a king and, though she had not lifted a finger in behalf of the Protestant community from which she sprung, had come to the aid of impoverished daughters of the nobility. The tragedy has only three acts, but they are lengthened by choruses. The structure is less strictly classical than in Racine's earlier plays and the presentation of the characters is hampered by respect for the Bible and for St.-Cyr. The chief value of the play lies in the style, which shows deep appreciation of Biblical verse and, especially in the choruses, gives the play a lyric flavor that puts it midway between classical tragedy and opera.

Encouraged by this venture, Racine composed *Athalie*, a much more impressive tragedy, written, like most of his plays, in five acts, but, like *Esther*, with a chorus. In the latter play he had dramatized, as Du Ryer had done before him, the rescue of the Jews. Now he celebrated the salvation of the race by showing how the seed of David was preserved in the person of Joas. While the latter gives, as he should, merely the impression of a boy brought up in an ecclesiastical sanctuary, the two leading characters, Joad and Athalie, are most effective, one a Hebrew prophet, inspired to save his people and turned aside from his purpose by neither considerations of personal safety, honesty, nor the social code of manners; the other, an old queen, seeking desperately to retain the power she had won by murdering her own grandchildren, vengeful and able, momentarily touched by the sight of the mysterious child she has found in the Temple. To these Racine added Mathan, traitor to his religion and his race, like Hitler's honorary Aryans, and Abner, the military leader who appreciates his duty to the queen, but is won over by Joad to more vital obligations. These characters, the profoundly religious inspiration of the play, the Hebraic note, mastered by Racine as by no one in France since d'Aubigné, the lyrical element in the choruses and in Joad's prophecy, the spectacle of the Temple, and the admirable structure have made many regard *Athalie* as Racine's finest play, though it lacks the intense inner struggles of several of his earlier tragedies.

Racine was little concerned with ideas and, except in *les Plaideurs*, limited himself to tragedy. His subjects are drawn from Greek mythology, ancient history, and the Bible, with the exception of *Bajazet*, for which, according to him, Turkish manners supplied the remoteness that the chronology of Turkish history lacked. He sought to portray in the characters supplied by his sources what he considered the essential human qualities of men and women dominated by fate, working through their passions, or, in his last two plays, by the God of Jews and Christians. He limited himself more than Corneille had done, both in his choice of subjects and in the manner of constructing his plays. He set an example that was more difficult to follow, for lesser men were hampered by restrictions that did not hinder him and were unable to reproduce his art of making his characters live and his ability at writing verse.

He accepted the classical system as he found it, departing from it, as many others had done, only in details. He differed from Corneille by narrowing the range of his interests, by producing much less, by placing in most of his tragedies greater emphasis upon love and upon the inner struggle, by seeking more frequently to rouse pity rather than admiration, by being less willing to accept the *vrai* as a substitute for the *vraisemblable*, and by paying greater attention to his style. He employs both the short, striking phrase and the elegant periphrasis, comes at times close to prose, but knows the secret of preserving the tragic tone. His work is the best defense of classical methods, as applied to tragedy. His genius as a portrayer of character, a creator of situations, and a poet could not have been learned in the school of d'Aubignac, but he would not have been the kind of dramatist that he was, if he had not had behind him, not only Euripides and Seneca, but Corneille, Rotrou, d'Aubignac, and other French authors, and various elements, Christian and pagan, that made up the culture of seventeenth-century France.

After 1663 tragedies were written, not only by Racine and by six authors discussed in the last three chapters—the brothers Corneille, Boyer, Quinault, and two women—but by amateurs, like Bidar, Blessebois, and Colonia, who did not write for the Parisian stage; by authors, like Aubry and Pader d'Assézan, who composed only one or two plays and whose work has little significance; by others, like Riupeirous, Belin, and Duché, whose plays composed in the seventeenth century are lost, or were not publicly acted till the eighteenth; by those primarily known as authors of comedy; and by ten whose chief concern was with tragedy. It is only the last two groups that require discussion here.

After writing plays for over twenty years, Boursault brought out his first tragedy, *Germanicus*, in 1673. It is chiefly valuable for the rôle of Piso, who nobly guides the action to his own destruction. Tiberius, strangely enough, fails to appear on the stage, the other characters are insufficiently active, and the style is marred by affectation. After attempting a tragedy with a modern subject, *la Princesse de Clèves*, the text of which is lost, he claims that he subsequently gave it the name of his earlier tragedy and was rewarded by its success—a commentary on the audience's dislike of the modern subject in tragedy. *Marie Stuard* presents a dramatic, if prejudiced view of Elizabeth and of the bastard Murray and has at least two good acts, the first and the second. Unfortunately the action subsequently lags and Mary is not given a large rôle. Boursault's comedies, novels, and letters show that his talents lay in other fields than the tragic, an impression that a reading of his tragedies does not dispel.

Actor-dramatists usually wrote comedies, but they occasionally rewrote for their colleagues earlier tragedies. This was the case with La Tuillerie, who adapted Scudéry's *Ibrahim* in his *Soliman* of 1680; Rotrou's *Hercule mourant* in his *Hercule* of 1681. In his lost *Nitocris* he probably treated in similar fashion the tragi-comedy of that name by Du Ryer. His work was largely that of improving his predecessors' technique, with some loss of spectacle and picturesqueness, which his audiences do not seem to have

missed. Dancourt, while in a provincial troupe, made further changes in
La Tuillerie's *Hercule*, having Dejanira only engaged to Hercules, who is
loved by Iole, while she is herself loved by Philoctetes, but these alterations
did not bring sufficient success to turn Dancourt from his career as an author
of comedies.

The only other author of distinction in the lighter *genre* who composed
a tragedy was Brueys. Combining his interest in the stage with his spiritual
profession, he brought out *Gabinie*, the best religious play among those that
followed *Athalie*. He imitated Father Jourdan's Latin *Susanna*, but
avoided the view of the martyr's severed head and connected the events
of the play with an important subject, the triumph of Christianity in the
Roman Empire. He improved the technique of his source and devised
a number of striking situations, but his art as a dramatist suffered somewhat from his respect for history and for Christian legend.

Of the ten dramatists who remain to be considered only two began to
write before *Phèdre* appeared, Abeille and Pradon. The first of these
composed three tragedies that have survived and two that are lost. In
Argélie he put on the stage, as Racine did not do, the rivalry of sisters,
one a violent and murderous person, the other active in her efforts to save
her lover. The author showed no special ability at characterization, but had
learned the art of working up situations and of creating suspense while
obeying classical rules. The tragedy is said to have suffered from the fact
that the protagonist was almost unknown. This cannot be said of *Coriolan*,
but the familiar subject was presented in such a way that, except for a few
proper names, it would be unrecognizable. The tragic nature of the
ancient tale is lost, largely out of the author's respect for the unities of
place and time, while the plot that Abeille invented centers chiefly round
Aufidius's Amazonian sister. The play shows how the rules could bring
a dramatist to sacrifice his subject in an effort to obey them. The third
tragedy, *Lyncée*, is the best of the three. The theme, already dramatized by
Gombauld in his *Danaïdes*, is presented with considerable skill. While
emphasizing the rôles of Hypermestre and her evil stepmother, Abeille
created a simple, unified, and psychological tragedy, but, like its predecessors, it did not long remain in the repertory.

Pradon is notorious for having dared to rival Racine and for exciting
the wrath of Boileau. He had certain merits that are often overlooked.
He wrote ten plays, all tragedies, that treated Asiatic, mythological, and
Roman themes and showed imitation of Corneille, Racine, and other dramatists. His first play, *Pirame*, combines two plots, one derived from Théophile's old play, the other and more important depicting a queen, intent on
holding her power, and her son, whose character develops somewhat as does

that of Attale in *Nicomède*. This tragedy was followed by *Tamerlan*, in which Pradon dramatized a Turkish subject, as Racine had recently done, and stressed the rôles of the Tartar conqueror and his royal captive. It is the latter's sacrifice of himself that induces Tamerlane to bring about the solution of the play. This tragedy, less successful than its predecessor, inspired Pradon's first remarks about a hostile cabal. There was, however, one that favored him and persuaded him to compose hurriedly a *Phèdre et Hippolyte* in order that it might be acted at the Guénégaud while *Phèdre* was being given at the rival theater. It is a pale imitation of Seneca, of Racine, and of two other Frenchmen who had treated the subject. Phèdre, now merely engaged to Theseus, is a caricature of Racine's heroine, while the dialogue and situations show none of the latter's dramatic power.

The defects of the play did not prevent its being well received in the winter of 1677. It turned its author into the field of ancient tragedy, from which he next derived an *Electre* that is lost and a *Troade*, based chiefly on Seneca and adding complications that deserve little praise. He then wrote *Statira*, derived from La Calprenède's novel, *Cassandre*, and containing certain effective scenes, but not combining happily the historical and novelistic elements of the story. After this he devoted himself to Roman history, from which he took four tragedies, of which two, *Tarquin* and *Germanicus*, are lost. A third, *Régulus*, written somewhat in the manner of *Horace*, is his masterpiece. It is a war play, with a patriotic theme, a minor love interest, and pathos produced by the introduction of a ten-year old boy, a rare figure in French tragedy. *Scipion*, with which his career ended, is distinctly inferior, a romanticized dramatization of Livy that does justice neither to Scipio, nor to Hannibal, nor to the historical forces they represented.

Pradon's best tragedies are *Pirame* and *Régulus*. Of the others only *Phèdre et Hippolyte* and *Scipion* deserved the severe criticism he received, unless his two lost plays were as absurd. He had little genuine originality, but he labored long to keep tragedy before the public, mastered the technical requirements of his day, and might have achieved some fame if he had not had the misfortune to be contrasted with Racine. There are interesting passages in several of his plays. It may at least be said of him that he was the only dramatist in the last third of the century who brought out in that period as many as ten tragedies that were acted at Paris.

It was the lack of such persistency that probably prevented other dramatists from making important contributions to French tragedy. Five of those that seem worthy of mention here wrote very few. Ferrier had at least enough originality to put on the stage a subject from national history. The title-rôle of his *Anne de Bretagne* is that of a woman enabled by the

great position she has obtained to conquer her love. Political questions
are discussed, as well as those of the heart, but the author failed to create
striking characters and situations and, though he imitated *Bérénice*, he
was not poet enough to make up for the scanty amount of material in the
subject he dramatized. His next play, *Adraste*, has a more conventional
subject, taken from Herodotus, but more striking characters. Its effectiveness was impaired by romantic elements and the alterations he made in
order to satisfy his critics. His only other play, *Montézume*, was not acted
until 1702 and is lost.

La Chapelle was a more talented author. His first tragedy, *Zaïde*, has
an unfortunate subject for a psychological play, that of a woman disguised
as a man, who gains great power in a Moorish state and is involved in
various sentimental complications. The theme called for a picturesque
production, but La Chapelle was prevented by the fashions of his time from
treating it in the only way that could make it acceptable. In his next
tragedy, *Cléopâtre*, he dealt with material that was better suited to the
classical system. The interest is centered on the two main characters,
gradually brought to their death. The simplicity of the language, the
excellence of the structure, and the pathos of the situations made this one
of the noteworthy tragedies of the period. *Téléphonte*, which followed,
showed the influence of Gilbert's play on the same subject and of Corneille.
The author emphasized recognitions and moral struggles, even paid a compliment to Louis XIV, but he should have made a more careful study of
his characters' motives and of the circumstances that led to his striking
situations. His last tragedy, *Ajax*, probably an adaptation of Sophocles,
is lost. The facts that it was never published and that the author wrote no
more plays are probably due to his political activities. His success with
Cléopâtre and with his one comedy makes it regrettable that he was diverted
from his career as a dramatist by the Bourbon princes to whom he was
attached.

The abbé Charles-Claude Genest also wrote four tragedies of which one
is lost. He began with a theme from Plutarch, reproduced certain historical
details, and made effective use of suspense, but there are important characters that do not appear and *récits* are too frequently substituted for action.
Pénélope is the tragedy for which he is chiefly known. Genest avoided the
mistakes of his earlier play, followed Homer, and arranged the scenes of
recognition so as to form a climax, but the play suffers from the decorum
which restrains Penelope from showing emotion over the return of her son
and her husband, makes of a herdsman a minister of state, and banishes
Homer's longsuffering dog. These objections may not have been raised
in the seventeenth and eighteenth centuries, when the structure, which seems

artificial to a modern reader, may have been appreciated, and the representation of Penelope, gazing over the sea, may have been considered daring. By 1764 it had been acted 158 times at the Comédie Française. His other plays were *Polymneste*, a lost tragedy, probably an adaptation of Euripides, and *Joseph*, which was not acted until 1710.

Péchantré's *Géta*, acted 146 times from 1687 till 1727, is superior to *Pénélope* and *Cléopâtre*. The four main characters, the mother, her sons, and the girl both men love, are all well drawn. The plot is simple, emphasis is laid on moral struggles, and the style is free from affectation. There is much pathos in the last act. The only criticism I would make is that we are not taken sufficiently into the emperor's confidence, so that we are not shown completely the steps by which he is brought to causing his brother's murder. This promising tragedy should have begun a distinguished career, but Péchantré's next play, *Jugurtha*, was not published, his *Mort de Néron* was not acted until 1703, and his only other contributions to drama were two school plays that have disappeared.

Longepierre, who had written in 1686 a *Parallèle de Corneille et Racine*, brought out in 1694 a *Médée* that is a modernization of Corneille's early tragedy, from which it differs chiefly by the suppression of much spectacle, the greater unity of structure, and the introduction of children on the stage. Though acted only twenty-three times in 1694-6, it was revived in 1728 and remained in the repertory of the Comédie Française until 1813, a tribute, perhaps, to Corneille rather than to Longepierre. His next play, *Sésostris*, failed and was never published. After it he wrote only *Electre*, acted privately in 1702, but not publicly until 1719. His record shows him to have been a critic and technician rather than a creative dramatist.

Far more important than any of these was Campistron, nine of whose tragedies were acted in 1683-93. His first play, *Virginie*, is a psychological tragedy built round Appius, with an idealistic treatment of the young hero, the heroine, and the latter's mother. It showed that he was already skilled in dramatic construction. It was followed by *Arminius*, a patriotic play, with love as a subordinate theme. Particularly impressive is the presentation of the two German warriors, Arminius and Segestes. Their attitude towards Rome resembles that of French leaders today in regard to Germany. Segestes, who had formerly resisted the enemy, would, like Pétain, submit to them in the futile hope that they would respect their promises, while Arminius, like de Gaulle, knowing that peace with them would be a " joug infaillible," would resist to the end. The second act, in which the ideas of these chieftains is brought sharply into conflict, recalls the political discussions of *Horace* and *Sertorius*. While the other acts are less effective, the play is well constructed and suspense is kept up until the decision is reached at the end of the play.

Further progress was made in *Andronic*, derived from Saint-Réal's account of Philip II, his wife, and her stepson. For some reason, perhaps because he did not wish to portray an ancestor of Louis XIV in an unfavorable light, Campistron disguised his subject by laying the scene at Constantinople in the time of John V Paleologus. The young hero is thoroughly tragic, as his outbreaking nature, wounded by wrongs he has received, brings about his death. He resists his passion for his young stepmother, whom he had loved before her marriage, and seeks to help his father's unfortunate subjects, but by offending both the emperor and his wily ministers he gets himself caught in a web from which he cannot escape. Interesting, too, are the suspicious, lonely, and vengeful emperor, the two politicians who forget their mutual enmity in order to work for their common advantage, and the pathetic empress, drawn from her home and obliged to sacrifice her love to interests of state. This appealing play is Campistron's masterpiece, one that had been acted 242 times before the end of the 1765.

The tragedy that followed, *Alcibiade*, was probably written essentially for Michel Baron, who had the title-rôle. It is less well constructed than the two earlier plays, for in the third act the chief decision is made, so that the rest of the tragedy has less to hold our interest. Love is so important a motive with the hero that it obscures his patriotism, while the other characters lack distinction. Baron, however, had a rôle in which he could display his seductive powers. He brought the play great, though temporary success.

The three tragedies that followed had no such good fortune. *Phraate* may have been a work of considerable merit, but its subject, which probably dealt with incest, put the author in danger of a trip to the Bastille. It was acted only three times, the second two and a half months after the first, the third nearly a month after the second, but such alterations as Campistron may have made did not convince the actors that it was safe to attempt it again. *Phocion* was entirely proper, but the title-rôle was statuesque and the minor characters were not sufficiently effective to overcome this defect. *Adrien* is a religious play, probably suggested by the success of *Esther*. The triumph of Christianity is indicated, as it was to be subsequently in *Gabinie*, and love has a part to play, but the hero is introduced too late and there is little action. Campistron had been unfortunate in selecting these three subjects.

In contrast with these productions, *Tiridate,* which followed them, is, next to *Andronic*, his most meritorious play. The subject of a brother's love for his sister is, of course, a difficult one to make acceptable, but Campistron presented it with great tact. He again concealed his source, now transferring the location from Palestine to Parthia. His leading character, torn between his love and his horror over it is a most dramatic creation, while his father, his sister, and even his confidant are well characterized. The play has effective situations and contains a bold warning to Louis XIV in regard to his prolonged military adventures. This tragedy was followed by *Aëtius*, which, though played fifteen times, was never published, and by *Pompeïa*, a tragedy on the theme that Caesar's wife must be above suspicion, which was never acted and has survived only in a form that is not thoroughly authentic. Campistron also began work on *Juba*, of which only two lines remain.

He imitated to a certain extent Corneille, Racine, and other dramatists, but not enough for one to say that he lacked originality. Some of his tragedies are heroic and patriotic; others, psychological and pathetic. *Alcibiade* combines the two kinds. A number of his characters are very well drawn. He depicts both victims and those who are responsible for their own undoing. He learned quickly classical rules and the art of exposition, preparation, and suspense. He was bold in his choice of subjects and in their presentation. While his second and third acts are apt to be more effective than his fourth, he is often able to hold our attention to the end. His weakness is in his style, which lacks the vigor and power of evocation to which Racine had accustomed his public. *Andronic, Tiridate,* and parts of *Arminius* and *Alcibiade* are, however, highly estimable. They show that classical French tragedy deserved to be written after Racine had abandoned it.

The best work of La Grange-Chancel was done in the eighteenth century. It is unfair to judge him by *Adherbal*, composed when he was thirteen, or even by the three tragedies that followed it in 1697-9. These three, however, possess some merit. In *Oreste et Pilade* he attempted the difficult subject of *Iphigeneia among the Taurians* and created several dramatic scenes, especially in Acts III and IV. While his play lacked the simplicity of its source and ended in an unsatisfactory manner, it showed considerable improvement in structure and style over his earlier play and supplied la Champmeslé with what was probably her last rôle. *Méléagre* was marred by its author's unwillingness to follow Ovid in making the mother guilty of her son's death. It is inferior both to *Oreste et Pilade* and to *Athénaïs*, which owes much to La Calprenède's *Faramond*, but is closer to ordinary life than La Grange's earlier productions. The study of moral problems in *Athénaïs* is quite detailed. While it lacks startling effects, it has various changes of fortune in the last act. There is, however, a certain smugness about the triumph of the mild and sensible emperor over his passionate Persian rival that interferes with its tragic effectiveness.

These plays should be judged chiefly as preparation for those that were to follow in the eighteenth century, especially *Amasis* and *Ino et Mélicerte,* which show at its best the skill with which La Grange-Chancel could keep his audience in suspense and create harrowing situations. He had the soul of a romantic dramatist, but he lived over a century too soon to acquire a suitable vocabulary for his imaginings.

Antoine de La Fosse, who was much slower in devoting his talents to drama, was more sober in his methods. While La Grange-Chancel began at thirteen, La Fosse brought out his first play in 1696, when he was forty-three. This was *Polixène*, a tragedy of love that is at variance with ties of blood and nationality. Though it is somewhat difficult to accept the data on which the work is based, or to consider the dénouement inevitable, it must be admitted that the author worked with great care, that his action progresses steadily, and that each act possesses at least two striking scenes.

This tragedy was followed by his masterpiece, *Manlius Capitolinus,* the first French tragedy that is based on an English play, Otway's *Venice Preserved.* La Fosse also utilized, as Otway had done, a *nouvelle* of Saint-Réal and, like Campistron, concealed his subject. As he transferred the location of his intrigue from modern Venice to ancient Rome, he borrowed from Livy certain necessary information. The sources of the play are consequently English, French, and Latin. It is the tragedy of Servilius, led by his wife to betray his friends and to cause the latter's conspiracy to fail. At its center is the moral struggle in the heart of Servilius, influenced now by the affection and gratitude he feels for Manlius and his loyalty to the group of conspirators he has joined, now by his love for his wife and his humanitarian objections to slaughter. Manlius is an interesting character, an ex-hero, restive under a dictatorship and seeking popular support for a change of government. In Valerius is portrayed a somewhat heartless aristocrat; in Rutile, an equally callous revolutionist. While the play is less picturesque than Otway's and less striking in its style, it has a more convincing ending. Like the English play, it illustrates the part played by personalities in national affairs and the pathetic results of political discord. It won great success and was acted at the Comédie Française until 1849.

The last of La Fosse's three seventeenth-century tragedies was *Thésée,* a tragedy of intrigue in which, after a large amount of information has been given, the action increases in rapidity to a thrilling fifth act, but, while the structure shows considerable skill, the interest shifts from one character to another and none of them makes a sufficiently vivid impression. In short, La Fosse's contributions were limited to one quite remarkable tragedy and to two which were composed with much ingenuity, but could not retain the interest of their audiences after they had ceased to be novelties.

From this review of tragedy in the time of Racine one can understand why he remained, with Corneille, the chief model for the eighteenth century. Boyer and Thomas Corneille were prolific enough, but they wrote plays of small importance after 1680, while Quinault's last tragedy was first brought out in 1670 or 1671. Of the younger writers Pradon, Campistron, and La Grange-Chancel alone wrote more than a few tragedies and only four composed by the last of these appeared before the end of 1700. Their contemporaries seemed to regard tragedy as a temporary diversion.

Novelty in the choice of subject-matter was seldom well received. Attempts to employ national history failed. The only successful play derived from English history was Thomas Corneille's *Essex*. Campistron and La Fosse disguised modern subjects in order to give them a Byzantine or a Roman setting. Racine desired that his biblical plays should not be acted at the Comédie Française and the three by his contemporaries that were acted there did not long remain in the repertory. The preference remained for ancient history and mythology. Classical technique was generally accepted. The choral and spectacular elements found in *Athalie* were not imitated on the popular stage. Children were introduced into *Régulus* and into Longepierre's *Médée*, but not into other tragedies that were publicly acted. Whether this unwillingness to experiment was due to the dramatists or to the actors at Paris, where, after August, 1680, there was only one troupe that acted tragedies, the result was that the new plays did not offer enough novelty to challenge the leadership of Corneille and Racine. However, a number of tragedies were produced that had an honorable history. Eleven written after 1670 by other authors than Racine were acted from 95 to 316 times at the Comédie Française. Of these *Ariane, Essex, Manlius,* and *Andronic* were the most frequently played. With these four I would put *Tiridate* and *Géta* as the best evidence that minor tragic dramatists are also worthy of our consideration.

CHAPTER X

MOLIÈRE

Molière's early years in the center of Paris and his venture with the Béjarts in the Illustre Théâtre gave him knowledge of metropolitan life, experience as an actor, and intimate acquaintance with French dramatic production and the needs of a troupe. His failure sent him to the provinces, introduced him to rural and village life, gave him additional experience in acting and in a troupe's business, and impressed upon him the need for fresh texts, which must have been difficult to secure outside of the capital.

It has often been asked why a man who was so productive between the ages of thirty-seven and fifty-one should have brought out his first play when he was thirty-three, but the fact is not surprising if one realizes that in the first half of the century it was most unusual for an actor to write a play and that the only prominent actor, among Molière's older contemporaries, who did so, Montfleury, merely made for his troupe an adaptation in verse of a prose play by La Serre. The remarkable thing is that Molière should have written at all. It is to his credit that he should have conceived the idea of writing plays while he was busy with acting and with managing his company. His residence at Lyons probably gave him more leisure than if he had been still paying only brief visits to provincial towns, while its many contacts with Italy may explain why he began his literary career by turning into French two Italian plays. If he also wrote short farces, they may have been inspired by the *commedia dell'arte*, as well as by provincial survivals of the Old French farce.

L'Etourdi combines farce with the methods of Italian literary comedy. It contains a series of farcical scenes, some of them requiring physical dexterity, minimizes women, and makes use of stock characters. Molière wrote for himself the long and brilliant rôle of Mascarille. The introduction of French as spoken by a German Swiss may have been suggested by Teutonic visitors he had encountered at Lyons. The play is now valuable chiefly for its style and for the evidence it gives that Molière was already fully consicous of his own histrionic powers. *Le Dépit amoureux* suffers from its complicated and unreal plot, but it shows a more equitable distribution of speeches among the characters, a steadier progress in the intrigue, and more ample participation allowed to women. Especially praiseworthy are the graceful scenes of the lovers' quarrels, finer in quality than the rest of the play or than any part of *l'Etourdi*.

It was not till he returned to Paris that he produced a masterpiece. Taking suggestions from Chappuzeau and Scarron and bearing in mind the talents of his troupe, he wrote *les Précieuses ridicules*, with its satire upon provincial imitation of an affectation that had been prevalent at the capital early in the century and had waned enough to enable Molière to attract most appreciative audiences. The plot is well constructed, the fun increasing as it progresses. Molière again took the rôle of Mascarille, wearing a mask and representing a valet who poses as a *bel esprit*, while Jodelet, the veteran of the farce who had recently joined him, appears as another valet, but pretends to be a veteran of military and courtly life. Madeleine Béjart and Catherine de Brie played the two *précieuses*, eager to make an impression in fashionable and literary Parisian circles, and contrasting with conservative, materialistic, and inelegant old Gorgibus and the maid who cares nothing for *le Grand Cyrus*, or for speech that is other than " chrétien." The play combines the traditions both of the farce and of the comedy of manners. In the simplicity of the plot it marked a revolt against comedies written under Spanish influence and a return to the example set by Desmaretz.

It was this play that enabled Molière to enter into serious competition with the actors of the Hôtel de Bourgogne, to whom he made a slurring allusion in his text. Somaize retorted by criticizing Molière and by attempting to publish his play, thus causing him to bring it out himself in January, 1660, an event that marks the beginning of Molière in book form and must have had much to do with establishing the custom of publishing one-act plays.

Sganarelle is inferior to *les Précieuses* in theme, plot, and characters. It belongs rather to the tradition of Scarron. The title-rôle, that of an uncouth, cowardly, and jealous husband, is, however, closer to reality than that of Mascarille. Molière played it without a mask. He next produced *Don Garcie*, read before the end of 1659, according to Somaize. It was, like *l'Etourdi* and *le Dépit*, an adaptation of an Italian play. It must have suffered from the fact that the great stress laid on jealousy was more to be expected in a comedy or farce than in a tragi-comedy, or, as Molière's editors called it, a " comédie héroïque." Its failure made Molière avoid this hybrid *genre* thereafter, but he did not give up the play altogether, for lines from it reappeared in *le Misanthrope* and *Amphitryon*.

The contrast between the failure of this play and the success of *Sganarelle* may have suggested to Molière that it would be advisable to put the leading character of the latter into another play, which, if in three acts, would give better opportunity for characterizing him. It is possible that his attention was called to Mendoza's *El Marido hace mujer* by the fact that Scarron, who left a dramatic fragment derived from this Spanish play, had attempted to turn it into French. With this play as his main source, but with considerable suggestions from Dorimond's *Femme industrieuse*, or Boccaccio's tale that he had dramatized, and with a few borrowings from Terence and others, Molière constructed *l'Ecole des maris*. Sganarelle is as crude as ever and as easy to deceive, but he is more insolent, more opinionated, and no longer cowardly. His conservativism shows itself especially in his views on costume and on women. If Molière had been writing a thesis play, he would have made him less unattractive and his adversaries less clever. The work is primarily a bright comedy of intrigue, with references to manners. It suggests ideas about the freedom women should be allowed when they select their husbands, ideas that are quite opposed to those suggested by *les Précieuses ridicules*.

Before continuing in the vein of *l'Ecole des maris*, Molière composed for the famous entertainment offered Louis XIV at Vaux by Fouquet a *comédie-ballet*, the first of its kind, though approaches to it had been made by French authors. Like *l'Etourdi*, it is a *pièce à tiroir*. It puts on the stage a series of bores, among whom stand out a pedant who wishes to be given the management of street-signs, a projector, and a hunter, this last a rôle that Louis XIV probably suggested. There are interesting references to dueling, card-playing, and to a young nobleman who makes himself a bore by his behavior on the stage. Molière had evidently grown bolder than he had been when he wrote *les Précieuses*, the absurd nobles of which are only disguised valets. The special novelty of *les Fâcheux* lies in the fact that each act ends in a ballet that fits well into the action.

After this interlude, he returned to the kind of subject treated in *l'Ecole des maris* and composed his first comedy of character, *l'Ecole des femmes*. He examined a tale that Scarron had derived from María de Zayas, discarded much of it, referred to certain incidents of the story as taking place before the action began, and had others occur during its progress, but behind the scenes. He emphasized the characters rather than the events. Many incidents that are not comic in María de Zayas or Scarron are made so in Molière's play by the fact that they are narrated by or to a certain person. In this way he rendered much the same service to classical comedy that Corneille, in *Horace*, had rendered to classical tragedy over thirty years before.

Arnolphe is not farcical like Sganarelle, but a prosperous and at times generous bourgeois, whose character is warped by his obstinacy and by his belief that woman is man's possession. Though he seems to have most of the cards in his hand, he is beaten by the girl he has tried to bring up in ignorance and by her rather simpleminded admirer. He suffers in his pride as a man and as an educator, but Molière is careful to see to it that the rôle never becomes tragic. The various mental stages through which Arnolphe passes are cleverly underscored by monologues. Agnès, too, has lines that contain considerable pathos, but she makes such rapid progress under the influence of love that we never doubt that a happy future awaits her. Horace by his naïveté, the servants by their stupidity, Chrysalde by his cynical comments serve to bring out Arnolphe's character and the comic failure of his plans. Only in the events related in the last hundred lines of the play, the fact that everything takes place in the street, and the lack of explanation for Arnolphe's frequent encounters with Horace do traces of intrigue comedy persist. This is the first five-act play in which Molière abandoned the comedy of intrigue that had flourished in his hands and in those of other Frenchmen under Spanish and Italian influence.

The quarrel over the play is almost as famous as that over *le Cid,* from which it differs by the fact that most of it is expressed in dramatic form— a happy circumstance to which we owe two of Molière's plays. His chief opponents were de Visé, Boursault, and Montfleury, son of the actor. They expressed the thoughts of jealous dramatists, of actors at the Hôtel de Bourgogne, of pious souls who were shocked by passages that bordered on indecency or seemed to satirize religion, of spectators who loved intrigue comedy with characters altogether good or evil. Molière was accused, not only of immorality, disrespect for religion, and destroying "la belle comédie," but of plagiarism, triviality, of attacking marquises, of being a pupil of Italian actors. The leading characters in *l'Ecole des femmes* were held to be unreal; Chrysalde and the notary, superfluous. The dénouement was found unsatisfactory and the charge was made that everything takes place in the street.

Molière's defense is contained in *la Critique de l'Ecole des femmes* and *l'Impromptu de Versailles.* Literary criticism had appeared in earlier French plays, but no play that we know to have been acted had been devoted to it almost entirely. Molière introduced a method of defense that consists of dividing his cast into two groups: the intelligent, who praise *l'Ecole des femmes,* and a disgruntled dramatist, a *précieuse,* and an empty-headed marquis who attack it. He not only introduced arguments against most of the criticisms made of his play, but he expressed the belief that comedy is more diffcult to write than tragedy, showed his respect for court opinion, indicated an independent attitude towards formal rules, and declared that the greatest of all rules is to please. He nowhere claimed that he had aimed to liberate women. His purpose was to " rendre agréablement sur le théâtre les défauts de tout le monde."

In the *Impromptu* he showed himself working with his troupe, giving some of his comrades excellent advice, holding Boursault up to scorn, and burlesquing the acting of Montfleury and other players of the Hôtel. Both this play and the *Critique* were criticized as well as *l'Ecole des femmes.*

Corneille, as the leading author of tragedies, was exalted, while Molière was accused of snobbery, of self-praise, of making personal attacks, and of being interested in cuckolds because he was one of the tribe.

The court sided, however, with Molière, the public favored his comedies, he was praised in a play by Chevalier, an actor of the Marais, and in a dialogue of 1664 by La Croix, which ended the controversy so far as *l'Ecole des femmes* was concerned. Apart from the personalities involved, the quarrel marked Molière's effort to establish comedy on an equality with tragedy and to replace intrigue by character. In these respects he was largely successful, as the subsequent history of comedy shows, but he never made peace with the actors of the Hôtel. The two troupes remained hostile throughout his lifetime and for several years after his death.

Far from being discouraged by this experience, Molière now entered upon the most productive years of his life, 1664-66. *Le Mariage forcé,* his second *comédie-ballet,* has a better organized plot than the first and a protagonist, Sganarelle, who resembles his earlier namesakes. Adultery had been feared without cause in *le Cocu imaginaire* and jests had been made about it in *l'Ecole des femmes*. In *le Mariage forcé* it will certainly be the lot of Sganarelle, obliged to marry clever and unscrupulous Dorimène, whose father and brother insist upon getting her off their hands. This theme might have lent itself to serious treatment, but Molière preserved throughout the tone of the farce, allowed the spectators no sympathy for his protagonist, and enlivened the whole by varying his scenes and by the use of ballet entries in which Louis XIV himself took part. Those who have so little appreciation of comedy that they find tragic elements in *George Dandin* will do well to learn from *le Mariage forcé* how humorously Molière could handle a similar theme.

He was invited to compose plays that might be intercalated into the festival called *les Plaisirs de l'Ile enchantée* that was given at Versailles in May, 1664. Both *les Fâcheux* and *le Mariage forcé, comédies-ballets,* formed part of the entertainment, as did a comedy that Molière wrote especially for it, *la Princesse d'Elide*. As the festival was given in honor of Louis's Spanish queen, Molière selected for adaptation a play by Moreto, but he was too greatly pressed for time to write in verse much more than one of his five acts. The portion in verse and the dénouement owe little to Moreto, but the prose in which the bulk of the play is written owes him much. The theme that love is inspired or cultivated chiefly by indifference is made comic mainly through the introduction of a court fool who takes a prominent part in the *intermèdes*. The characterization is superficial. The play was well adapted to outdoor performance at Versailles, but little else can be said in its praise. Written to honor the queen, it was not intended, as some have supposed, to excuse the king's love for Louise de La Vallière. Molière probably did not take the work very seriously, for he was occupied with more important matters.

He had already begun to work on *Tartuffe* and had gone far enough to have the first three acts played as part of this Versailles entertainment. He subsequently altered these three acts considerably, but, though their original form is not accurately known, it is clear that they contained enough satire of the *dévots* to frighten the Compagnie du Saint-Sacrement, an organization that had enough influence with the queen-mother to prevent further performances of the play, with the exception of one on Aug. 5, 1667, until Feb. 5, 1669, when Anne of Austria was dead and the play was allowed to begin its first long run. The dramatist's purpose was not to attack religion, or even hypocrisy, but to write a comedy in which the central character, Orgon, is misled by religiosity as Arnolphe is by his masculine egotism, with the result that he allows himself to be utterly deceived by a hypocrite. The latter brings disorder into Orgon's home, causes his son to be ordered out of it, seeks to prevent his daughter's marriage, attempts to seduce his wife, and, when he fails in the latter undertaking, threatens to take possession of the house. Orgon is backed by his mother, even more obstinately credulous than he. His undertakings are opposed by his wife, his children, his brother-in-law, and a clever and devoted *suivante*. They succeed in restoring family unity by unmasking the villain, but only the king's interposition can finally dispose of the impostor.

In no previous play had Molière shown so many interesting characters. Orgon, Tartuffe, Elmire, Dorine, and Mme Pernelle are admirably presented, while the young lovers and the outbreaking son produce interesting scenes and Cléante served to protect Molière against his critics. He gives an excellent picture of a seventeenth-century household and makes other references to manners. While the structure can be criticized for admitting characters not essential to the plot and for the king's unprepared intervention, it is admirable in its animated exposition, careful preparation, and excellent use of suspense. The scenes are varied and there are highly comic situations, especially in Acts III and IV. Molière skillfully prevented the play from becoming a *drame* by such devices as the concealment of Damis in a closet or of Orgon under a table. He brought it closer to life than any of his previous plays. Its comic qualities, its solid structure, its excellent rôles, its quotable lines, and its ending in the triumph of the family made it the most popular of all French plays if we may judge by the number of times it was acted at the Comédie Française.

As this triumph was far from apparent in 1665, Molière was obliged to compose a five-act play to replace *Tartuffe*. He selected a familiar theme, that of Don Juan, which had already tempted Spanish, Italian, and French dramatists. The haste with which he composed his own *Don Juan* is shown by the fact that he wrote in prose and that the last three acts, though they contain admirable scenes, read like a collection of *morceaux choisis*. A number of scenes give evidence of hasty composition and no unity is achieved except that all parts of the play are related to the presentation of the central character. However, the comedy has many fine qualities: the portrayal of the protagonist, a seducer, slayer, and atheist, constantly in search of new sensations; the celebrated peasant scenes of the second act, the only one that seems quite finished; the presentation of bourgeois Dimanche, thrifty and obsequious; and the observations of humorous, cowardly, and orthodox Sganarelle, constantly contrasting with his master and commenting comically upon his views and deeds. Nobility, bourgeois, and peasants appear. There are references to costume, meals, and the monastic system. The supernatural element, reduced to a minimum, adds a touch of spectacle and is given a comic flavor by the valet's reaction to his master's death. Such merits did not protect the play from attacks by the devout, shocked by Don Juan's atheistic remarks, his scene with the pauper, and the fact that the principal defender of orthodoxy is Sganarelle. Though the play had been quite successful, Molière withdrew it and refrained from publishing it. Except in a milder form, provided by Thomas Corneille, it was not acted again at Paris till the middle of the nineteenth century.

Instead of writing other plays to which the pious might object, Molière now turned to medicine, already mentioned incidentally in *Don Juan*, for to be "impie en médecine" was safe enough. *L'Amour médecin* of 1665 and *le Médecin malgré lui* of 1666, each in three acts, drew their comic material primarily from that subject. The first is a *comédie-ballet*, highly farcical in tone, that introduces four physicians, two of whom have special mannerisms in speech, while all are mercenary, obstinate, and guided by authority rather than by observation. Sganarelle, now the head of a family, represents the respectful public, while the maid is delightfully incredulous. M. Josse, a goldsmith, has given his name to those who are primarily influenced by what is to their professional advantage. The lovers illustrate the comic triumph of their feeling for each other over pedants and their dupes.

Le Médecin malgré lui introduces no physicans, but shows how a man may become one in the eyes of the unwary public, if he uses unfamiliar terms and wears the proper costume. Sganarelle, who had once served a physician, but has become a chopper of wood, has the selfish materialism of his namesakes, but is clever both in his speech and in his adaptability. He accepts the profession that a quarrel with his wife has caused to be thrust upon him, diagnoses with brilliant nonsense, deceives peasants who come to him for treatment, and finally, when he learns that his patient is neither ill nor mute, helps in her elopement. It is chiefly this character and gullible Géronte, the mingling of comic effects derived from character, manners, and gestures, and the inexhaustible flow of wit that made this play, despite the carelessness of the structure and the improbability of the situations, second only to *Tartuffe* in number of performances at the Comédie Française.

Meanwhile Molière had been at work on a play that is usually held to be his masterpiece, *le Misanthrope.* He seems to have desired to compose a comedy that would enable him to utilize verses he had written for *Don Garcie.* He wrote the first act of it in 1664 and may have finished the whole by the end of the following year, but it was not presented to the public till June, 1666. It is a comedy of *la société mondaine,* represented by a coquette, a prude, a sincere woman, a would-be poet, two young fops, a compromiser, and Alceste. The latter was intended to be a comic figure, one whose love of truth would act somewhat as did Orgon's love of religion, but the author, like the women of his play, became so deeply interested in him that we all champion his cause and many of us overlook his comic characteristics. The case is comparable to Shakespeare's presentation of Shylock.

Here there is no question of life and death, as in *The Merchant of Venice,* nor, since Célimène is a widow and the other characters are unmarried, of danger to a family, as in *Tartuffe.* Molière represented an elegant and symbolic salon, where men and women talk of love in its various aspects, describe many social types, dabble in poetry, boast of their attainments, discuss their chances of winning law-suits, bring out the difficulties encountered by a man unwilling to accept society's compromises. The play is rendered comic by the contrast between Alceste and the company that surrounds him, by the wit and poise of Célimène, by the hypocrisy of Arsinoé, by the scene of the sonnet with Alceste's recitation of a folk-song, by the infatuation of the young nobles with their own charms, by the humorous comment on society that runs throughout the play, and by a farcical situation introduced to keep the dialogue from seeming too serious. The material is excellently distributed. There is little plot, but enough to involve the characters in difficulties from which they are finally freed, so that the play practically ends where it begins. The brilliant style, the clever repartee, the striking characters, the glitter of the costumes, and the unity of the tone brought the play success from the first, if we take into consideration the fact that it began its career in the summer season. It was Molière's greatest and most complete example of high comedy.

He showed his versatility by bringing out shortly afterwards *le Médecin malgré lui* and by composing three brief additions to the *Ballet des Muses,* presented at Saint-Germain-en-Laye in December, 1666, and the first two months of 1667. The first of these was *Mélicerte,* derived from *le Grand Cyrus* and containing only two acts, apparently because Molière did not have time to complete it. It is a conventional and somewhat insipid pastoral, to which a touch of comedy is added by the rôle of Lycarsis, probably played by Molière. The second production, which has survived only in a libretto, was probably written chiefly to introduce singing and dancing. The third, more important than the others, is *le Sicilien,* a farcical *comédie-ballet,* with a jealous protagonist, outwitted by young lovers. The use of *lingua franca,* of fanciful scenes, of music, dancing, and rhythmic prose adapted it well for introduction into a spectacular ballet.

These pieces, while suitable to the entertainment for which they were written, added little to Molière's reputation, but this cannot be said of *Amphitryon,* which ranks high among Molière's comedies. The *Ballet des Muses* may have made him think of writing for his own theater a " machine " play, but he did not at the time have a large enough stage to rival the elaborate performances given at the Marais. Rotrou's adaptation of *Amphitruo* had given rise to a work of this sort called *la Naissance d'Hercule.* There was no reason why Rotrou's comedy should not be similarly used again. Molière imitated both Rotrou and Plautus and introduced " machines " into the prologue and the third and last act. He selected what the seventeenth century called " vers libres " as the form in which he was to present his fanciful theme, a form that Corneille had recently employed for *Agésilas* and which they were both to use in a later " machine " play, *Psyché.* He wrote verses of 12, 10, 8, and 7 syllables, two more kinds than are found in *Agésilas,* and adapted them to the tone of the passages in which they occur. The charming lightness with which they are composed should, without other evidence, have convinced readers that no such serious purpose as defending the moral of Louis XIV was intended.

The play is a delightful fantasy in three acts, varied in form and in spectacle, concerned with the affairs of a divine and urbane philanderer, a baffled husband who has tact enough to remain silent at the end of the play, a virtuous heroine, an immortal messenger and bully, and a comic pair of servants, who contrast with their aristocratic employers and give the play much of its humor. The comic effect is heightened by the playful anachronisms and the irreverent treatment of mythology. It became the most frequently acted of all " machine " plays and made a distinct addition to the many varieties of comedy that Molière produced.

A few months after this play appeared, Molière was again serving the court, for which he wrote *George Dandin*, a *comédie-ballet* with music by Lully. For the three acts he employed a tale found in many works, including a *novella* of Boccaccio and *la Jalousie du Barbouillé*, long attributed to Molière, but probably another author's imitation of *George Dandin*. The subject is a mésalliance, produced by the marriage of a wealthy peasant to the daughter of proud and impecunious arisotcrats. Dandin, who cares nothing for his wife and has married her in order to better his condition, is made the butt of jests, is tortured by his jealousy of the young noble who courts his wife, and is treated with contempt by the latter's parents. In Act I he is forced to apologize to the lover; in Act II he is told that he ought to thank his wife for her fidelity; in Act III he is tricked into a false position and obliged to kneel and beg his wife's pardon for harboring suspicions of her virtue that are only too well founded. His floundering deeper and deeper into the morass is emphasized by monologues that recall a similar usage in *l'Etourdi*.

Dandin, his fossilized parents-in-law, his wife, her lover, and the peasants are excellently portrayed. The play is well constructed and mingles a penetrating study of manners with elements of farce. To find the leading character "douloureux" as Michelet did, one has to have little sense of humor to start with, to read the play superficially, and to forget that it was accompanied by a ballet and composed in the seventeenth century for a courtly entertainment.

Molière's next play, first acted in his own theater, was *l'Avare,* derived in the main from Boisrobert's *Belle Plaideuse,* but with farcical additions from Plautus's *Aulularia* and suggestions from Chappuzeau's *Dame d'intrigue* and other plays. The failure to fuse completely elements from various sources and the use of prose may be explained, as in the case of *Don Juan* and much of *la Princesse d'Elide,* by the author's desire to hasten the completion of the play. Though *l'Avare* has greater unity than *Don Juan,* the principal unifying agent is again the protagonist's character. Harpagon is a prosperous bourgeois, dominated by avarice, spiritually starved in the midst of plenty, a solitary figure, but presented too comically to become tragic. His penuriousness has made of his son a spendthrift, of his daughter a girl whose impertinence was more striking in the seventeenth century than it is today. Next to Harpagon the leading character is Frosine, a matrimonial agent who makes her way by flattery, specious arguments, and clever intriguing. Maître Jacques with his double personality of coachman and butler, the valet La Flèche, and other servants add to the comic interest. There are many references to manners, extremely comic scenes such as those between Harpagon and his son, or Harpagon and Frosine, and farcical scenes such as the one occasioned by the loss of the *cassette.* The first act is marred by the tedious opening scenes; the last act, by the weakness of the dénouement; but the other acts are among Molière's most highly comic achievements.

In the three and a half years that followed, Molière brought out only *comédies-ballets* and a " machine " play. The first of the former is *Monsieur de Pourceaugnac*, in three acts and in prose. It introduces satire of provincials, physicians, and lawyers into a farcical plot, concerned with the breaking of a projected marriage. Pourceaugnac, a native of Limoges, is badgered by the girl he hopes to marry, her lover, a professional intriguer, and persons who assist them. Especially amusing are the scene of diagnosis, the scene of Pourceaugnac's appeal to the law, and the scene in which a supposed Languedocienne and a supposed Picarde, while speaking their patois, try to foist on him children they claim he has fathered.

This play is greatly superior to *les Amants magnifiques*, the subject of which was selected by Louis XIV. It was written, like *la Princesse d'Elide*, for performance at court and makes some use of " machines." The comic element is largely confined to comments on astrology and to the rôle of Clitidas, played by Molière. Its inferiority may be explained by the king's special interference rather than by the fact that it was a *comédie-ballet* written for the court, since this is true also of Molière's next play, which is one of his greatest.

Le Bourgeois Gentilhomme combines in most amusing fashion a comedy of character with a burlesque upon Turkish manners. For the latter Molière was advised by d'Arvieux, who had lived in the Near East, while the music of the play was composed by Lully. Monsieur Jourdain, the immortal parvenu; his excellent wife, who has no use for her husband's social ambitions; Dorante, a clever and tricky aristocrat; Cléonte, an admirable young bourgeois; charming Lucile, a rôle probably written for Molière's wife; and merry Nicole, one taken by la Beauval, about to begin her long and distinguished career at Paris—these characters could have been given scenes that would have made an excellent comedy of character. As Molière was, however, writing a *comédie-ballet*, he provided scenes that would occasion ballet entries and altered his tone to match, so that passages illuminated by deeply comic observations alternate with farce. Such contrasts and the careless structure might have injured the play, if it had been composed by a lesser dramatist, but in Molière's hands the work became, not a comedy of character degenerating into farce, but a *comédie-ballet* that entertains us, not only with music, dancing, and a burlesque ceremony, but with excellently drawn characters and a delightful dialogue.

Psyché is altogether a " machine " play, but not altogether Molière's. He devised the plot and the spectacular features. He composed the prologue and the first scenes of Acts I, II, III. The rest of the work was written by Corneille, with the exception of the songs, the work of Quinault. The play contains several charming passages, but is chiefly noted for the spectacle it presented and for the use of the verse form employed in *Amphitryon*.

In the two years that remained to Molière he produced plays that recall his earlier tastes. *Les Fourberies de Scapin*, partially derived from Terence, but with suggestions from French plays, emphasizes the valet as in *l'Etourdi* and pays as little attention to verisimilitude. Amusing situations are found in each of the three acts, but there are no genuine studies of character and few striking phrases other than " Que diable allait-il faire dans cette galère? " borrowed from Cyrano. However limited Boileau may have been in insisting that Molière should have refrained from writing farces and however uncritical his opinion of Terence, it must, indeed, have been hard for him to recognize in Scapin's sack the author of *le Misanthrope*.

La Comtesse d'Escarbagnas formed part of the *Ballet des ballets*, which included portions of other plays by Molière. It was written primarily to introduce ballet entries, but Molière succeeded in making of it a comedy of provincial manners. In so doing he probably drew upon his memory of earlier wanderings. The chief character is a pretentious countess, probably of humble origin, who is courted by a rough tax-collector and a mild lawyer. She has selected an obsequious tutor to instruct her son and she amuses the hero and heroine by her social mistakes. If we consider the brevity of the play, the study of rustic manners is remarkably large and makes us regret that Molière did not pay more attention to this rich source of comic material. A reference to the press is novel, but tantalizingly brief.

In the last years of his life Molière seems to have had in mind the composition of another comedy in five acts and in verse that would not be a *comédie-ballet* or a " machine " play. He realized this project by the production in March, 1672, of *les Femmes savantes*. While it echoes to a certain extent *les Précieuses ridicules*, it has more fully developed characters and a broader study of feminine affectations. It gives no evidence of hasty composition and produces a greater effect of harmony than his earlier five-act plays, with the possible exeception of *le Misanthrope*. If the unity is that of character and ideas, rather than of plot, it is because Molière deliberately accepted this form of structure.

There is no character so striking as Alceste or Tartuffe, but there are many of great interest: the henpecked husband; his dominating wife, who has the courage to live according to her principles, such as they are; her elder daughter, who poses as shunning matrimony, but who is jealous of her sister; the latter's aunt, a *précieuse* grown old and ridiculous; Henriette, whose good sense does not destroy her charm; her lover, Clitandre, a manly young nobleman, quite able to cope with his prospective mother-in-law; the pet poet, Trissotin; his blundering and learned colleague, Vadius; and the outspoken maid. The characters are divided sharply into two camps, opposed almost to the end of the play.

Molière depicts, as in *Tartuffe* and *l'Avare*, a seventeenth-century household and echoes various ideas of the day: the interest in science and philosophy that was beginning to enter salons, monastic views about matrimony, the effort of literary men to seek patronage from prosperous women, the struggle of feminists and the resistance it was encountering. The comic element comes primarily from the contrast between reality and the aims of the *savantes*. One may suppose that Molière sympathized with the views expressed by Clitandre rather than with the aspirations of Philaminte or the anti-literary opinions of Chrysale and Martine, but he was not writing a thesis play. He was composing a delightful comedy that drew its effects from a sharp conflict between would-be reformers and those who realized how disastrous they would find the consequences of their reforms.

A few days before his death Molière produced *le Malade imaginaire*, as if he defied the illness that was to take him off after its fourth performance. It is, like *le Bourgeois Gentilhomme*, a *comédie-ballet*, with large elements of a comedy of character. In earlier plays he had laughed at physicians, real or pretended. He now put them on the stage again, but he selected for his principal character a patient, one who today would be sent to a psychiatric clinic, but whose malady in Molière's time was a subject for laughter.[1] He is thrifty and at times shrewd, with some affection for his daughters, but his monomania has bred in him an absurd reverence for physicians, so that he insists on marrying his elder daughter to one of them and finally seeks to become one himself. His intriguing second wife and the physicians take advantage of his peculiarities, while the maid, Toinette, a younger and more violent Dorine, supports the lovers. Physicians are more amply treated than in earlier plays. The most memorable of them is the young pedant, Thomas Diafoirus, who seeks instruction from his father even when he is courting the heroine. Louison is the most admirable child that appeared on the seventeenth-century stage. The farcical element supplied by Toinette and the physicans leads us to the final *intermède*, in which Argan is initiated into the medical profession by druggists, physicians, and surgeons who sing, dance, praise the neophyte's Latin responses and wish him many years of eating, drinking, bleeding, and killing. The first victim, however, was not Argan's patient, but his creator.

More than anyone else Molière represents the spirit of comedy. He was the leader of a successful troupe that he had helped to form and that

---

[1] Cf. the title of Dufresny's *Malade sans maladie,* also called *la Malade imaginaire.*

became, when combined with its rivals, the Comédie Française, the world's most longlived company of actors. He was himself a great actor of comedies, whose eminence was admitted even by his enemies. He was the author of a large variety of celebrated comedies. Like most actor-authors of his century, he avoided the composition of tragedies, unless one considers that *Psyché*, part of which he wrote, is a tragedy. His one attempt at tragicomedy was a failure. His pastorals, written for special occasions, were not expected to live. He devoted himself almost entirely to comedy, emphasizing character or manners, writing high comedy or farce, forgetting neither music, nor dancing, nor spectacle, but concerning himself primarily with the art of dramatizing in comic fashion the errors of mankind.

It is difficult to fit Molière into any definition of classicism. Does he portray only essential human traits? Many of his characters are as living as if they were our neighbors, but others bear only the slightest resemblance to our contemporaries. Does reason dominate his imagination? Read *Amphitryon*, his *comédies-ballets*, or many farcial portions of his other productions. He had a sense of form, but he was willing to abandon regulations if they interfered with his desire to please his audience. So we find him violating the unities of time and place in *Don Juan* and *le Médecin malgré lui*; the unity of action in a number of plays, though he could keep all three when he chose to do so, as he did in *les Précieuses, Dandin,* and *l'Ecole des maris*. He often preferred to unify through character, rather than through action.

It has been held that Molière was primarily a moralist. Men have believed that he defended the family, social stratification, common sense, love of truth; others, that he argued for a belief in nature and attacked religion and morality. One can hardly defend both points of view. Let us see what can be said for either.

If he was bent on defending the family, it is remarkable that he gave only one example of a congenial married couple—Monsieur et Madame de Sotenville! The question whether a girl or her guardian should choose her mate is answered in one way in *les Précieuses*, in another in *l'Ecole des femmes*. Chrysalde's smiling support of *cocuage* did not impress Bossuet with Molière's interest in the family. If one sees in *le Bourgeois Gentilhomme* and *George Dandin* a desire to uphold aristocracy, one has only to remember Dorante and the Sotenville couple to abandon the idea. Molière boasted that he had made a comic type of the young marquis, while many of his bourgeois are sympathetically presented. To look upon him merely as a representative of common sense is to forget the fancifulness of *l'Etourdi, Amphitryon,* and *Pourceaugnac*. Nor would Alceste have approved of the deceptions practised by persons with whom we sympathize when they bring about the dénouements of *les Femmes savantes* and *le Malade imaginaire*.

The scarcity of Christian references in his plays does not argue that Molière believed in natural religion, for they would have been quite out of place in his comedies. M. Mornet [2] has recently held that his lay morality contradicted Christian and that certain of his plays show nature as good or indifferent. In support of his position he cites Agnès's asking how one can resist " ce qui fait du plaisir," the scene of the beggar in *Don Juan* and the protagonist's disdain for his humble petitioner, the imbecility of Orgon and Madame Pernelle, and the defense of Louis XIV's adultery in *Amphitryon*. But there is no more evidence that Molière was seeking to defend Louis XIV than that Plautus and Rotrou were trying to do so in plays on the same subject.[3] Orgon and his mother are, of course, ridiculous in their religiosity, but so is Alceste when he wants to tell the whole truth in social gatherings and Philaminte when she puts philosophy and literature above the concerns of her household. As we do not sympathize with Don Juan, it is not to be supposed that Molière approved of his attitude towards the beggar.[4] As for Agnès, her line is comic in showing the result of Arnolphe's educational system. To pick out a line regardless of the context and argue from it about a dramatist's general ideas is a method worthy of the Compagnie du Saint-Sacrement rather than of a twentieth-century critic. There is nothing in these examples that cannot be explained by Molière's devotion to his art.

Molière understood what many of his contemporaries and many of his critics have not understood, that one may become ridiculous by exaggerating what is good in itself and that we may laugh at a man with whom we may sympathize. He did not restrict himself to making fun of avarice, debauchery, gluttony, and the like, but included in material for comedy religion, zeal for the truth, love of learning, and love of correct expression. The fact that he thus enlarged the field of comedy does not mean that he was himself irreligious, untruthful, ignorant, or a careless writer. His plays may encourage a reader or a spectator to shun various vices, but his primary purpose, the one that gives unity to his work, was that of an artist rather than that of a moralist.[5]

Lanson exaggerated the influence of farce on Molière. That there was such influence and that it helped him break away from Spanish and Italian complications of plot cannot be denied, but the true descendant of the farce

---

[2] *Histoire de la littérature française classique*, Paris, Armand Colin, 1940, pp. 272-3.
[3] Cf. above, Part III, pp. 517-9.   [4] Cf. above, Part III, p. 642.
[5] The only case I find in which he forgets his art to express a personal bias is the speech of Filerin to his fellow physicians in *le Malade imaginaire*. In *la Critique*, *l'Impromptu*, and *les Précieuses*, when he ceased to be an artist, it was only to defend his work as a dramatist, or to attack his rivals. The speeches of Cléante in *Tartuffe* and the intervention of the king, as well as Don Juan's hypocrisy, were devised to make the production of *Tartuffe* possible. This means merely that Molière was a producer as well as an author, and it must be remembered that both professions are necessary to the life of drama.

is Poisson. If one compares him with Molière, one can see how much the latter owed to other forms of comedy. Molière wrote comedies of character, making his persons live as they had not done in earlier attempts at this form. The best examples are *l'Ecole des femmes, Tartuffe, le Misanthrope, l'Avare,* and *les Femmes savantes.* Their excellence is illustrated by the fact that, if we leave out of consideration *le Médecin malgré lui* and *les Plaideurs,* they are the five plays that were most frequently acted at the Comédie Française between 1680 and 1920. *Don Juan* would probably rank with them, if Molière had had more time to compose it and if it had not long been presented in a form for which Molière was not responsible. He also composed fanciful *comédies-ballets,* of which the best examples are *le Bourgeois Gentilhomme* and *le Malade imaginaire;* a "machine" play, *Amphitryon,* and part of another, *Psyché;* comedies of intrigue, *le Dépit* and *Scapin; pièces à tiroir, l'Etourdi* and *les Fâcheux;* comedies like *la Princesse d'Elide* and *les Amants magnifiques,* written for outdoor entertainments at court; plays in defense of his art, *la Critique* and *l'Impromptu;* farces that introduce references to manners, like *les Précieuses, Sganarelle,* and *le Médecin malgré lui.*

This variety in the types of play he favored was accompanied by greater variety in the means he employed to produce comic effects. His wit was not applied externally, but came from intimate knowledge of the persons he created. It ranged from the polished thrusts of *le Misanthrope* to the horseplay of *Scapin.* He could be imaginative, fanciful, and charming, as well as cynical and uproariously amusing. He surpassed in comedy all writers before or since his time, made it the most popular *genre* in France, and profoundly affected the dramatic production of the years that followed.

CHAPTER XI

MOLIÈRE'S RIVALS

When Molière began to write, the principal authors of comedy were Boisrobert, Quinault, and Thomas Corneille. These, as well as others who preceded Molière, but continued to write comedies after he had begun, have been discussed in Chapters V, VII, or VIII. Those who began to write in the period of Molière's productive activity, 1655-72, form the subject of the present chapter.

The earliest of them is Chappuzeau, whose life and writings show him to have been the first cosmopolitan among French dramatists. He composed two tragi-comedies, one of which is the first French play located in China, a patriotic school-play for children of Geneva, and six comedies, several of which influenced Molière. The first of these, *le Cercle des femmes*, is composed of material from five colloquies by Erasmus. The play ridicules feminism and snobbishness, retains much of the great humanist's wit, and, though loosely put together, is important in introducing, before *les Précieuses* did, studies of manners into a one-act play. In 1661 he republished this prose play in verse, changing its title to *l'Académie des femmes*, the peasant to a clever valet, and adding new references to manners, including an account of a pretended noble who misbehaves on the stage. This was followed by a pure farce, *Colin-Maillard*, derived from a folk-tale; a comedy of intrigue, *le Riche mécontent*, that presents as its leading character a parvenu tax-collector, the most ample portrait of a businessman given up to that time; another comedy of intrigue, *l'Avare duppé*, which emphasized a miser and a "femme d'intrigue," as did subsequently *l'Avare*, which owed it suggestions; and *les Eaux de Pirmont*, the first extant French play of which the scene is laid at a watering-place.

He paid much attention to manners, dwelling upon costume, food, books, genealogy, alchemy, medicine, and behavior at a resort. His chief character is his tax-collector, but his *savantes*, miser, matrimonial agent, cook (*Colin-Maillard*), and other persons are distinctly entertaining. He wrote with considerable humor and liveliness. With his knowledge of the theater, shown by his *Théâtre françois*, and his talent for comedy, he might have gone far, had he not divided his life among many countries, his literary activities among many kinds of work.

Another early rival was Lambert, whose *Magie sans magie* and *Sœurs jalouses* were probably acted at the Hôtel de Bourgogne in 1656-8. They were both comedies of intrigue, the second derived from a play by Calderon. They combine romance with comic observations and are agreeably written.

Jests about aerial transportation, the reawakening of a man's love, an early example of social protest on the part of a valet, and a reference to music are points in them that deserve notice.

Neither of these authors was an actor, but five actors began to write plays not long after Molière did, one for a provincial troupe, two for his comrades of the Hôtel de Bourgogne, two for the Marais. Dorimond, who acted during most of his life in the provinces, has left us two full-length comedies and five farces. His *Rosélie*, which recalls Scarron, but is much less amusing, has a romantic plot with comic passages relating to avarice and pedantry. His *Festin de Pierre* served as an intermediary between Italian imitators of Tirso and Molière. His other plays are much less pretentious. *L'Inconstance punie* presents a philanderer and a series of girls who punish his fickleness by abandoning him. *L'Ecole des cocus* is the first play to use *école* in a title as Molière and Sheridan were to use it; derived, like *l'Ecole des femmes*, from Scarron's *Précaution inutile*, it keeps the coarser side of the tale and introduces the conventional figures of a braggart and a pedant. These reappear in *la Femme industrieuse*, which probably passed on to Molière incidents narrated by Boccaccio. The situations in this play are cleverly arranged, there is a curious passage related to the *Carte de Tendre*, and the author's wit has a finer quality than in the two earlier farces—an improvement that is also shown in the two others, *l'Amant de sa femme* and *la Comédie de la comédie*. The first of these depicts a wife who, by wearing a mask, attracts her husband's wandering attention and finally succeeds in winning him back; the second puts on the stage an interesting account of life as seen by the doorkeeper of a theater. Dorimond's work shows the continuing popularity of farce in the provinces. His gay and amusing style, as well as his sketches of manners, compensates to a certain extent for his carelessness in dramatic structure, character-study, and details of composition.

Villiers, though he acted chiefly at Paris, had somewhat the same tastes, for he brought out both farces and a *Festin de Pierre*. The latter play resembles Dorimond's, but it is more brutal, better written, and introduces a cleverer valet. One of Villiers's farces is lost. *L'Apoticaire dévalisé* puts on the stage an irascible druggist, who has given up medicine for a humbler, but more lucrative profession. It is a racy and somewhat brutal play that satirizes both law and medicine. It contains entertaining allusions to manners and ends in spectacular fashion. *Les Ramonneurs* is more conventional except in the introduction of chimney-sweepers, whose costume and whose cries of "Haut à bas" have a definite function in the play.

Villiers was surpassed as a dramatist, and probably as an actor, by his comrade at the Hôtel, Raymond Poisson, whose first play, *Lubin ou le sot vengé,* continues the style, material, and meter of the Old French farce. The protagonist is a forlorn cuckold who is persuaded that, if he recites a magic formula while applying a certain cudgel to his wife's back, she will give up her lover and become docile. The success of this scheme, a list of children's games, and other references give the play a flavor of folk literature. Poisson's second and much more ambitious play was the celebrated *Baron de la Crasse.* The life here described is that of a château in southern France, the property of a baron who had once taken an unhappy trip to Fontainebleau and who now entertains his neighbors with a performance by a strolling troupe. Poisson describes this rustic nobleman, his guests, his untrained servants, and the troupe, which has a repertory of old plays, a leader who may well be intended to represent Molière, and gives an inner play in verses of eight syllables that combines the characteristics of Old French farce with those of the *commedia dell'arte.*

Four plays in one act followed. *Le Fou raisonnable,* which suffers from an excess of material, is to be remembered for the disguise of the hero and his valet as persons who think they are Alexander and Hephestion; for the rôle of Crispin, now, not a servant, but an amiable innkeeper; and for a passage showing how escaped criminals were denounced at Madrid. *L'Après-soupé des auberges* has so little plot that it may be called a " slice of life " as experienced by a mixed company at a Parisian inn. The guests include an affected viscountess, who gives, so far as I can tell, the first recorded evidence that uvular *r* existed at Paris; a Gascon, a Norman, and a Fleming, each of whom talks the French of his home; and an ignorant marquis, who attempts to analyze Corneille's *Othon.* The conversation of these persons is supplemented by marionettes that dance a ballet and play a farce. *Le Poète basque* shows the stage of the Hôtel before the audience arrives and introduces a number of well-known actors, an importunate and naïve Gascon, and a Basque dramatist. The latter, who converses with a friend in his native language, brags about his productions and finally gives one of them that recalls the gymnastics of Italian actors. A few months after *le Poète basque* appeared, Poisson brought out the first French play to be inspired by the visit of ambassadors. As the Russian envoys who had visited the two rival theaters failed to come to the Hôtel, Poisson supplied in their place thieves who pretend to belong to their suite. We are shown a Parisian tavern, hear the thieves prepare their intrigue, are told about the bustle in the street when the Russians arrive, and see a peddler disguised as the ambassador. A trivial plot joins together highly farcical scenes.

Poisson next attempted a five-act play, *les Femmes coquettes,* a comedy of manners satirizing women who gamble. The main character is that of the heroine, selfish and unintelligent, but able to deceive a naïve old man and for a while to get the better of her longsuffering husband. We are shown her women friends, who come to gamble with her, her servants, two card-sharpers, and a valet who disguises himself as a veteran. There are references to the amusements of idle Parisians, to war, to actors, and to localities in Paris. The plot is more carefully constructed than those of the earlier plays. It was followed by *la Holande malade,* a dull piece of political propaganda, and *les Foux divertissans,* a three-act comedy inspired by Cervantes and Beys, but largely original in both plot and form. The insane persons, their unprepossessing keeper, the young man who pretends to be mad in order to elope with the latter's fiancée, and the kindly soldier, quartered on the establishment, make up most of the cast. Opportunity is given for amusing episodes and for comment on opera. The musical entertainments that follow the acts correspond to the ballets of Molière's *comédies-ballets.* Subsequently reduced to one act by Dancourt, the comedy became, next to *le Baron de la Crasse,* the most popular of Poisson's plays.

He had a decided talent for farce. He knew the audiences for whom he had so often acted and realized what hits would be effective. He presented samples of low-class Parisian manners, those of actors, both when they were wandering through the provinces and when they were preparing to play at the Hôtel de Bourgogne, those of a minor inn at the capital, of gamblers, of an insane asylum. He was quick to make use of such recent happenings as the visit of ambassadors or the invasion of the Low Countries. He was especially interested in comic varieties of speech. His work bears a more marked imprint of his personality than that of most of Molière's rivals. He won a great reputation as an actor and left descendants who followed in his steps. Four of his nine plays, one of them in the form that Dancourt gave it, were acted in the eighteenth century. It is surprising that he has received so little attention from students of the drama.

Brécourt, who acted successively at the Marais, the Palais Royal, the Hôtel, and the Comédie Française, wrote a play or two for each theater, ten in all, of which four are lost. Of those that remain, *la Feinte Mort de Jodelet* and *la Régalle,* which is connected with gambling, are extremely slight, while *Timon,* his last work, is strangely gloomy, but may have pleased by its spectacular features. Of greater interest are the comedies inspired by Molière. The lost *Grand Benest* was probably suggested by a line in *les Fâcheux; l'Ombre de Molière* praises the great dramatist and consists largely of conversations carried on in Hades by some of his characters; while *les Apartemens,* which has survived only in an analysis of it, brought together at Versailles important characters from seven of Molière's comedies. More original is *la Nopce de village,* a purely peasant play with little plot, amusing in its portrayal of customs and its use of patois. Very different in

9

tone is the three-act *Jaloux invisible*, which draws comic effects from the portrayal of a jealous husband, from the introduction of a supposedly magic hat, and from verses that parody *le Cid* or are written in *lingua franca*. Brécourt was unable to compose satisfactorily a play of any length, but he had a considerable variety of devices for amusing an audience. None of his plays was acted after 1698.

Unlike Brécourt, Chevalier wrote only for one theater, the Marais. He produced five farces in verses of eight syllables, three comedies of intrigue, and two of manners. *La Désolation des filoux* gives a glimpse of the Parisian underworld and refers to a performance of Corneille's *Toison d'or*. *Le Soldat malgré luy* draws comic effects from military preparations. Chevalier's best work is found in *l'Intrigue des carrosses à cinq sous*, which dramatizes Pascal's invention of the omnibus in a double plot that illustrates the opportunities offered by the new conveyances for robbery and flirtation; and in *les Amours de Calotin*, which describes a scene on the stage of the Marais just before a performance is to begin. In the latter play nobles discuss Molière, Poisson, and Chevalier himself. They are joined by Arnolphe, Mascarille, and the Baron de la Crasse. The farce that constitutes the inner play ends in a ballet. Chevalier showed little ability at portraying character or constructing plots, but he knew how to draw comic material from the life about him, as he showed by his quick response to the appearance of the first Parisian omnibus, and he wrote wittily, making more use than anyone else in his century of animal comparisons, referring to various authors, books, and songs, to food, to disease, and, like Scarron, indulging in word-creation.

More prolific than any of these dramatists was the younger Montfleury, not himself an actor, but the son of one and the son-in-law of another. He composed a tragi-comedy, *Trasibule*, which, thanks to a common source in Belleforest, has some resemblance to *Hamlet*, four comedies in one act, one in three acts, and eleven in five. Seeking to rival Molière, he imitated him extensively.[1] Like him he illustrated the waning influence of Spain, to which he owes only about a fifth of his total production: two comedies and an *intermède* taken from *comedias*, and a third comedy derived from a tale by Castillo Solórzano.

The four one-act plays are a farce in which a pedant is caught by the ambiguous use of the word *rien*; another inspired by Gelli's interpretation of the Circe myth, arranged to celebrate the greatness of Louis XIV; the cleverest of the playlets that attacked Molière in the quarrel over the *Ecole des femmes*; and a defense, in the manner of *la Critique*, of his own *Femme juge*. The third of these plays introduces actors of the Hôtel under

---

[1] Cf. above, Part III, pp. 271-2.

their own stage-names and refers to plays of the day, while the fourth discusses the difference between comedy and tragedy. The longer plays are all comedies of intrigue with some references to manners and considerable use of disguise. Special emphasis is laid in them on brutal and jealous husbands, guardians, and lovers. Among other characters are peasants, a country nobleman, and a man disguised as an abbé. Montfleury introduces Teutonic French, *lingua franca*, imaginary Turkish, a parody of *Britannicus*, a lottery, recruiting, satire of medicine and law. He showed considerable constructive ability and sought to vary his form, especially in *l'Ambigu comique* and *le Comédien poète*.

The subject of the former play is the death of Dido, to which its three acts are devoted, but each act is followed by an *intermède* that has no relation to the Carthaginian queen. One of them discusses the drama of Montfleury's day; one is a farce that bears some resemblance to *Pourceaugnac*; and the third, though Spanish in origin, portrays the life of a French village. *Le Comédien poète* contains an outer play, in which an author and actors meet for a rehearsal, and two inner plays, one borrowed from Plautus, but with spectacular additions, the other a comedy of intrigue that is often farcical in tone. The whole is an interesting study of dramatic production, ending in the triumph of the actor-author over the poet who insists on imitating the ancients. It is in these two plays that Montfleury appears most original, though they were not acted so frequently as *la Fille capitaine* and *la Femme juge*, which were last performed, respectively, in 1789 and 1863. He had considerable talent for dramatic structure and some gift for characterization in a limited field, but he never drew characters of large significance or wrote a play that could seriously compete with Molière.

Boursault, who began to write not long after Montfleury, ultimately proved himself to be an abler dramatist, but this fact was not at first apparent. As he composed novels, letters, tragedies, a " machine " play, and an opera, he had less time than Montfleury for comedies, yet he managed to bring out ten of them. A farce in which a wife is rescued from a jealous husband was followed by a playlet both imitating Molière's *Critique* and replying to it, and by three mediocre comedies. He first showed that he was capable of better work by his clever attack upon Boileau, entitled *la Satire des Satires*. Though the satirist had referred to Boursault as a " froid rimeur," he was sufficiently heated by the announcement of this play to take steps that kept it from being acted.

In the fourteen years that followed Boursault abstained from comedy, but he enriched his life sufficiently to produce a play in 1683 that was far superior to its predecessors. The *Comédie sans titre* or *Mercure galant* is the first French play to discuss the business of an editor's office. We are shown thirteen separate affairs with which the editor's substitute has to deal, each giving a sketch of Parisian manners. The author derives comic material from snobs, lawyers, talkative girls, a dishonest tax-collector, a printer, a teacher, a veteran of the navy, even from French grammar. The play is a clever comedy of manners in which a love-affair acts as a frame for a great variety of comic scenes. It met with great success, holding the stage as late as 1905.

Esope is built on somewhat the same plan, consisting of scenes in which the fabulist is consulted by a series of persons, including a *précieuse*, a genealogist, children, peasants, and actors. Into the interviews are introduced fables that owe something to La Fontaine and are written with some of the latter's skill. Æsop endeavors to teach his visitors to know themselves, sympathizes with some, and condemns others. There is again an extensive study of manners, but the modern reader finds the play, despite the excellence of certain scenes, moralistic and mechanically constructed. In its own day it met with such success that the author returned to the subject early in the eighteenth century and composed *Esope à la cour*. Before doing so, he brought out *Phaëton*, written in what was known as " vers libres " and introducing considerable spectacle in its last two acts. Especially amusing are the verses assigned to Momus, held by J.-B. Raisin to be worthy of Molière. Boursault also composed *les Mots à la mode*, in one act, concerned with aspiring bourgeoises, affected in speech and costume, and their sensible relatives. The play can still be read with pleasure, though many of the words on which the jests depend have ceased to exist.

As he was attacked by both Molière and Boileau, Boursault has found little appreciation among modern critics. It is true that his early work merits little praise, but *la Satire des Satires, Esope, Phaëton,* and *les Mots à la mode* contain much that is amusing, while *la Comédie sans titre* is one of the best comedies of manners written during the century.

A word may be said of two of his early contemporaries, Somaize, a talentless author, whose attacks on Molière brought him notoriety, and La Forge, who composed a dialogue, *le Cercle des femmes sçavantes*, in praise of distinguished women from Sappho to Mme de Sévigné, and, as if he thought he was in danger of becoming a feminist, *la Joueuse dupée*, which demonstrates the unhappy effect on a family of women's gambling, shows a game in progress, and points out methods employed by cheats of both sexes.

De Visé began to write about the same time as these authors. His *Zélinde* attacked both *l'Ecole des femmes* and *la Critique*, but with little cleverness. It was followed by his more personal *Réponse à l'Impromptu de Versailles,* implications in which he had to explain. Apparently he made his peace with Molière, for the latter produced his *Mère coquette*, a comedy that marks a new departure in French comedy by presenting as rivals a mother and daughter. This play would have attained greater fame if Quinault had not written a cleverer, but less original work on the same subject and even with the same title. As if in preparation for his comedy, de Visé had probably composed *les Costeaux*, primarily a satire of impecunious guests, but containing a mother who is constantly scolding her daughter.

De Visé wrote two little plays concerned with death and birth: *la Veuve à la mode*, a comic presentation of a hypocritical widow and the customs associated with the death of an unloved husband; and *l'Embarras de Godard*, a still more amusing account of circumstances surrounding an *accouchement*. He also composed three longer comedies: the lost *Maux sans remèdes; les Intrigues de la lotterie*, in which manners connected with a lottery are portrayed; and *le Gentilhomme Guespin*, in which we meet provincial society at the home of a jealous husband and the young wife he has brought from Paris. These were followed by a pastoral, three " machine " plays of his own, and three, including *la Devineresse*, written in collaboration with Thomas Corneille. With the latter he also wrote a lost comedy of manners, *l'Usurier*. His only other play that has survived is *les Dames vangées*, acted in 1695. Some of the characters are of distinct interest: a hero who through love loses his cynical attitude towards women, an appealing heroine whose interests are sacrificed to those of her brother by their aristocratic mother, and entertaining servants. The play lacks, however, highly comic scenes, a fact that may be due in part to alterations that suppressed a part of the play and gave it an unhappy and unsatisfactory ending.

De Visé was an unequal writer, who spent much of his life as a journalist. His early antipathy to Molière was probably due to his desire to get his name before the public. When he had achieved a certain reputation, he became careless about preserving his plays by publication. He showed ability in devising elaborate spectacles, in presenting farces dealing with domestic life at Paris and in the provinces, and in characterization, so far as *la Mère coquette* and *les Dames vangées* are concerned. He produced, however, no thoroughly effective play when something more was required than spectacle, farce, and sketches of manners.

It was probably several years after de Visé began to write that Saint-Evremond composed in England *Sir Politick Would-be*, the first French play to show the influence of an English play. He is said to have been assisted by d'Aubigny and the Duke of Buckingham. They borrowed a number of details from Jonson's *Volpone*, but added much new material, especially the part of the play that is concerned with the idiosyncracies of persons when abroad. A pompous and unpractical English gentleman who dabbles in statesmanship, an obsequious French bourgeois with financial theories, their wives, a boastful French marquis, a sightseeing German, a wily Italian, and Tancrède, amused by his neighbors' follies, are the principal characters. Unfortunately Saint-Evremond was not a sufficiently gifted dramatist to make the most of his conceptions, but his study of cosmopolitan manners is of considerable interest. Besides the part he took in composing *la Comédie des Académistes*, his only other contribution to drama is *les Opéra*, composed in 1676 and expressing the author's objections to this new art. Not only the opera, but rural nobles, law, medicine, and even the church are satirized. There are references to Molière, Poisson, Cambert, and Lully, with specific criticism of various operas. If the theologian had been suppressed, the play might have succeeded at Paris, but the author made little effort to have it acted. As, like *Sir Politick*, it was not published until 1705, neither play influenced the general course of French comedy.

It was in 1668 that *les Plaideurs*, Racine's one comedy, was acted at the Hôtel de Bourgogne and at Versailles. Making use of two great humorists, Aristophanes and Rabelais, he satirized delightfully the ways of the law, putting on the stage a sleepy judge, litigants ever ready to discuss their suits, grandiloquent lawyers, and self-seeking minor officials. The farcical tone should prevent the play from being considered a serious attack upon the administration of justice, but many of Racine's satirical thrusts can still be applied. The skill with which the telling scenes are placed, the gaiety of the style, and the excellence of the verse have made this the most frequently performed of all one-act plays at the Comédie Française.

Despite the large number of plays that were being produced at Paris, provincial actors still found it desirable to write comedies for the troupes to which they belonged. One of these was Du Perche, who wrote a farce, *l'Ambassadeur d'Affrique*, that is an abbreviated transposition into French surroundings and eight-syllable verse of Boursault's *Mort vivant*, and a brief comedy of manners, *les Intrigues de la Vieille Tour*, that describes life at Rouen as it was known to a dealer in old clothes and other merchants and artisans. Nanteuil, who acted abroad as well as in the provinces, produced a large number of plays. The first three, apparently written in the Low Countries, are unpretentious farces. At the court of Celle he composed a three-act play in " vers libres " called *le Campagnard dupé* that has an allegorical prologue in honor of the Dukes of Brunswick-Luneburg; two romantic plays derived from *le Roman comique*; and his most effective production, *l'Héritier imaginaire*, a *comédie-ballet* inspired by an amusing episode in a novel by Boursault. Strangely enough, after this work, which is written with spirit, he seems to have ceased to write plays, though he was only twenty-four when it appeared.

There was another actor who began to write while playing in the provinces, Rosimond, whose *Duel fantasque* is reminiscent of Chevalier's first productions. Joining the troupe of the Marais, he composed a Don Juan play, to rival those given at the Hôtel and at the Palais Royal. In this work he imitated Molière, made his protagonist more brutal than ever, and increased the spectacular element, but he avoided language that might give rise to objections based on religious grounds. His most successful play was *l'Avocat sans étude*, in which the law is satirized and a cobbler, disguised as a lawyer, indulges in gymnastics worthy of the Théâtre Italien. *Les Trompeurs trompez* is a farce with symmetrically arranged characters, including two wives who get the better of their philandering husbands. In *la Dupe amoureuse* a rich old man is deceived by the girl he loves, his nephew, and clever servants. In *les Qui pro quo* the chief characters are two valets, one of whom is punished for his avarice and treachery, while the other lies cleverly in order to serve his master and is rewarded by the latter's favor and by the hope of winning the maid he loves. Rosimond's last play, *le Volontaire*, written apparently after he joined Molière's troupe and succeeded to many of his rôles, is chiefly remarkable for the fact that the young hero is a thief and for a passage in which law is preferred to service in the army. Rosimond's contributions to the French stage are of no great importance. He stressed situations rather than manners and made much use of servants. He is principally to be remembered as the author of a Don Juan play and of *l'Avocat sans étude,* with its lively and farcical satire of the legal profession.

Among Molière's rivals the one who came closest to the master, if we consider the number of plays composed as well as their quality, was Hauteroche, who took his profession as an author more seriously than did Poisson, was closer to reality than Montfleury, and wrote far more comedies than Racine did. In his first play, *l'Amant qui ne flatte point,* he attempted to create a character who would resemble Alceste in his frankness of speech, but Hauteroche was unable to do justice to the rôle, became more interested in the rival, and developed the plot in such a way that frank Géraste turns out to be a hypocrite. The first two acts are well written and contain a good deal of social satire, but the tone is not sustained in the rest of the play. Hauteroche wisely began to compose shorter plays, which soon established his reputation.

He selected a simple theme for his *Souper mal apprêté,* the situation of a young man who cannot pay for the meal to which he has invited friends.

There are few characters, no serious conflict, only a misunderstanding, humorously presented, with perfect unity of tone and an effect of reality that is found in few one-act plays of the period. *Crispin médecin*, which followed, is a prose comedy in three acts, chiefly remarkable for the scene in which a physician proposes to dissect a valet, posing as a corpse. The physician's gleeful anticipation of this opportunity to show his prowess, the maid's desperate efforts to divert him from his purpose, and the complete silence of the valet make this a most remarkable scene of comic suspense. In publishing the third of these plays, *le Deuil*, Hauteroche expressed the belief that shorter comedies should be composed with the same care as those in five acts, a theory illustrated by this one-act comedy, which has a simple and unified plot and realistic characters that include a farmer and his helper.

His reputation made by these prose comedies, Hauteroche wrote in verse *les Apparences trompeuses*, a study of jealousy which his colleagues refused to produce. They may have considered it dangerous to act in a play that included a protest against convents and a satire of *abbés galants*. Hauteroche accepted their decision and wrote *Crispin musicien*, a companion piece to his greatest success, *Crispin médecin*. The new play has no such striking scene as that of the operating table in the older one, but there are a number of amusing characters and music is extensively employed, so extensively, indeed, that the music of the intermissions is incorporated into the action, so that there are no intervals between the acts. This fact, references to opera, the presence of a professional musician, of a valet who pretends to be one, and of other persons who like to play or sing acquired for the work the sub-title of " l'Opéra de l'hôtel de Bourgogne." Its popular qualities won over the actors, despite a slurring reference to convents, and the public supported their judgment of the play.

Les Nobles de province describes the manners of aristocrats in Vivarais, who cherish their vendettas and the memory of their ancestors, have great regard for precedence, look to Lyons as the center of culture, and are shown in relation to their neighbors and their peasants. The presentation of rural life is excellent and there are highly comic scenes, but the plot is less satisfactory, a fact that may explain why the play was not long produced. The next two plays, one concerned with the vogue of newspapers, the other with that of a card-game, are lost, but the two that followed had qualities that not only preserved them, but made them highly successful. *La Dame invisible* is a comedy of intrigue derived partly from Calderon and partly from his imitator, d'Ouville. It is cleverly constructed and has amusing scenes in which the valet is terrified by the invisible lady. The other is *le Cocher*, in one act, also Spanish in origin and showing the same structural qualities.

His last two plays met with no success. *Le Feint Polonois* was acted only once, perhaps because the two parts of the plot were not in harmony with each other. *Les Bourgeoises de qualité* was acted nine times. It presents an interesting household and entertaining comments upon manners, but the intrigue lacks probability and the resemblance to *les Femmes savantes* and *les Précieuses* invited comparisons that were not in Hauteroche's favor.

He had excellent ideas about dramatic structure, which he sometimes put into effect, but sometimes failed to practise. He created no great comic characters and relied too much upon his valets, perhaps because such rôles were taken by his colleague, Poisson. He wrote readily, created many comic situations, gave in several plays a strong impression of reality, and often depicted manners effectively. Though several of his thirteen comedies failed, seven of them were so highly successful that, if we leave out of consideration plays written in collaboration, the only French authors who surpassed him in the number of times their comedies were acted at the Comédie Française were Molière, Regnard, Dancourt, and Marivaux. Neither he nor any other author mentioned in this chapter could approach Molière, however, in the variety of their comedies, their ability to characterize, or their sustained comic power. *Crispin médecin* and *le Deuil*, like *les Plaideurs*, might surpass certain of Molière's plays, but they could not enter into serious competition with his masterpieces.

CHAPTER XII

MOLIÈRE'S SUCCESSORS

For ten years after Molière's death comedies were written chiefly by Thomas Corneille, by some of the men studied in the last chapter, and by a few new authors, the only one of whom to write several was Champmeslé. Before 1673 he had composed only one comedy, *les Grisettes*, a sprightly imitation of *les Précieuses* that he rewrote, probably in 1673, as *Crispin chevalier*. Not long afterwards he composed *les Fragmens de Molière*, a comedy in two acts made up chiefly of passages from *Don Juan* and *Scapin*. He then wrote *la Bassette*, which is lost, but was apparently a comedy of manners centered round the playing of a card-game. *Le Parisien* is a witty comedy in five acts that portrays a miserly Parisian father, his silly wife, and their spendthrift son. Champmeslé employed in it various comic devices: parody of tragedy, a scene entirely in Italian, a forfeit, threats of arrest and of law-suits, references to recruiting, to the exploitation of distant countries, etc. This play was quickly followed by *la Rue S. Denis*, the first French comedy to introduce as an important theme fraudulent bankruptcy. It is an amusing playlet with several persons that have peculiar habits of speech and with many references to Parisian localities.

Champmeslé's plays of 1683, *les Joueurs* and *le Divorce*, are lost. *Ragotin*, which appeared the following year, is derived from *le Roman comique*, but with considerable alterations in characters and plot. It contains an amusing parody of La Chapelle's *Cléopâtre* and interesting references to the habits of a troupe. *Le Florentin*, Champmeslé's most successful comedy, resembles *l'Ecole des femmes*, but has only one act. It depicts the triumph of a clever girl and her lover over a tyrannical guardian, who becomes the victim of his device for ensnaring his rival. *La Coupe enchantée* was also very well received. Derived from two *contes* by La Fontaine, it presents in charming fashion naïve lovers, assisted by kindly peasants and at odds with an embittered guardian. Patois adds to the comic effect, while the magic cup that indicates fidelity or the lack of it lends grace to the story. *Le Veau perdu*, also derived from La Fontaine, is lost. An account of it that has survived indicates that the wit displayed in it was coarser in quality. *Je vous prens sans verd*, written to celebrate May-day, introduces songs, dances, a fable, dramatizes a game called " au verd," and suggests, as does *la Coupe enchantée*, a doctrine of tolerance. Finally, *la Veuve*, written not long before the author's death, resembles de Visé's *Veuve à la mode* in describing a widow's efforts to fend for herself, but it is much less dramatic and shows a distinct decrease in Champmeslé's talents.

He imitated Molière extensively. His use of La Fontaine's *contes* and the advertising instinct of a Dutch publisher resulted in the attribution of five of his plays to the fabulist, an error that has been corrected only in the last decade. His early plays have no moral content. There is no condemnation, for instance, of fraudulent bankruptcy. Subsequently the only virtue he suggested was tolerance towards a wife's unfaithfulness, one that he must have needed in his own household. He employed in some of his plays a great wealth of comic devices, but he had little ability at constructing a full-length play. His best work is consequently found in his shorter productions. He often wrote cleverly and was interested in portraying gamblers, actors, discontented wives, and unpleasant guardians. He showed distinct ability as a parodist and knew how to lighten his effects with dancing and song. *Le Florentin* has genuine comic force; *la Coupe enchantée*, a great deal of charm. These two plays, acted in our own time, possibly because they were attributed to La Fontaine, are among the best one-act comedies of the century.

Only two other authors who wrote before 1680 need be mentioned. We know little of Denis, whose only play that seems worthy of performance may not have been acted. It is *les Plaintes du palais*, a comedy of manners that deals with a hardfisted lawyer, his family, his clerks, and his clients. Both the lawyer and his wife are well drawn, while comic scenes are devoted to bewildered peasants and to the economies of a thrifty household. The other author was Poisson's son-in-law, La Tuillerie, who wrote two little comedies concerned with Crispin, a rôle that must have been played by the old actor. In each of them Crispin pretends to have a profession that is not his and meets a genuine member of it with comic results. *Crispin précepteur* introduces a boy, brought up as a peasant, who has to study Latin under Crispin's supervision, while *Crispin bel esprit* has in its cast a lady who dabbles in verse, a veteran, and a young hero who makes effective use of disguise. The latter play, much the better of the two, has amusing passages when Crispin poses as an authority on verse and especially when he tries to describe his imaginary campaigns to the veteran. When his military terms fail, he falls back upon borrowings from *le Cid*.

Eight plays of decided interest were produced in 1680-6, each of them its author's only contribution to the comedy of the century. The best of the eight is La Chapelle's *Carrosses d'Orléans*, a comedy of wayfaring life, in which a Parisian gets the better of a young provincial and we are shown the confusion of an inn at Chambord, which harbors a jealous coachman, an energetic cook, an affected *provinciale*, a *plaideuse*, and a Dutchman. Well constructed, it has a lively dialogue, an entertaining study of seventeenth-century travelers, and a spectacular scene to cover the lovers' retreat at the end of the play. Fontenelle's *Comète* is arresting on account of its theme. It is the first French play to be inspired by a contemporary astronomical event. Saint-Glas dramatized the craze over *bouts-rimés*. Robbe showed in *La Rapinière* the business of the *douane* at Genoa, as carried on by dishonest officials. Sévigny described life in a frontier town in time of peace, including the business of the commissariat, the hazing of recruits, and sentry duty.

Campistron, like La Chapelle, devoted himself especially to tragedy, but he brought out in 1684 *l'Amante Amant*, a comedy of intrigue that shows he had talent for repartie and contains an entertaining passage devoted to the behavior of young nobles on the stage. Saint-Yon described in his *Façons du tems* amusing incidents connected with the decay of morals often associated with the Régence, apparently the result of a long war. It is unfortunate that we do not have the text of the play at the time it appeared, December, 1685, for the work has survived only as *les Mœurs du tems*, played in 1694 and published in Holland in 1696. It is possible that the text did not originally include passages concerned with manners that would have been more novel in 1685 than a decade later. Another play concerned with the effects of war is Desmares's *Merlin Dragon*, a lively farce in which a miserly owner of property is bullied by soldiers quartered on his estate in compliance with the wishes of his son. All of these eight plays were acted at Paris and prepared the way for the extensive revival of interest in comedy that took place with Baron, Dancourt, and later authors.

Michel Baron, a very celebrated actor of tragedies, wrote only comedies, most of which are studies of fashionable Parisian society. His reputation as an author was made by the five that were first acted in 1685-7. *Le Rendez-vous des Thuilleries* has a prologue in which actors discuss their affairs and three acts that show the life of a household, whose mistress and her friends gamble, converse, intrigue, amuse themselves at the theater or the opera, while the servants neglect their work and imitate the habits of those they serve. The decay of manners is indicated by what we hear of young nobles. The first act begins in an unusually striking fashion, but the play becomes less interesting as the action develops. It was followed by *les Enlèvemens*, a comedy in one act, with a somewhat mechanical plot, but with an attractive presentation of rural life as led by impecunious aristocrats, their servants, and peasants.

After this excursion into the country, he returned to high society at Paris and produced his most celebrated play, *l'Homme à bonne fortune*, a comedy of character, the incidents of which are skillfully arranged so as to bring out the protagonist's characteristics rather than to assist in the progress of the action. Moncade, a brilliant adventurer, who makes his living by dazzling women with his costumes and his fashionable bearing, is excellently portrayed, but the other characters, with the exception of the servants, are not given sufficient individuality. It is a play for a star, with an entertaining study of a society in which love has become largely a matter of fashion. The tone is well adapted to the theme. *La Coquette*, acted less than a year later, at the end of 1686, has no such central character, but a greater variety of persons. It depicts an aristocratic society, into which bourgeois who can pay their way are admitted. Like the earlier comedy, it has in its cast the rôle of a precocious boy, taken by Baron's son, Etienne, and apparently written for him. In *le Jaloux* he sought to write a second comedy of character, employing verse as the principal medium for the first time. He presented as his hero the most violent person in seventeenth-century comedy, but there is too little progress in the incidents that reval his characteristics, there are melodramatic tendencies, and the ending is unsatisfactory. Though an interesting play, it does not rank with the two that preceded it. The three that soon followed it are lost, but their titles suggest that Baron continued to interest himself in costume, actors, and fashionable society. When he wrote again for the stage, early in the eighteenth century, it was only to produce two adaptations of Terence.

Baron's work owes much to Molière, especially to *le Misanthrope, Don Garcie*, and *l'Impromptu de Versailles*. He was skillful in creating an atmosphere in harmony with the trivial aristocrats he wished to emphasize. He studied in detail the manners of a restricted group of persons. He deserves credit for seeking to revive the comedy of character, neglected since the time of Molière, though the only memorable character he created was that of Moncade. His portrayal of peasants and children enlarges his field of observation, but it remains very small in comparison with Dancourt's. He is usually thought of as the author of one play, just as that play is remembered as a frame for one character. While his work deserves consideration for other reasons, it is true that his chief title to fame as a dramatist is that he composed *l'Homme à bonne fortune*.

While Baron, who belonged to a family of actors, was dramatizing aristocracy, Dancourt, a nobleman, was devoting himself especially, though not exclusively, to persons of the middle class. Before he came to Paris as an actor, he wrote a farce that shows interest in newsmongers, in wars against the Turks, and in comic varieties of French. His first Parisian play, *le Notaire obligeant*, has too much symmetry in the choice of characters, too little reality in the plot, but it gives evidence of the author's ability to write spirited dialogue. After bringing out two farces that satirize operas and parody lines from them, he wrote his first comedy of manners, *la Désolation des joueuses*, with a rudimentary plot and a thorough study of gambling and its effects on various social types, both noble and bourgeois, whom the passion for lansquenet brings together and who are angered by the official prohibition of the game. Sinister figures hang around, an upstart who has made his way by cheating at cards and a pawnbroker, eager to spy out an opportunity of lending to desperate losers.

Dancourt now ventured upon longer plays without abandoning those in one act. In five years he wrote five plays in five acts, two of them in collaboration with Saint-Yon, and nine plays in one act, one of which was the result of collaboration and two were reworkings of plays written by others. The finest of them all is *le Chevalier à la mode*, a comedy of manners that describes the struggle between the impecunious or eccentric aristocracy and the crude, but substantial bourgeoisie. The chevalier himself may be an aristocrat, but he has become merely an adventurer, living by his attraction for women. The marquise, who forces Mme Patin's elegant equipage to recoil, is desperately poor. The baroness cherishes a law-suit more than a century and a half old. Mme Patin, widow of a tax-collector, would use her immense wealth to secure social recognition, were it not for her rough brother-in-law and the intelligent lawyer, Migot, who will see to it that the money remains in the family. The conflict of the classes, the pretentious folly of Mme Patin, the schemes of the chevalier and his valet, and the absurdities of the baroness give excellent comic material, presented in a brilliant dialogue.

Two of the longer plays, *la Dame à la mode* and *le Carnaval de Venise*, of which the latter contained political satire, are lost. *La Femme d'intrigues* introduces a more resourceful Frosine, who makes her living by aiding all sorts of people honestly and dishonestly and is finally disappointed in a matrimonial venture of her own. The play consists of a long series of incidents that show her various activities. *Les Bourgeoises à la mode* has a more substantial plot, which may be due to Dancourt's collaboration with Saint-Yon, and contains excellent comic scenes, but its cynical tone may have diminished its success, while the story of the stolen diamond savors of melodrama and a number of questions are left unsolved at the end.

Of the nine one-act plays, *Merlin déserteur* is lost; *la Folle Enchère* is an intrigue comedy composed with Mme Ulrich and having little semblance of reality; *l'Impromptu de Garnison* is a play by an anonymous author that Dancourt adapted to the stage; and *le Bon Soldat* is Poisson's *Foux divertissans*, reduced to one act. On the other hand, *la Maison de campagne*, Dancourt's first country play, presents a highly amusing picture of a lawyer who has sought peace in rural surroundings, but is harassed by his family and their visitors until he gets out of the difficulty by turning his home into an inn. *L'Eté des coquettes* gives us a view of fashionable girls at Paris in summer, when they have to console themselves for the absence of genuine officers by receiving those of dubious reputation, financiers, abbés, and music teachers. The study of manners and the clever dialogue are made more effective by the slightness of the plot. *La Parisienne* has somewhat the same qualities, but it is less sophisticated and has more resemblance to earlier farces in representing a girl's efforts to handle a series of lovers. *La Gazette de Hollande* gives an interesting picture of recruiting, book-selling, and the functions of a correspondent, who sends items of interest from Paris to a Dutch journal. Finally *l'Opéra de village* is peculiar in its large use of music and in the fact that the hero does not appear on the stage. Like *la Maison de campagne*, it introduces peasants into the cast. It is with this play that the vogue of the *comédie-vaudeville* begins.

The success of these comedies seems to have made Dancourt limit himself for several years to one-act plays. They vary considerably in quality. *La Baguette* is lost. The scene of only two of the other thirteen is laid at Paris, a fact that distinguishes Dancourt from most of his contemporaries who wrote for the Parisian stage. He prefers to locate his plays in the suburbs of Paris, but may go as far as Péronne or Bourbon. It is in this period that he begins to bring out seasonal plays, written to seem appropriate to the time of the vintage, of fairs, or of vacations. The two Parisian plays show us the interior of a fair or the operation of a lottery. Three comedies are primarily concerned with peasants, three with Parisians who have gone to the suburbs for amusement, while the scene of one is laid at a watering resort. Several are connected with war. While *le Tuteur* exists chiefly for one situation, most of the plays give an ample picture of manners. The plots are usually slight and the characters only sketched, but the dialogue is excellent, the effects are varied, and there is a definite impression of reality. The best of them are probably *les Vendanges de Suresnes*, which has an interesting collection of knaves, makes effective use of songs, and was the most frequently acted at the Comédie Française of all Dancourt's plays; and *le Mari retrouvé*, which is based on a contemporary murder trial and has amusing situations and an entertaining display of peasant psychology.

The plays of 1699-1700, with the exception of *la Fête de village*, are inferior to these. *Les Fées* echoed the contemporary taste for fairy-tales, but had a theme too far from reality to suit Dancourt's talents. *La Famille à la mode* suffers both from imitating *l'Avare* and from not possessing its comic power. *L'Opérateur Barry*, written for a private performance, is chiefly valuable as an attempt to revive interest in a charlatan and in the type of farce that had flourished early in the century. *Les Trois Cousines* is a peasant play with an interesting prologue, devoted to the customs of an audience, but with few striking scenes elsewhere. In contrast with these four plays, *la Fête de village* gives an amusing picture of village life with its petty rivalries and aspirations, a *tabellion,* obsequious before a shrewd Parisian attorney, the wives of rural magistrates who long to escape from the boredom of life in Brie, and a *greffière,* who, as she expects to be a countess, disdains her sister and her cousin till the impoverished young nobleman she had hoped to purchase eludes her grasp.

Dancourt was eminently a man of the stage, an actor, the husband and father of actresses, next to Hardy the most prolific dramatist who wrote in the seventeenth century, often the spokesman of his troupe. In *le Chevalier à la mode* he gave an excellent model of the full-length comedy of manners, not only in its surface manifestations, but in the deeper significance of the social struggle that was going on around him. While his other plays do not equal this one in value, they constitute an extensive and detailed account of French society, city and country, in peace and in war, at work and on vacation. Dancourt's verse is inconsequential and the structure of his plays often leaves something to be desired, but he was able to breathe life into a very large variety of characters and to present them to the public in a racy dialogue and cleverly devised situations. He knew his audience so well that his plays long remained popular. Among all French authors who devoted themselves chiefly to comedy he stands next to Molière in the number of times his plays were acted at the Comédie Française.

While Dancourt was making his reputation, a different type of comedy was becoming more and more important in the life of Paris, that of the Théâtre Italien, which began to include French scenes of some significance in 1681 and continued the practice till 1697, sometimes producing plays that are entirely in French. Over fifty such comedies, written partly or wholly in French, have survived. The chief authors were Fatouville, Delosme de Monchesnay, Regnard, Dufresny, Louis Biancolelli, Palaprat, and Lenoble. Their comedies were constructed without regard for classical regulation concerning verisimilitude, unity, and propriety. Tales may break off without being completed. The tone is that of highly exaggerated farce. The actors, who often appeared under their stage-names, collaborated with the authors, altering their lines as the occasion suggested. Gherardi compares them to nightingales, as opposed to the parrots of the Comédie Française. While nightingale was hardly the word to employ, he was right in emphasizing the actors' resourcefulness and agility.

Under the farcical tone, one detects no genuine study of character, but an extensive representation of manners. The authors portrayed nobles, bourgeois, workmen, peasants, men of various trades and professions, parodied *le Cid, Bérénice,* and other French plays, as well as operas, answered a satire of Boileau, burlesqued the acting of Baron and la Champmeslé. While they influenced certain authors who wrote for the Comédie Française, they received far more suggestions than they gave. This was partly because one of their aims was to present the life of Paris in their peculiar manner and French plays and operas formed part of that life. Their chief aim was to startle their audience by the variety and extravagance of their inventions. For this purpose they mingled mythological and exotic elements with those found in ordinary life, combined business transactions, love scenes, and military references with buffoonery and gymnastic exploits, made sudden use of spectacle, and shifted from prose to verse, from French to Italian and other languages.

Fatouville established their type of play and made more contributions to it than anyone else. With him the Italian element, at first predominant, diminished until it disappeared altogether. He is at his best in *Arlequin Procureur*, which satirizes law, and in *le Banqueroutier*, with its exposé of big business. Delosme de Monchesnay's originality is chiefly shown by his writing a dramatic critique of a longer play he had composed, a novelty for the Théâtre Italien, though not for French actors. The most important contributor after Fatouville was Regnard, as he showed especially in his *Divorce, Coquette, Arlequin Homme à bonne fortune*, and *Foire S. Germain*. He manifested interest in other antiquities than Greek and Roman by writing *la Naissance d'Amadis* and *les Momies d'Egypte*. Dufresny, who collaborated with him in four plays and with Louis Biancolelli in two, displayed his originality chiefly by the brevity of the plays he wrote without a collaborator, his emphasis on village life, and his use of song. He satirized fairy-tales with Biancolelli. The latter, possibly under the influence of his sister Colombine, defended women. He showed his originality by representing Harlequin as a misanthropist. His most artistic production was *le Tombeau de maître André*, which combines a picture of domestic difficulties occasioned by a supposed death with a quarrel over a bottle of wine, a parody of *le Cid*, and an amusing spectacle. Lenoble and Palaprat left each only two contributions to the Théâtre Italien: the former, a play inspired by Boursault's *Esope* and a farce dealing with identical twins; the latter, *la Fille de bon sens* and *Arlequin Phaéton*. This last play has a remarkable scene in which Phaeton and Momus look down upon the city of Paris as it awakens in the morning, a scene that combines effectively spectacle with social satire.

The popularity of this Italian troupe shows that the tastes of the Parisian public were not limited to the enjoyment of classical productions. The company was well established before Molière returned to Paris and was still playing there after he and Corneille had died and Racine had ceased to write plays. They were so well known that the term Comédie Française seems to have arisen in an effort to distinguish the French actors from those of the Comédie Italienne. Yet their methods were utterly different from those of their French colleagues and showed none of the qualities ordinarly ascribed to *classicisme*. Nor did they long abandon Paris after Louis XIV drove them out, for they returned in 1716 to amuse the descendants of those who had been entertained by Scaramouche, Harlequin, Colombine, and their comrades.

One of the French authors who contributed to the Théâtre Italien, Palaprat, wrote many more plays for the Comédie Française, several of them in collaboration with Brueys. The two friends began with *le Concert ridicule,* which introduces a sergeant who composes songs and a parody of verses from a recent opera. This last device was developed by Palaprat in his *Ballet extravagant,* which outlines an opera on Roman history and puts into action an attempted rape of the Sabines. The next play written by both authors was *le Secret révélé,* developed from a story told by the actor J.-B. Raisin, but requiring his talents, of which they were deprived by his death, to keep it long in the repertory. The masterpiece of the collaborators was *le Grondeur,* a three-act comedy of character in which the protagonist is a physician who opposes all suggestions that are made to him, merely because they come from others than himself—a new vice in French comedy, as the authors point out, and one that was to reappear in a play by Dufresny. Clever servants, a boy, his pedantic preceptor, and a man who speaks largely in monosyllables add to the comic effect, while references to Madagascar reflect the expanding interests of the French. In order to help the play succeed, Palaprat composed a prologue in "vers libres" which sought to forestall criticism of the play by putting it into the mouths of the actors. A few months later the two authors brought out *le Muet,* an adaptation of Terence's *Eunuchus,* with a pretended mute substituted for a pretended eunuch, a seacaptain for a *miles gloriosus.* They modernized the manners and added an entertaining medical passage, but the play remains, like its model, a comedy of intrigue.

With this play Palaprat's good fortune ended. His *Saturnales,* a poorly constructed comedy that lacks highly comic scenes, was a failure. His *Hercule et Omphale,* acted only four times, is lost. Three other plays that he wrote for the Comédie Française not only are lost, but were never acted. He probably wrote with Brueys *le Sot toujours sot,* which was played, but has not been preserved in its original form, and *les Embarras du derrière du théâtre,* which gives an entertaining account of the world behind the scenes, but was, for some unknown reason, never acted, though on June 9, 1693, the actors paid for the copying of its rôles.

Unlike Palaprat, Brueys continued to compose. He brought out *l'Important de cour, les Empiriques,* a religious tragedy, and several plays that appeared in the eighteenth century, among which *l'Avocat Patelin* was enormously successful. *L'Important,* which owed only a few suggestions to Palaprat and Raisin, is, like *le Muet,* a prose comedy in five acts. A pretentious upstart is its chief character. There are clever scenes in which a child takes part. Despite its title, the play is a comedy of manners rather than of character. *Les Empiriques,* in which the protagonist resembles Argan, ridicules quacks. The latter, their victim, and those who rescue him, including a worthy Swiss who speaks French with difficulty, supply the comic material.

The two authors composed several clever plays in one act, portrayed manners in considerable detail, and sought to continue Molière's comedies of character. In this ambition they succeeded only with *le Grondeur.* Palaprat seems to have had flashes of comic inspiration and to have been more closely in touch with the actors than his colleague, who probably supplied the more substantial portions of the work they did in common. Left to his own devices, Palaprat had only one success, *le Ballet extravagant,* while Brueys wrote without his friend several plays that were well received. It is unfortunate that they did not collaborate over a longer period, for their farces and *le Grondeur* show genuine talent for comedy that might have produced a series of excellent plays if they had continued for more than a few years to unite their forces.

The only other men who won a prominent place among authors of comedy were Regnard and Dufresny, who wrote for both the Comédie Française and the Théâtre Italien. After contributing extensively to the latter company, Regnard wrote his charming *Attendez-moi sous l'orme,* with a flavor of *Robin et Marion* and the triumph of peasants over an officer, who is attempting to restore his fortune by marriage. The simple plot, the peasants' songs, and the ironical use of the elm give the play a very distinct character. *La Sérénade* is less simple in plot and more conventional in the devices employed, but its animation, its music, and its racy dialogue made it more successful in the eighteenth century, though it was not revived, as *Attendez-moi* was, in the last half of the nineteenth. The third play, *le Bourgeois de Falaise* or *le Bal,* made much less of a hit than either, though its amusing figures from Normandy and Gascony and the dance that brings about the dénouement deserved a more satisfactory reception than was accorded it.

Regnard next produced *le Joueur,* which he had begun in collaboration with Dufresny, but which he finished without his assistance. It is a comedy of character in verse, in which the hero oscillates between gambling and love, finally losing at both games. The fancifulness of the presentation, the sparkling verses, the characters of the gambler, his valet, the pretended marquis, and Mme La Ressource, the pawnbroker, made this Regnard's masterpiece. His *Distrait* was less successful, though it has in the absent-minded hero, the impertinent young chevalier, and Widow Grognac characters that are fully as interesting. Its weakness lies in its form, for the events of the play are not affected to any great extent by the hero's absent-mindedness. *Démocrite* is peculiar in the choice of an ancient period for the time of the play and in the violation of the unities of time and place. The author makes much use of contrast, but he would have given us little more than a romantic tragi-comedy if he had not introduced the delightful scenes between Strabon and Cléanthis and the excellent rôle of the peasant, Thaler. Regnard's final contribution to seventeenth-century comedy was *le Retour imprévu*, a modernization in one act of Plautus's *Mostellaria*, which he was so eager to have the actors play that he agreed to accept no share of the receipts.

In the early years of the eighteenth century he brought out three comedies that were highly successful, but he did not alter the general impression produced by his seven earlier plays, which showed that he took suggestions from Plautus and Dufresny, as well as from Molière, whose depth and variety of interests he lacked. He was far more limited in his outlook than Dancourt and paid much less attention to manners. He helped reinstate verse, however, as a medium for longer comedies, wrote with much gaiety and humor, and succeeded in his professed aim of diverting "les gens d'esprit avec art." *Le Joueur* is one of the best comedies written after Molière's death, while *Attendez-moi, le Distrait,* and *Démocrite* still possess much to delight the reader.

Dufresny's plays that were interpreted by French actors fall mainly in the eighteenth century. Most of those he wrote in the seventeenth were poorly received. His *Chevalier Joueur*, which could not compete with Regnard's *Joueur*, was acted only once. The actors could not finish their one performance of *la Malade sans maladie*. *Sancho Pança*, which was played five times, is lost. His three remaining comedies have, however, decided merits. *Le Négligent* has an interesting form. In the prologue, which refers to Molière and to the state of the drama when the play was written, it is proposed that a comedy be composed about the characters that have already appeared or been mentioned. The three acts that follow are the result of this suggestion. Unpractical Oronte, a poet, a marquis, an old maid, and her niece and rival are presented in entertaining fashion, while there are many references to manners. It probably suffered from its lack of unity, but it had some influence on Regnard. *La Nopce interrompue* is a pleasing peasant play in which love triumphs over the lord of the manor. It ends in dancing and singing like one of Dancourt's *comédies-vaudevilles*. Finally, *l'Esprit de contradiction*, the great triumph of Dufresny's career, proved to be one of the most popular plays of the century. The leading character is the feminine equivalent of the protagonist in *le Grondeur*. She, her mild husband, the peasant gardener in whom he confides, his very clever daughter, and the wealthy upstart who courts her are admirably characterized, while the comedy has the rare quality of showing in its cast neither valet nor *suivante*. In structure and in dialogue it is a fine production, one that showed what its author was able to do when his constructive ability did not fall short of his powers of observation and expression.

Three other Parisian dramatists contributed to seventeenth-century comedy. Jacques Raisin wrote for his more distinguished brother four playlets, of which only one has survived, *Merlin Gascon*, a one-act play concerned with a miser and the manner in which his daughter is rescued from his clutches. The clever dialogue emphasizes the comic rôle of a valet who pretends to be a Gascon, the rôle that J.-B. Raisin must have taken. Perrault composed two little plays that are not highly comic or dramatic, but possess a quiet humor that is not without charm. Known for his fairy-tales and for his part in the quarrel of the Ancients and Moderns, he created for his first play a valet who acts the fairy godmother and enables his young master to get ahead of his miserly father, while in the second he held up to ridicule a studious young man's absurd admiration for ancient authors and heroines. The plays give a study of middle-class life, including references to *fontanges* and *oublieux*, from which they derive their titles.

The third of these authors, Jean-Baptiste Rousseau, ultimately famous for his odes, wrote three comedies in the seventeenth century, the best and least pretentious of which is *le Caffé*, a one-act study of guests in an establishment where coffee is sold. He then attempted comedy of character, but was not equal to the task. Though there are interesting characters and situations in *le Flatteur*, it is a comedy of intrigue, paying some attention to manners, and borrows too obviously from *Tartuffe* to escape a damaging comparison. *Le Capricieux* has a most involved plot that fails to keep the promise of the title. It is a dull production that does not make us regret the author's exile, which put him out of contact with Parisian actors.

There were two authors who, before the century ended, had composed a few plays for provincial troupes. Marc-Antoine Legrand, subsequently most prolific, wrote in his youth six comedies for the troupe with which he had gone to Lyons. Two are lost. The others are short comedies that reproduce phases of life in this provincial city. A considerable portion of one is a parody of Quinault's opera, *Phaéton*, with local applications. In another the value of opera is discussed. A third brings in an *opérateur* and a little dancing-girl. A fourth refers to a provincial troupe and to well-known dramatists. They show already some of the qualities for which Legrand was subsequently to be famous. The other dramatist, François Passerat, is less interesting. Attached, as Nanteuil had been, to the troupe of the Dukes of Hannover, he wrote two comedies, as well as a tragedy and a brief pastoral. *Le Feint Campagnard* is a dull production in one act, but *l'Heureux Accident* gives a pleasant picture of life at a château, with talk of love, food, and books, an entertainment that is violently interrupted, and an ending made gay by three ballet entries.

Finally, there were a number of comedies whose authors are unknown or about whom we know little. Those that are the most meritorious are *la Bourgeoise Madame*, in five acts, especially remarkable for the lively scene in which a number of bourgeoises gossip about their affairs and various customs of the day; the *Batteau de Bouille*, which describes the bustle about a boat that is on the point of leaving Rouen for a trip on the Seine; *les Petits-Maîtres d'été*, which describes the manners of fashionable youths and suggests the general decay of Parisian society; *la Chasse ridicule*, derived from La Fontaine, but adding a protest against the treatment of peasants by a self-made aristocrat; and *le Quartier d'hiver* with its many echoes of the relations between warriors and civilians near the end of the century.

It can be seen from this and the preceding chapter that Molière, when he died early in 1673, had by no means said the last word of the century in regard to comedy. None of his contemporaries or successors approached him in genius, but they added much, in regard to characters, form, and especially manners, to what he had achieved. Chappuzeau, Montfleury, Boursault, Hauteroche, Champmeslé, the Théâtre Italien, Baron, Dancourt, Palaprat, Brueys, Regnard, and Dufresny have a great deal to offer that is often overlooked by students of Molière. It was especially between 1683 and the end of the century that comedy, after losing its greatest master, was definitely on its feet again, in a sense that was not true of other *genres*. The proof of this fact lies not only in the large number of comedies that were then written, but in the excellence of such full-length plays as *la Comédie sans titre, l'Homme à bonne fortune, le Chevalier à la mode, le Grondeur*, and *le Joueur*, of such one-act masterpieces as *la Maison de compagne, l'Eté des coquettes, le Mari retrouvé, le Florentin, la Coupe enchantée, Attendez-moi sous l'orme*, and *l'Esprit de contradiction*.

CONCLUSION

In the seventeenth century France produced one of the world's four leading dramas, a corpus of plays that long dominated European production. Its eminence in the eighteenth century led to bitter resentment and to a reaction that caused it to be attacked both at home and in other countries. It has suffered from its friends, eager to attribute to it their own aspirations, as well as from enemies, moved by patriotic and personal, rather than aesthetic reasons. It has been misunderstood by those who have been unwilling to relate it to the life around it, who have considered it primarily imitative of other literatures, or have studied only a small portion of the texts that have survived. A reexamination of the evidence may bring us to conclusions that are less prejudiced and more satisfying.

One would judge from the silence of certain writers that there was little connection between the work of the dramatists and the times in which they composed it. But the crude plays that appeared early in the century corresponded to the condition of French society, not yet recovered from the Wars of Religion and from the poverty and neglect of education that they caused. It was when conditions improved under Richelieu's guidance that marked progress was made in drama, that authors began to discuss standards of dramatic art, while Mme de Rambouillet was organizing polite society and writers were grouping themselves in anticipation of the French Academy. The participation of France in the Thirty Years War did not seriously affect the prosperity of the country, roused it to patriotic effort, made it the first power in Europe. At the same time the dramatists worked out their methods and established the general principles of their art, as especially exemplified by the tragedies of Corneille and his early contemporaries.

Then came the Fronde with its sufferings and disappointment. A new society asked for comedy rather than tragedy, for emphasis on character and manners rather than upon complex action, for subtle analysis of emotion rather than for heroic idealism. Molière was then able to do for comedy what Corneille had done for tragedy, and Racine was helped to create his own variety of the latter *genre*. The years 1659 to 1672, years of peace broken only by brief minor wars, was the greatest period in French drama. The destructive wars that occupied much of the period that ran from June, 1672, to the end of the century were certainly among the elements that caused a decline in drama, though there was some compensation in the fact that social changes produced by war supplied authors of comedy with new types and new customs to be portrayed.

It is unnecessary to repeat what has been said in regard to connections

143

between the court and the stage, efforts to please Louis XIII, Richelieu, Mazarin, and especially Louis XIV, the latter's patronage of Molière and Quinault, his suppression of the Marais and of the Théâtre Italien, his putting the interests of Lully above those of Molière, Mme de Maintenon's inspiring *Esther* and *Athalie*. The stratification of French society was reproduced on the stage. Certain religious taboos affected dramatists. Without the church we should have neither *Polyeucte*, nor *Tartuffe*, nor the *abbés galants*. While school plays rarely influenced popular drama, the education given by Jesuits and Jansenists, including discussions of " cas de conscience," must have been one of the foundations on which rested much of the psychological analysis found in French plays. Authors of comedy owed a large debt to the society in which they lived for providing them with a great variety of manners and customs to reproduce. Nor were they oblivious to events and inventions of the day.

French drama could not have been what it was without the theaters of Paris and the actors who played in them. Strolling troupes were not a substantial reliance. It was when Paris began to dominate the dramatic world and when a troupe was regularly established there that the classical movement got under way. The existence of a second theater may well have helped dramatists break with older habits. When three troupes were acting, each had as specialties tragedies, comedies, or "machine" plays. The suppression of the Marais may have been a cause of difficulties that soon beset drama. The union of the two remaining troupes prevented further competition between rival companies in tragedy and in high comedy. Nor is it hard to establish a direct connection between the special gifts of such actors as Montdory, Molière, and la Champmeslé and the composition of rôles in which they acted.

Knowledge of Parisian theaters and of those who attended performances in them should dispel the idea that French drama was written for an élite. As a mater of fact, the parterre was at times considered the most influential part of the audience, while the number of persons who attended was far too large to allow us to think that only the leisure class was represented. Dramatists were obliged to take this fact, as well as the police, into consideration. French drama of the seventeenth century is not a place to look for ideas held only by a minority, for social or religious protests of which most of the audience would have disapproved, or for subtle theories in regard to the nature of man that would not have been appreciated by highly mixed spectators. *Tartuffe* was kept off the stage by a small minority—an élite, according to some definitions. As soon as the government allowed it to be played freely, it began its career as the most popular of French plays.

Since it is obvious that many dramatists employed sources, only a super-ficial scholar will ignore them, but merely to indicate a source tells us little. France has been for centuries a center of European thought and taste, receiving from many countries and giving in many directions. It is consequently natural that many influences should be exerted upon its drama, which would not be truly national if this were not the case. As I have shown in Chapter III, the most extensive direct influence was that of works written in French, plays, novels, tales, etc. Latin literature came next, then Greek. The influence of all three was felt from time to time through-out the century. Spanish influence was exerted chiefly between 1629 and 1670. Despite the fact that *le Cid, Venceslas,* and *Saint Genest* have Spanish sources, it was exerted chiefly upon comedy. While imitation of Spanish plays produced good results in *le Menteur* and in comedies by Scarron, the general effect of it was to delay the creation of classical comedy. Italian influence was limited largely to the pastoral, where it was dominant, to a few comedies and tragedies produced by French actors, and to the Théâtre Italien. Biblical and hagiographical writings inspired a great many amateur plays, but were chiefly of value in the use made of them in a few tragedies written around 1640 and around 1690. English plays supplied material only to *Sir Politick Would-be* and to *Manlius Capitolinus.*

While French plays were occasionally close adaptations of others written in a foreign tongue or in French, most of the dramatists altered freely the material they borrowed. This always happened when the source was not a play, or when the foreign play imitated was written in accordance with different ideas of structure, manners, or dramatic effects from those favored by Frenchmen. It is easy to illustrate this statement by citing the well-known examples of *le Cid, l'Ecole des femmes,* and *Phèdre.* Corneille emphasized the inner struggle of his hero and heroine in a way that Guillén de Castro had not dreamed of. Molière made a series of profoundly comic scenes out of a narrative that was hardly meant by María de Zayas to be amusing. Racine developed his heroine in a manner that was only suggested by Euripides and Seneca.

The century produced a considerable variety of dramatic *genres,* more than one who reads merely Racine's tragedies and Molière's leading comedies, would suspect. Before 1634 five were in favor, if farce is included. The pastoral, of which the best representatives are *les Bergeries* and *Sylvie,* remained popular until that date, when most authors ceased to cultivate it. Subsequent attempts to revive it produced only a few plays, none that had more than brief success. Tragi-comedy, whose characteristics were fixed by Hardy, was the leading *genre,* so far as numbers are concerned, from 1628 to 1642. Its masterpiece was *le Cid.* Soon after that play appeared,

Du Ryer led a movement to apply classical standards to what had been an unrestrained type of play, with the result that it came to resemble tragedy more closely. Then Corneille brought out *Cinna*, with its happy ending, which further reduced the difference between the two *genres*, while his tragedies of 1640-2 made such an impression that in 1643-8 more tragedies were written than tragi-comedies. The latter type of play steadily diminished in popularity until 1666, after which, even if we include *comédies héroïques* among tragi-comedies, few were composed.

Meanwhile the " machine " play had come into existence, supplying the spectacle that was lacking in classical tragedies. It flourished chiefly between 1648 and 1681, by which time opera had been well established. Farce, which probably existed throughout the century, was seldom considered worthy of publication before 1655. *Les Précieuses ridicules*, printed early in 1660, gave the signal for greatly increased publication of farces. A special variety of farce is found in the French scenes written for the Théâtre Italien. These existed as early as 1681, but few were published before 1694.

In 1630 a Parisian spectator might see a tragedy, a tragi-comedy, a pastoral, or a comedy, and each of these might be followed by a farce. In 1660 he could find similar offerings, but with a " machine " play substituted for the pastoral, except that it was not followed by a farce. In 1690 he could see at the Comédie Française no new plays except tragedies, comedies, and farces, but he could witness the productions of the Théâtre Italien, or of the opera. He would have been surprised to learn that a day would come when the dramatic output of his century would be remembered as limited to tragedy and comedy.

It is true that more comedies and tragedies were produced in the century than plays belonging to other *genres*. If we follow the indications given in over eleven hundred of the plays that have survived from 1610-1700, we find that about 42 per cent of them are comedies, 30 per cent tragedies, 20 per cent tragi-comedies, and 8 per cent pastorals.[1] But such predominance of comedy and tragedy does not hold for the first half of the century. In 1610-34 about 34 per cent of the plays are tragi-comedies, 27 per cent tragedies, 26 per cent pastorals, 13 per cent comedies. In 1635-51 about 41 per cent are tragedies, 37 per cent tragi-comedies, 20 per cent comedies, and 2 per cent pastorals. It was the triumph of comedy and tragedy in the second half of the century, as well as the fact that the most celebrated plays belonged chiefly to those *genres*, that has caused the real importance of others in certain periods to be neglected.

---

[1] Among comedies are included farces and plays of the Théâtre Italien; among tragi-comedies, *comédies heroïques*; among pastorals, plays called *tragi-comédies pastorales, comédies pastorales*, etc. " Machine " plays are usually called tragedies by their authors; sometimes comedies.

It is well to bear these facts in mind when one considers the introduction of classical rules, for, though drama ultimately contributed the chief French works of the imagination that were classical, it also produced many that were not. The rules were at first unknown. After their introduction, they were not applied to all *genres* and for several years were not dominant in any. They were applied chiefly in tragedy, less so in tragicomedy, pastoral, and high comedy, little in "machine" plays and in farces written for French actors, not at all in plays of the Théâtre Italien. Even in tragedy they were not so strictly followed as is often supposed.

They had the effect of making dramatists concentrate their attention upon analysis of emotions and causal sequences of events, so that they produced, on the whole, finer plays than those that remained irregular. They had some unfortunate effects. They caused certain subjects to be avoided or to be altered in such a way that essential qualities were lost. They made difficult the development of character. The decorum they recommended smothered emotion at times and restricted vocabulary. But writers like Racine drew tragic effects from decorum, as it enabled them to contrast the surface appearance with the emotions it attempted to conceal. The rules diminished melodramatic, sentimental, and moralistic passages. They helped the author put drama first, instead of substituting for it lyrical and epic developments. Those who claim that it substituted reason for imagination seem to be unable to appreciate the fact that as much imagination may be shown in the subtler effects of classicism than in those of other systems. A classical tragedy in the hands of Racine may be compared to a Petrarchan sonnet, composed by a great poet whose technical skill enables his emotion to express itself with the help of his form rather than in spite of it.

Finally, the appreciation of French seventeenth-century drama has been diminished by those who write only of Corneille, Molière, and Racine. These are, of course, the greatest, but their work is far from telling the whole story, nor can it be fully appreciated if we know nothing of their fellows. Corneille excelled in his broad conception of drama, his skill at dramatizing general principles, in the effort he brought to establish French classicism; Racine, in his keen analysis of emotion, his poetic style, his gift at depicting appealing characters; Molière in his great variety of comic devices, his humanity, his unfailing wit. But admiration for them should not make us overlook Théophile's genuine emotion, Mairet's early efforts at introducing art into drama, the contribution made by Rotrou, Du Ryer, Tristan, and La Calprenède to French tragedy and tragi-comedy while classicism was on trial; the work of Thomas Corneille and Quinault in the time of Racine; that of Campistron and La Fosse after Racine had ceased to write for the popular stage. Nor should it keep us from enjoying the amusing qualities of *les Visionnaires*, the abounding cleverness of Scarron,

Poisson, and Hauteroche, Dancourt's extensive study of manners, Regnard's fancifulness, the humor of Palaprat, Brueys, and Dufresny.

Molière's slight pastorals tell us little about that *genre*. Tragi-comedy is a much larger subject than one would suppose who read only Corneille. One would not suspect the existence of "machine" plays, if one read only Racine. To limit one's knowledge to three leading writers is comparable to the old method of studying history only in its wars, its political negotiations, and the private lives of its kings and queens. The approaching triumph of democracy in war and government should coincide with willingness on the part of scholars to hear the claims of minor authors, who complement the work of greater men and with them reflect the aspirations in art and in life of a century when the French government refused to yield to foreign encroachment and enabled French authors to dramatize what is stimulating or pathetic, admirable or laughable in the behavior of mankind.

SUPPLEMENT TO PARTS I, II, III, AND IV

Two books have recently appeared that indicate the principal characteristics of certain seventeenth-century authors: D. Mornet's *Histoire de la littérature française classique, 1660-1700. Ses caractères véritables. Ses aspects inconnus* (Paris, Armand Colin, 1940. 427 pp.), and H. Peyre's *Le Classicisme français* (New York, Editions de la Maison française, 1942. 281 pp.). In 1941 the Johns Hopkins Press published my book entitled *The Comédie Française, 1680-1701. Plays, Actors, Spectators, Finances,* which gives the daily record of plays performed in those years and adds information about French actors; to this volume are due the corrections made below in regard to the amounts received by authors for their plays. My *Adventures of a Literary Historian* (Baltimore, Johns Hopkins Press, 1942) contains an article describing my experiences in composing and publishing Parts I-IV of the present work, one concerned with the effect of war on seventeenth-century French drama, one on relations between comedy and opera (originally published in *Essays and Studies in Honor of Carleton Brown,* New York, New York University Press, 1940), one on la Du Parc, and one on J.-B. Raisin (published in somewhat different form in *MP,* February, 1941). My study of "The Horse in French Plays of the Seventeenth Century" is shortly to appear in a volume in honor of Professor Feuillerat. The Johns Hopkins Press published, late in 1940, E. E. Williams's *Racine depuis 1885, bibliographie raisonnée*; in 1941 Maurice Baudin's *The Profession of King in Seventeenth-Century French Drama*; in 1942 Sister Maria Loyola Coffey's *Adrien Jourdan's Susanna* (1653) and M. I. Protzman's *Les Illustres Fous of Charles Beys.* It has in press a bibliography of Molière by Saintonge and Christ.

Jean Boorsch published "Remarques sur la Technique dramatique de Corneille" in *Studies by Members of the French Department of Yale University* (New Haven, Yale University Press, 1941). J. R. Kleinschmidt showed in *MLN,* LV, 575-8, that Rutter's translation of *le Cid* was published in 1638, not, as often supposed, in 1637. W. L. Schwartz brought out in *PMLA,* LVI, 395-427, an article based on Hubert's *Registre,* to which reference will be made below. J. Scherer discussed in *MLN,* LVII, 407-20, a variety of title employed by Molière and many other dramatists for their plays. Pierre Mélèse published in 1940 an edition of three comedies by de Visé, *la Mère coquette, la Veuve à la mode,* and *les Dames vangées* (Société des textes français modernes). R. C. Knight advanced a theory concerning "The Evolution of Racine's 'Poétique'" in *MLR,* XXXV (1940), 19-39. Sister Marie Philip Haley published in *PMLA,* LV, 426-39, an article on "Peripeteia and Recognition in Racine." Dr. E. Creore has called my attention to articles by Emile Dacier in the *Revue de l'art,* Vols. XLIV and XLIX, on pictures representing scenes from certain plays of the seventeenth-century Théâtre Italien.

Part I, pp. 20, 76, L. E. Dabney showed in *MLN,* LVI, 431-2, that Thillois's *Solyman II* was probably written, not in 1608, but between 1612 and 1617. P. 198, n. 2, add *Osman* has been studied in detail by Elizabeth Marshall, *op. cit.*; the play, which concerns the murder of Osman II, has choruses like other Belgian tragedies of its time. P. 283, n. 8, read *Richecourt, Niobé,* and *Palemon.* P. 452, as Antoine Adam showed in the *Revue d'Histoire de la philosophie,* V (1937), 25-37, that the chief source of *le Prince déguisé* is the story of Sidonio in Canto XIV of Marino's *Adone,* delete Juan de Flores (l. 1), add a fifth on the *Adone* of Marino (l. 5), change five *to* four (l. 9), six *to* seven (l. 11). Pp. 481-2, correct in accordance with the fact that the main source is Marino's *Adone.* P. 484, n. 1, *for* July 30 *read* July 20.

Part II, p. 20, W. L. Schwartz, *op. cit.,* p. 399, is unwilling to accept Sauval's statement that the larger hall held three or four thousand persons, because " such large audiences cannot be reconciled with what is known of the total receipts from ticket sales." Need I remind Mr. Schwartz that the number of tickets sold does not indicate the number that were not sold? His figures show merely that it was the larger, not the smaller, of the two halls that Molière used. It seems probable that, before Molière began to play at the Palais Royal, the staircase which reminded Sauval of a Roman theater was torn down, diminishing the capacity of the hall by about 1200 places and leaving the total number of persons that might enter it at about 1800, not many more than Fritsche's 1450, which Schwartz seems inclined to accept. There is, then, no reason to discredit Sauval. Pp. 128-44, Antoine Adam, *op. cit.,* VI (1938), 29-52, makes suggestions as to the authorship of pamphlets in the *Cid* quarrel. P. 235, n. 18, correct the second and third sentences in accordance with Part IV, pp. 186-7. P. 299, Roy, *Sorel,* p. 422, claimed for Sorel the authorship of the *Comédie de chansons* on the ground that an analysis of the play is given in the 1623 ed. of *Francion* (Roy ed., IV (1931), 63-6). It is true that a comedy composed entirely of popular songs is there described, that the name Alidor appears in a song mentioned in the novel and is that of the play's hero, and that a good many of the songs quoted in the novel reappear in Acts I and IV of the comedy, so that there is certainly some connection between the two, but it is impossible to be sure just what that connection was. The play may have been written first, before 1623, and have influenced Sorel, or Sorel may have developed the play from the sketch he had given in *Francion,* or someone else may have imitated Sorel's novel. The date of the first ed. of the *Comédie de chansons* and the reference in it to the siege of La Rochelle argue for one of the last two hypotheses. Cortland Eyer, *RR*, XXXII, 329-38, pointed out further debts of Boisrobert to Vergil and Ovid, but he claimed that his chief sources were two early Spanish dramatists, intermediaries between him and Justin; I showed in the same journal, XXXIII, 72-3, that there is no evidence that Boisrobert made use of the Spaniards and that Justin remains his chief source, though he followed Vergil to a greater extent than I had previously indicated. P. 559, l. 29, *for* younger *read* Michel. P. 593, n. 13, l. 10, for *Frédéric* read *Fédéric*. P. 605, n. 3, *substitute for the last sentence* For his other plays cf. below Part III, p. 167, Part IV, pp. 95-7, 217-8. P. 617, l. 2, *read* a hint from Aristotle's *Poetics* or from the scholiast. P. 682, l. 17, *for* 1693 *read* 1683. P. 783, first item, *Solyman* is by La Tuillerie; *italicize* Appius, *but not* Aristotle. P. 803, l. 6, *for* P. 25 *read* P. 250.

Part III, p. 27, l. 9, *for* she and her niece were *read* her niece was. P. 29, l. 24, *for* 1687 *read* 1685. P. 34, l. 4, *for* 1773 *read* 1673; l. 10, *delete* one of. P. 38, l. 9, *for* November 4 *read* October 28. P. 157, l. 6, *for* properties *read* proprieties. P. 187, n. 6, *add* d'Aubignac (*Pratique*, Martino ed., p. 140) declared that the last act was condemned on account of "Discours inutiles." P. 220, for the hypothesis that Molière was attacking Mlle de Scudéry and her friends cf. Antoine Adam, *op. cit.*, VII (1939), 14-46; his work, highly conjectural, does not take into consideration objections to his hypothesis that I have mentioned. P. 267, n. 27, l. 12, *read* Paul Lacroix. P. 280, l. 34, *for* ten *read* eleven. P. 281, l. 12, *for* five *read* four; n. 18, *Timon* should be among the extant plays. P. 282, l. 38, *delete* the last. P. 372, l. 9, *for* Mlle *read* George. P. 447, l. 21, *for* 1647 *read* 1648. P. 451, running title, *read* Boyer's. P. 519, ll. 36-7, Schwartz, *op. cit.*, p. 411, gives reason for believing that La Thorillière played Amphitryon; in that case Jupiter was probably acted, as in *Psyché*, by Du Croisy. P. 536, l. 2, *for* two *read* seven; n. 3, l. 2, *for* Jan. 7 *read* May 31. P. 543, ll. 14-5, *for* by Molière's troupe *read* at Paris. P. 560, l. 7, *read* accusations. P. 617, l. 28, *for* Act I *read* Act II. P. 619, l. 22, *for* boar *read* bear. P. 652, l. 26, *for* da *read* de. P. 660, cards and tobacco were required for the play in 1693, as shown below, Part IV, p. 35. P. 704, n. 24, *add* as *le Bonnet enchanté*, it was played six times at the Comédie Française, Oct. 14 to Nov. 13, 1692, but "le Jaloux" of Oct. 22, 1673, was Montfleury's *Semblable à soy-mesme*; cf. Part IV, p. 442. P. 752, n. 22, for IV read V. P. 810, J. F. Privitera holds, in *MLN*, LVI, 211-4, that Th. Corneille drew most of his source material for Acts IV and V of *la Comtesse d'Orgueil* and some for the other acts from Moreto's *El lindo Don Diego*. P. 893, l. 6, *for* republished *read* announced the republication of; n. 1, *for* Pasco *read* Pascoe. P. 894, remark on Part I, p. 482, Antoine Adam has shown that Miss Matulka was mistaken and that the source of the play is Marino's *Adone* (cf. above, remark on Part I, p. 452); remark on Part I, p. 756, for *Primaleón* read *Adone*, by Marino. P. 895, l. 46, read *Sallengre*.

Part IV, p. 3, l. 10, *read* Bourdet. P. 15, n. 2, Schwartz, *op. cit.*, p. 406, argues that Jean de Villiers was the *gagiste* who played for Molière in 1672, after Easter. I called his attention to a document published by Liebrecht which shows that Jean de Villiers had signed a contract to act in another troupe at that time. Schwartz then suggested that there was a *lettre de cachet* which forced the actor to break his contract and referred to Monval's *Chronologie moliéresque*. Monval, however, does not speak of a *lettre de cachet*, but of an *ordre*, and does not say by whom it was given. If he knew there was a *lettre de cachet*, why did he not mention it, as he did in the case of Baron? The *Chronologie* is not a collection of documents, but a list, unsupported by evidence, of supposed events, some of which certainly never occurred. Until documentary evidence to the contrary is discovered, one must hold that the *gagiste* was another Villiers. It would, of course, be strange that a *sociétaire* of one troupe should be forced to become merely a *gagiste* in another. Schwartz's remark that Villiers had only half a share when he joined the Comédie Française has no significance, as that represented normal remuneration for a young actor. La Bellonde, according to Tralage (P. Lacroix, *Notes et Documents*, Nouvelle Collection moliéresque, 1880, p. 3), though born in Paris, had acquired through acting in the provinces a provincial accent "approchant du gascon." P. 19, n. 11, *add* Tralage (*op. cit.*, p. 4) calls Le Comte a "fort honeste homme," a poor actor in serious rôles, forgetful, but tolerated in comedy, where he played the part of a *conseiller, commissaire,* or "gentilhomme de campagne, gardeur de dindons"; n. 12, *add* Tralage (*op. cit.*, pp. 2, 3) notes the great popularity of the younger La Thorillière, who "gourmande le parterre," but is its "délices"; he calls him a spendthrift, but indicates that his wife, Colombine, has a saving disposition, like her parents. P. 20, l. 1, *for* Aug. *read* July; l. 3, *add* except when fractional shares, set aside to meet extra expenses, raised it higher, once to 25½ (cf. my *Comédie Française*, p. 10). P. 22, n. 20, *add* Tralage (*op. cit.*, p. 2) calls him "le bon homme du Perier, avec son air doucet," and states that he played George Dandin and was hissed; n. 21, Tralage (*op. cit.*, p. 9) reports that he saw Rosélis as Polyeucte and Sévigny as Sévère in April, 1688, "applaudis d'une grande assemblée"—a reference to a performance of *Polyeucte* on April 3, 1688, when 713 persons paid admission. P. 23, l. 15, *for* his brother Jacques *read* Sévigny; l. 16, *for* as did Sévigny later in 1694, la Le Comte in 1695 *read* as did Jacques Raisin in October, 1694, la Le Comte at Easter, 1695; n. 23, la Duclos is called by Tralage (*op. cit.*, p. 4) " une grosse fille qui se porte bien, aimant la joye . . . assez bien faite, la peau fort blanche. . . . C'est une actrice de génie médiocre. Elle n'a point la timidité de Mme Clavelle." Pp. 23-4, *for* The following year *read* In 1694-5. P. 24, n. 24, according to Tralage (*op. cit.*, p. 2), Du Mont de Lavoy was about forty when he joined the troupe and played in a manner " trop rustique, brusque, et qui n'est bonne qu'au village." P. 34, ll. 20-2, the identification of Laurent as Champagne is confirmed by Bapst, *Essai*, p. 392: " Laurent, dit Champagne . . . vint à Versailles et à Fontainebleau avec les comédiens en 1697." P. 37, last line of text, *for* 1685 *read* 1684. P. 39, n. 13, l. 7, *for* 2675 francs, 4 sous *read* 2718 francs, 6 sous; l. 8, *for* 6 sous *read* 10 sous. P. 40, last line of note, *read* 937 francs, 2½ sous. P. 41, ll. 23-4, *for* those . . . nothing *read* while the shares of the others were kept by the treasurer and credited to the actors against what they owed the sinking-fund. P. 42, n. 15, the last sentence should be changed to *read* The largest number of paid admissions was 1123, on Feb. 8, 1688. P. 43, n. 16, l. 7, *for Chevalier à la mode read Curieux de Compiègne.* P. 44, l. 20, *read* rarely more; l. 21, *for* or *read* rarely. P. 47, l. 6, de Vergnette was probably J.-B. Rousseau, cf. my review in *MLQ*, II, 343. P. 49, n. 30, Tralage (*op. cit.*, p. 62) quotes a poster announcing a performance of the Italian troupe on Sept. 1, 1688, when admission to the parterre was 15 sous, to the third tier of boxes one franc, elsewhere three francs, while a lower box sold as a whole for 3 louis; ll. 10-12, change this sentence to *read* When the *Cause des femmes* was first produced, a lower box cost 3 louis.

P. 52, l. 14, *for* She and her *read* Her. P. 61, l. 8, read *Andromaque.* P. 238, n. 2, l. 11, *for* 6 sous *read* 10 sous, *for* 2230 *read* 2210; l. 13, *for* 1512 *read* 1612. P. 338, l. 22, *for* 13⁷⁄₁₂ *read* 14. P. 401, n. 2, l. 3, *for* 1828 francs, 6 sous *read* 1832 francs, 17 sous (cf. my *Comédie Française*, p. 155); l. 8, *for* 228 *read* 226. P. 434, l. 20, *read* âne. (I, 8); l. 23, *for* 8 *read* 10. P. 470, last line, *for* Hévart *read* Hervart. P. 547, n. 23, for further information about Crosnier cf. C. D. Zdanowicz in *MLN*, LVII, 245-52. P. 579, l. 18, *for* Le *read* La. P. 587, l. 9, *for* fourteen . . . erroneously *read* fifteen . . . correctely. P. 598, l. 1 and end of n. 15, read *Titapapouf*; n. 15, l. 4, *for* 2672 francs, 4 sous *read* 2718 francs, 6 sous; *for* 1796 *read* 1791; l. 6, *for* 19 *read* 19½; l. 16, the amount assigned to *la Désolation des joueuses* does not include the author's share for Aug. 26, 1687, probably about 35 francs, as the film representing the record for that day was not made; l. 17, *for* 409 francs *read* 424 francs, 14 sous; l. 21, *for* 8 sous *read* 17 sous; l. 23, *for* 188 francs, 10½ sous *read* 201 francs, 6½ sous; l. 28, *for* 56 francs *read* 55 francs. P. 600, l. 24, *for* Giratoni *read*

Giaratone. P. 605, n. 20, *add* Moreover, a fashionable woman's day had been described as early as 1662 in Gilbert's *Intrigues amoureuses* (cf. above, Part III, p. 696). P. 616, l. 18, *read* No recent French play; l. 21, *read* dramatist of the 1680's. P. 618, n. 24, *for* Constantini, known as Mezzetin *read* Lolli, known as Baloardo (cf. Tralage, *op. cit.*, pp. 5-7). P. 628, n. 36, read *Descente*. P. 633, l. 14, *delete* a seat in *and* an unusually high price. P. 695, n. 19, it was also published as *Les Souffleurs ou La Pierre Philosophale d'Arlequin*, Amsterdam, Adrian Braakman, 1695 (a copy of this illustrated ed. was acquired by the Johns Hopkins University in 1941). P. 708, n. 5, for the next to last sentence *read* The authors earned from the production of the play 581 francs, 1 sou. P. 724, n. 32, *add* On June 9, 1693, the actors paid 2 francs, 5 sous for "les roles de la petite piece intitulée Le derriere du theatre" (cf. my *Comédie Française*, p. 138). P. 748, n. 29, *for* Isabelle *read* Ismène. P. 754, n. 38, l. 4, *for* 156 francs, 7 sous *read* 150 francs, 17 sous, *for* 132 francs, 11 sous *read* 133 francs, 1 sou; ll. 4-6, for support of this suggestion, cf. my *op. cit.*, p. 190. P. 758, n. 9, l. 4, *for* ½ *read* ⅙. P. 817, n. 13, l. 2, *for* 1892 *read* 1898; l. 7, *for* 947 francs, 3½ sous *read* 937 francs, 2½ sous; l. 8, *for* 805 francs, 5 sous *read* 804 francs, 1 sou; ll. 9, 10, *for* 497 francs, 1 sou, *read* 475 francs, 15 sous; ll. 10-1, *for* 325 francs, 14½ sous *read* 326 francs, 11 sous; l. 12, *delete* ½; l. 14, *for* ¾ *read* ¼, *for* 48 francs, 15 sous *read* 41 francs, 3 sous. P. 829, l. 34, *add* It was given on May 1 in 1693, 1694, 1695, 1698, and 1700. P. 847, for J.-B. Rousseau cf. H. A. Grubbs, *J.-B. Rousseau*, Princeton, 1941, who notes that in the original ed. of *le Caffé* Coronis was given Gascon characteristics in his speech and that the dialogue of *le Flatteur* was lengthened and made less vigorous in its later form. P. 862, n. 6, l. 10, *for* 19 sous *read* 18 sous; l. 14, *for* ½ *read* ¹⁄₁₂; l. 15, *for* 99 francs, 19 sous *read* 106 francs, 14 sous. P. 878, n. 7, l. 10, *for* 1681 *read* 1678. P. 884, the last stanza quoted is, with slight changes, vv. 5-8 of Boileau's translation of Sappho (*Traité du sublime*, ch. 8, pub. 1674). P. 929, l. 16, *for* he *read* she. P. 979, transfer *Pattes de mouche* to the Sardou item.

Addenda. Marc Denkinger has prepared for publication a book on the "forme des salles de théâtre à Paris sous Louis XIII." Part II, pp. 38, 407-8, Part III, pp. 178-9, Roxelane is the name given the Sultana by Mairet, Scudéry, and Jacquelin; I referred to her by her historical name, Roxana or Roxane.

SUBJECT INDEX OF PARTS I, II, III, IV, AND V

155

298, 335, 367, 376, 401, 414-908, 912-24, 926-8, 933-5, 939-41, 943-50, 983-4; V,
    3-6, 11, 14-5, 17, 23, 27-32, 34, 36, 38-40, 42-7, 49, 53, 57-60, 62-3, 66, 68-71, 73-
    85, 88, 93-4, 102-47, 149-50, 152.
comet, IV, 484, 536-9, 944, 948-9; V, 9, 11, 132.
confidant (including *suivante*), I, 20, 56, 239, 268, 295, 363, 484, 533, 563-4, 601,
    603, 605-6, 615, 617, 633, 664, 676, 758; II, 32, 101, 132, 140, 155, 157, 191, 213,
    229, 240, 261-2, 337, 377, 384, 398, 409-11, 429, 433, 459-61, 528, 534-5, 542, 549,
    581, 590, 609, 717, 728, 734, 760; III, 57, 66, 72, 74, 84, 93, 110, 118, 136, 159,
    165, 198, 201, 231-2, 281, 304, 316, 321-2, 329, 331, 338, 346, 361-2, 437, 460,
    481-3, 541, 563, 565, 572, 575, 582, 601, 611, 655, 679, 687, 786, 792; IV, 28, 74,
    83, 96, 98-9, 103, 120, 147, 149, 159, 166, 168, 170, 172-3, 197, 200-1, 203, 207,
    213, 216-8, 236, 241, 256, 262, 265, 268, 271-2, 274, 276, 282, 285-6, 311, 360-1,
    379, 381, 402, 407, 412-3, 420, 454, 507, 511, 516, 519-20, 600, 605, 613, 657-8,
    690, 713, 723, 727, 759, 765-6, 799, 800, 809, 811, 833, 845, 850, 854, 872, 889,
    902-3, 905-6, 910, 918, 930, 936; V, 24, 59, 107, 141.
Confrérie de la Passion, I, 15, 18, 573, 710-1, 713-4, 717, 727, 729, 742; V, 13, 23.
convents, abuse of, I, 204, 629; II, 478, 654, 764; III, 329, 779-80, 834; IV, 9, 414,
    420, 433, 440, 459-60, 466, 471-2, 474, 530, 666, 676, 744, 763, 774, 776, 781, 797,
    811, 822-4, 828, 843-5, 854, 872, 930-1; V, 128.
costume, I, 30, 76, 90, 96, 132, 136, 140, 188, 200, 223, 238, 261, 277, 297, 323, 329,
    342, 345, 350, 362-5, 391, 404, 423, 437-8, 440, 443, 448, 460, 465, 481, 492-3, 511,
    513, 519, 549, 566-7, 582, 587, 591-2, 602, 618-9, 650, 652, 655-7, 666, 676, 678,
    724-6, 728, 730-1, 733-7, 746; II, 25, 30, 32, 46, 57-8, 80, 93, 101, 112-4, 165-6,
    172, 180, 240, 250, 268, 270, 272, 291, 295, 298, 323, 376, 379, 397, 404, 411, 413,
    419, 432, 437, 440-1, 446, 454, 461, 471, 476, 484, 486-7, 490-1, 497, 516, 533, 537,
    541, 545, 549, 568, 571, 574, 580, 619, 621, 647, 649, 675, 716, 730, 738, 747, 753,
    761; III, 39, 44, 58-9, 63, 66, 68, 71-2, 77, 99, 101, 104, 115, 124, 137, 144, 150,
    161, 191, 198, 201-2, 215-6, 221, 225, 230, 232, 236-40, 242-3, 245, 249, 255, 262,
    264, 270, 276, 278, 283, 292, 298-9, 305, 308-9, 317-9, 325-6, 330, 332-3, 340-1,
    343-4, 357-8, 362, 380, 397, 414, 421-2, 463, 541, 544, 558, 615, 628-9, 636-8, 640,
    643, 648, 652-3, 657, 662-3, 668, 670-1, 673, 675-6, 678, 683, 686, 689, 691, 695-6,
    702-3, 707-8, 713, 717-8, 725, 730, 743, 752, 761, 765, 771, 775-6, 783-6, 791, 797-
    8, 805-6, 808, 814, 819, 821, 823, 825-7, 829-30, 832, 837; IV, 8, 35, 48, 82, 124,
    152-3, 168, 194, 198-9, 205, 228, 285, 312-3, 341, 343, 360-1, 418-20, 427, 433,
    436-8, 444-5, 452, 467, 471-2, 477, 492, 497, 501, 506, 508, 514-5, 518, 520, 522,
    524, 526, 539, 546, 551, 557, 559-60, 562, 565, 569-71, 580, 592, 609-12, 614, 618,
    620-1, 624, 627-9, 632, 635, 638, 650, 652-6, 660, 662, 666-7, 669, 671, 673, 676-9,
    684, 688, 691, 693-4, 700-1, 703-4, 709-10, 720, 725, 733-4, 737-8, 744, 750, 758,
    760, 766, 772, 779, 787, 789, 793, 803, 809, 814-5, 826, 828, 830, 838-41, 858-60,
    863, 875, 877, 879-81, 883-4, 887, 890, 898, 902-3, 910, 916, 935, 945, 948; V, 21,
    104, 108-9, 118, 122, 124, 126, 133.
court performances, I, 14, 68-9, 160, 169, 233, 243, 280, 476, 512, 530, 552, 582, 592,
    623, 658, 711, 748; II, 6-9, 95, 97-8, 103, 114, 129, 204, 207, 210, 225, 376, 390,
    408, 475, 512, 559, 677-9, 682; III, 6, 22, 53, 57, 95, 150, 192, 217, 238-9, 243-4,
    253, 262, 366, 373, 378, 383-4, 447, 483, 503, 518, 520, 534, 540, 545, 583, 590,
    607, 614, 616-7, 620-2, 624, 631, 648, 650-1, 662, 674, 707, 709-10, 713, 718-9,
    722, 724, 730, 736, 745, 752, 768, 803, 807, 819, 827, 836, 861; IV, 5, 7, 29, 35,
    40-1, 53, 69, 76, 88, 94, 146-7, 196, 199, 205, 207, 211, 214, 217, 220-1, 228, 232,
    235, 237, 256, 264, 271, 278, 299, 300, 313, 324-5, 335, 338, 358, 364, 382, 401,
    437-8, 467, 485-6, 510-2, 517, 522-3, 532, 541, 563, 566, 571, 573, 576, 593, 595-6,
    598, 600, 643, 718, 721, 726, 754, 761, 764, 766, 775, 777, 809-10, 812-3, 817, 825,
    827, 831, 841, 846, 848, 857, 862, 869, 872, 887, 927, 984; V, 14, 16, 19, 87, 106-7,
    110, 153.
crawfish, I, 652; III, 97; IV, 794, 833, 896.
curtain, stage, I, 714-7; II, 18, 20, 52, 90, 317, 359, 375-6, 576, 603, 622, 680, 682;
    III, 42-3, 457, 774, 893; IV, 42, 46, 317, 461, 623, 715; V, 16-7.

dedications criticized, II, 293, 722, 737; III, 198.
deer, I, 98, 100, 162, 187, 200, 228, 417, 680; II, 175, 226, 243-5, 365, 400-1, 417,
    737; III, 145, 209, 241, 288, 422-3, 472, 845-6; IV, 89, 282, 525, 593-4, 596, 641,
    667, 883, 925.
democracy, I, 74, 83, 94, 136, 452, 489, 529, 544, 654, 726, 758; II, 59, 60, 169, 200,
    236, 402, 636, 684-5, 702; III, 37, 170, 550; IV, 227, 802, 808, 822-3, 834.
disguised subject of a play, III, 566; IV, 140-2, 193, 252, 257, 264, 276, 350, 383,
    391, 941-2; V, 46, 98, 100-1.
dog, I, 27, 37, 61, 71, 84, 97-8, 172, 318, 380, 425, 428, 438, 518, 653, 677, 681, 724;
    II, 23, 89, 117, 244, 261, 275, 278, 412, 462, 489, 659, 734, 756; III, 59, 61, 72,

national characteristics, I, 278, 327, 425, 480, 519, 544, 555, 657; II, 270, 382, 384, 492; III, 83, 123, 241, 264-5, 276, 588-9, 697, 829, 842-3; IV, 11-3, 69, 468-70, 586-7, 746, 849, 885-8, 916.

nature, feeling for, I, 26, 61, 91, 96-7, 130, 167, 171, 175-8, 210, 215, 224, 239, 272, 297, 313, 319, 325, 391-2, 396, 403, 420, 442, 463, 537; II, 101, 250, 276, 664-5, 717; III, 367-8, 386, 412; V, 50.

newspapers, newsmongers, etc., referred to in plays, II, 117, 294, 436, 446, 476, 734; III, 542, 736; IV, 5, 415, 465, 485, 523-7, 578-9, 605, 607, 670, 682-3, 690, 714, 728, 780-1, 832, 876, 879, 894, 896, 944, 946; V, 76, 113, 128, 133, 135.

nobility investigated, II, 24; III, 7, 685-7, 809, 822; IV, 281, 480-1.

noble, comic country, II, 429, 466-70, 728, 755-7, 770; III, 46, 58-9, 80-3, 287, 290-4, 675-6, 712, 719-21, 754, 809-11, 819-21, 838-9, 856-8; IV, 26, 415, 435-6, 462-4, 469, 471-3, 481-2, 484, 530-1, 593-4, 736-8, 753, 825-6, 944, 984; V, 4, 30, 75, 80-1, 111, 115, 120, 123, 125-6, 128.

noble, comic young, I, 588; III, 23, 221, 242-3, 254, 257-64, 266-7, 269, 298-9, 327-8, 342, 545, 613, 655, 660-1, 664, 667-9, 672-4, 688-92, 728, 766-7, 778, 786, 791-2, 801, 857; IV, 435-6, 484, 564, 576, 633, 654, 656-7, 673-4, 690, 715, 722, 724, 733, 740, 742-3, 746, 751-3, 755-6, 769, 815, 818; V, 4, 85, 104-5, 109, 115, 118, 120, 126, 132, 140.

nurse, I, 20, 24, 49, 50, 56, 71, 76-7, 86, 108, 112, 123, 158, 175-6, 184, 196, 232, 284, 289, 317-9, 372, 484, 487, 492, 494, 498, 533-4, 556, 563-4, 578-9, 594-7, 603, 606, 645, 693-4, 730, 758; II, 14, 32, 38, 52, 240, 287, 337, 479, 514, 520, 525; III, 51, 102, 354, 397, 399, 425, 463, 731; IV, 101, 109, 112, 129, 290, 303, 440, 497, 611, 711, 720, 930-1; V, 91.

nursing, evils of, IV, 428-9, 778.

Odéon, II, 550; III, 644, 690; IV, 116, 593.

omnibus, III, 7, 322-5, 336, 857; V, 9, 10, 122.

opera, I, 58, 242, 352-3, 453, 512; II, 6, 16, 20, 154, 171, 173, 175, 240, 312, 386, 413, 677-8, 681, 719, 727, 748, 762, 774; III, 6, 39, 92, 101, 498, 500, 520, 704, 860-1; IV, 6, 8, 16-7, 42, 88, 121-2, 172, 185, 202, 211, 232, 243, 245, 251, 261, 292, 299, 325, 349, 352, 361, 364, 378, 398, 403, 415-6, 435-6, 457, 459, 461, 470-4, 484, 488, 505-6, 534-5, 541, 547, 549, 556, 562, 565, 568-9, 571, 573-4, 581-4, 604-5, 612-4, 616-7, 621, 626, 629-30, 634-6, 638, 645-8, 650-1, 653, 655, 657-9, 663-7, 670-1, 675-6, 678-80, 683-4, 686, 691, 696, 702-5, 709-12, 715, 731, 736, 752, 755, 757, 770, 778-9, 782-3, 791-4, 805, 816, 818-20, 836, 838, 848-9, 857-8, 860, 863-70, 872-3, 875-6, 890, 892, 895-6, 909, 918-9, 922-4, 926, 934, 944, 946; V, 7, 10, 14, 16-7, 28, 33-4, 45, 58, 66, 84-6, 91, 121, 123, 126, 128, 132-3, 136-8, 142, 146, 149.

opéra comique, II, 294, 804; III, 816; IV, 732, 935.

opérateur in plays, II, 92, 746; III, 648, 651; IV, 461, 597, 636, 812-3, 870-1, 881; V, 135, 142.

otter, II, 275.

oyster, I, 652.

Palais Royal (Cardinal), I, 716; II, 8, 20, 359, 363, 367-8, 375, 381, 390, 444, 678; III, 22, 29, 30, 234, 243, 253, 262, 267-8, 327, 523, 616, 639, 709, 713, 778, 843, 852; IV, 16, 40, 43, 45, 170, 599, 909; V, 6, 12, 14, 16-7, 20, 22-3, 121, 127, 150.

palmistry, III, 58-9, 61, 807-8.

panther, I, 172, 201, 266; III, 61, 506, 530.

parasite, I, 72, 143, 579, 624-5, 657; II, 110, 260, 264-7, 269, 429, 437-8, 457, 479, 481, 490, 534, 770; III, 50-1, 91, 102-3, 628; IV, 419, 421, 511, 719.

Paris, comment on, I, 597; II, 261, 272, 430, 434, 443-4, 487, 744; III, 216, 222, 252, 697, 735; IV, 513, 644, 657, 887; V, 9, 63.

Paris, localities (other than shops, taverns, and theaters) in or near, I, 14, 35, 37, 39, 67-8, 133, 139, 150, 152-3, 155, 160, 163, 169, 220-2, 229, 233, 235, 278, 298, 303, 309, 314, 334, 341, 352, 354, 379, 385-6, 407, 426-7, 437, 453, 463-4, 469, 476, 485, 512, 516, 519, 522, 533, 543-4, 581, 584-5, 587-8, 591-2, 601, 605, 610, 614-5, 620-2, 627, 629-32, 643, 649, 652, 658, 671, 676, 691, 706, 709-11, 714-6, 719, 729-30, 742, 746; II, 8, 9, 17, 20, 46, 88, 95, 97-8, 100-1, 103, 109, 112, 114-5, 117, 129, 163, 204, 207, 269-70, 293, 329, 340, 430-1, 433-5, 444, 446, 452, 482, 487-8, 492-7, 559, 587, 620, 665, 676, 735, 744, 746-8, 758, 763, 804; III, 5-7, 21-2, 48, 52-3, 55, 57, 60, 62, 97, 108, 150, 192, 219-20, 238-9, 244, 253, 255-6, 259, 262, 264-6, 276, 285, 292, 298, 302, 309-10, 323-5, 338, 360, 366, 373, 375, 378, 383-4, 447, 470, 483, 520, 540, 545, 583, 590, 616-7, 620-4, 631, 648, 650-1, 662, 670-1, 673-4, 686-7, 690, 694, 702, 707, 709, 713, 718, 722, 730, 736, 745, 761, 763-4, 768, 773, 803, 819, 821-2, 826-7, 836, 841, 851, 861; IV, 9, 16-7, 21-3, 25, 29-30, 35, 40, 42, 47, 50, 53, 69, 84, 94, 146-7, 196, 199, 205, 207, 211-2, 214, 217, 221-2,

804, 809, 812, 815, 820, 829, 833, 836, 850, 858, 864, 870, 889, 893-4, 897-8, 900-1, 904, 911, 914, 920, 925-7, 929, 935-6, 943, 947, 984; V, 31, 36, 38-9, 41, 43-4, 48-51, 58, 66-7, 77, 82, 86, 110, 113, 120, 122, 124, 126, 138, 140. (See also lyric monologue.)
Vesuvius, III, 577.

war, influence of, or allusions to recent or contemporary wars, I, 13, 66, 143-4, 201, 206, 226-7, 309, 334, 395, 449, 490, 584-5, 588, 681, 729; II, 1, 5, 6, 12-3, 105, 107, 114-7, 121, 149, 172, 175, 269-70, 290, 301, 306, 338-9, 373, 383-4, 429, 432-3, 442-3, 446, 475-6, 487, 489, 492, 556, 572, 676, 699, 700, 707, 713, 727, 731, 733-5, 762-3, 765; III, 5, 7, 21, 59, 152, 167-8, 175, 187, 195, 222, 279, 286-7, 302, 334-6, 338, 351-4, 374-5, 384-5, 392, 429, 471, 496, 503-5, 510, 526, 529, 543, 593, 626, 629, 671, 687, 709-10, 712, 760-2, 764, 803, 811, 824-6, 840, 843, 849; IV, 1, 5, 18, 29-31, 34, 41, 44, 84, 88-9, 193, 228-9, 269, 305, 314, 317, 349, 351, 354, 400, 415, 425, 451, 455, 460, 478, 480, 483, 485, 493, 506, 508, 518, 525, 529, 535-6, 545-6, 556, 558-61, 578-9, 588, 605, 627-8, 630, 634-6, 644-5, 647, 653-4, 657, 659-60, 663-4, 667-8, 670, 677, 681-2, 684, 686-8, 690-1, 697, 708-11, 714, 716-8, 722, 724, 726, 728, 733, 746-7, 756, 769, 773-5, 777-81, 790, 793, 795, 797-8, 800, 802-4, 818-9, 828, 849, 852, 855, 857-60, 864-5, 876, 878-9, 884-90, 916-7, 923-5, 931, 937-8, 940-1, 945-6, 948, 950; V, 3, 4, 11, 17-9, 64-5, 83-4, 90-1, 121-2, 132, 135-6, 142-3, 149.
watches, I, 583, 588-9, 621, 634; II, 733, 735; III, 324; IV, 506, 569, 612, 692, 717, 744, 763, 799, 901, 915.
water, speculation in, IV, 622-3, 696.
watering resorts, I, 591-2; III, 7, 87, 803, 840-4, 857; IV, 684, 769, 796-7, 819; V, 118, 135.
weasel, I, 81; IV, 832.
whale, I, 139, 694; IV, 651.
wig, I, 183, 671, 726; II, 277, 288; III, 266, 333, 340-1, 676, 686, 691, 762, 771, 786, 791, 814; IV, 20, 35, 48, 281, 471, 562, 565, 569-70, 621, 632, 655, 666, 676, 694, 725, 772, 774, 860, 883, 887, 890, 902.
wildboar, I, 47, 52, 77, 102, 190, 228, 470-1; II, 42, 169, 483, 582; III, 79, 383, 386, 499, 524-5, 617-9, 722-3, 846; IV, 183-5, 376-8, 660, 737; V, 151.
wolf, I, 27, 132, 136, 149, 196, 201, 333-4, 400, 429, 443, 448, 680; II, 174-5, 250, 275, 294, 365, 660, 737, 745; III, 60, 321, 323, 325-6, 352, 390, 422-3, 660, 811, 842; IV, 282-3, 492, 641, 701, 833, 852, 931-2.
woman's rights, I, 758; II, 591, 648, 751-2; III, 7, 64, 123-4, 208, 235-6, 251-2, 283, 288-9, 297, 740, 742, 776; IV, 637, 651, 676-8, 682, 685, 883-4; V, 114, 118.
women who wrote plays or operas, II, 95, 197-8, 278, 657, 671-4; III, 24, 30, 125-6, 142, 157-60, 457-9, 500-2, 544-8, 559-61, 665-7, 679-80, 861; IV, 186-8, 235-9, 355-8, 638, 724-5, 771-3, 928-33; V, 86-7.
workmen's compensation, IV, 35.
worm, I, 37, 40, 114.

FINDING LIST OF PLAYS[1]

Abraham sacrifiant, Bèze, I.
Absalon, Duché, IV.
Absent chez soy, d'Ouville, II; III.
Académiciens, see *Académistes*.
Académie burlesque, see *Femmes co- quettes*.
Académie des dames, see *Coquette*, Re- gnard.
Académie des femmes, Chappuzeau, III; V.
Académistes, Saint-Evremond, I; II; III; V.
Accouchée, see *Embarras de Godard*.
Acero de Madrid, Lope, III.
Achab, Marcée, I.
Achille, Mort d', Benserade, I; II; IV; V.
Achille, Mort d', Corneille, T., IV; V.
Achille, Mort d', Hardy, I.
Achille victorieux, Borée, I.
Acoubar, Du Hamel, I.
Adelphes, Baron, IV.
Adelphoe, Terence, III; IV.
Adherbal, La Grange-Chancel, IV; V.
Adieu du trône, Dubosc de Mont-André, III.
Adieux des officiers, Dufresny, IV.
Adolphe, Le Bigre, II.
Adonis y Venus, Lope, III.
Adraste, Ferrier, IV; V.
Adrianus, Cellot, II.
Adrien, Campistron, IV; V.
Advocat duppé, Chevreau, II; III; V.
Aëtius, Campistron, IV; V.
Affaires sont les affaires, Mirbeau, III.
Agamemnon, Æschylus, IV.
Agamemnon, Arnaud, II.
Agamemnon, Boyer, II; IV; V.
Agamemnon, Seneca, II; IV.
Agarite, Durval, I; II; III; V.
Agathocle, Aubry, IV.
Agathonphile, Pascal, Françoise, III.
Agésilan de Colchos, Rotrou, I; II; III.
Agésilas, Corneille, I; III; IV; V.
Agimée, Basin, I.
Agioteurs, Dancourt, IV.
Agis, Desjardins, III.
Agis, Mort d', Guérin de Bouscal, I; II; V.
Agnès de Méranie, Ponsard, I.
Agrippa, Riupeirous, IV.

Agrippa, roy d'Albe, Quinault, III; IV; V.
Agrippine, Cyrano de Bergerac, II; III; V.
Aïeux chimériques, Rousseau, J.-B., IV.
Ajax, La Chapelle, IV; V.
Ajax, Sophocles, IV; V.
Alboin, Billard, I.
Albouin, Chrestien des Croix, I.
Alcaide de sí mismo, Calderon, III.
Alcée, Hardy, I.
Alceste, Hardy, I.
Alceste, La Grange-Chancel, IV.
Alcestis, Euripides, I; II; IV.
Alcibiade, Campistron, II; IV; V.
Alcide, Mage, I, 18.
Alcide, Mort d', see *Hercule, Mort d'*.
Alcidiane, Desfontaines, II; III; V.
Alcimédon, Du Ryer, P., I; II; III; IV; V.
Alcimène, Bompart de Saint-Victor, III.
Alcionée, Du Ryer, P., I; II; III; IV; V.
Alcméon, Hardy, I; II; II, 803.
Alexandre, Godinot, II.
Alexandre, le grand, Racine, II; III; III, 896; IV; V.
Alexandre, Mort d', Hardy, I.
Alexandre, Mort d', Louvart, IV.
Alidor et Oronte, see *Célidée*.
Alinde, La Mesnardière, II.
Alizon, Discret, II; III; V.
Alphée, Hardy, I.
Alphonce, Lapoujade, IV.
Alzire, Voltaire, IV.
Amalasonte, Quinault, III; IV.
Aman, Montchrestien, I.
Aman, Rivaudeau, I.
Amant de sa femme, Dorimond, III; V.
Amant douillet, Claveret, I; III, 701-2.
Amante Amant, Campistron, IV; V.
Amante courageuse, see *Isolite*.
Amante ennemie, Sallebray, II; V.
Amante invisible, Nanteuil, III; IV.
Amantes, Chrestien des Croix, I; III; V.
Amante victorieuse, see *Sélidore*.
Amante vindicative, Baro, I; II.
Amant indiscret, Quinault, III; IV; V.
Amant libéral, Guérin de Bouscal, I; II.
Amant libéral, Scudéry, I; II; V.
Amant masqué, Dufresny, IV.

---

[1] Plays whose authors are known are listed under the names of the latter in the indices of Parts I, II, III, IV, and in the General Index of Part V. Such plays, with the exception of *proverbes dramatiques* (see Part IV, pp. 929-32), are entered in this finding list under their own titles, which are followed in most cases by the author's name and an indication of the Part or Parts in which the plays are mentioned. Sub-titles of plays, most of which have been previously omitted, are included, with a reference to the main title. The Roman numerals, if followed by a period or a semicolon, refer to the indices of the Parts they indicate. The first item above means that *Abraham sacrifiant* is listed under Bèze's name in the index of Part I. If the Roman is followed by an Arabic numeral, the reference is to the Part and page so indicated; such references usually have to do with material in the supplements.

Amant parfait, Palaprat, IV.
Amant qui ne flatte point, Hauteroche, III; V.
Amant ridicule, Boisrobert, I; III; IV, 983; V.
Amants brouillés, see *Mère coquette*, Quinault.
Amants brouillés, see *Mère coquette*, Visé.
Amants infortunés, Montfleury, IV.
Amants magnifiques, Molière, III; IV; V.
Amaranthe, Gombauld, I; II; V, 70.
Amar después de la muerte, Calderon, III.
Amarillis, Du Ryer, P., I; II; III.
Amarillis, Passerat, IV.
Amarillis, Tristan l'Hermite, I; II; III.
Amar sin saber a quién, Lope, II; III.
Amasie, Racine, III; IV; V.
Amasis, La Grange-Chancel, II; IV; V.
Ambassadeur d'Affrique, Du Perche, III; V.
Ambigu comique, Montfleury, III; IV; IV, 984; V.
Amélie, Rotrou, I; II; III.
Ami de tout le monde, see *Maris infidèles*.
Amie rivalle, see *Galerie du Palais*.
Aminta, Tasso, I; II; III; IV; V.
Aminte, Dalibray, I.
Aminte, Rayssiguier, I.
Amis Ennemis, see *Armetzar*.
Amnon et Thamar, Chrestien des Croix, I.
Amo criado, see *Donde hay agravios*.
Amor al uso, Solís, II.
Amore opera a caso, Bartolommei, III.
Amor médico, Tirso de Molina, IV.
Amor y Amistad, Tirso de Molina, III.
Amour à la mode, Corneille, T., II; III; IV; V.
Amour apotiquaire, Denis, IV.
Amour Berger, IV, 924-6.
Amour caché par l'amour, Scudéry, I.
Amour contraire, see *Philine*.
Amour de la Patrie, see *Judith*, Bouvot.
Amour desplumé, Moucque, I.
Amour divin, Gaulcher, I.
Amoureuse vaine, Pascal, Françoise, III.
Amoureux extravagant, Pascal, Françoise, III.
Amoureux extravagant, see *Place royale*, Corneille.
Amour extravagant, see *Agimée*.
Amour fantasque, Fiot, IV.
Amour Médecin, Molière, III; IV; V.
Amour Peintre, see *Sicilien*.
Amour sanguinaire, see *Charite*, M. H. L.
Amours contraires, Du Ryer, Isaac, I.
Amours d'Alcippe et de Céphise, see *Cocue imaginaire*.
Amours d'Angélique et de Médor, Gilbert, II; III; V, 76.
Amours de Calotin, Chevalier, III; V.
Amours de Diane et d'Endimion, Gilbert, II; III; IV; V.
Amours de Didon et d'Enée, see *Ambigu comique*.

Amours de Germanicus, see *Germanicus*, Boursault.
Amours de Merlin, Rosidor, III; IV; IV, 984.
Amours de Néron, see *Arie et Pétus*.
Amours de Phélidon et Polibelle, see *Urnes vivantes*.
Amours de Trapolin, see *Comédie de la comédie*.
Amours de Vénus et d'Adonis, Visé, III; III, 896; IV.
Amours d'Ovide, Gilbert, II; III; III, 896; V.
Amours d'Ovide, Racine, III.
Amours du Soleil, Visé, III; III, 896; V.
Amour sentinelle, Nanteuil, III; IV.
Amour téméraire, see *Cléonice*, P. B.
Amour triomphant, Troterel, I; V.
Amour tyrannique, Scudéry, I; II; III; III, 895; V.
Amour vengé, see *Amour victorieux*.
Amour victorieux, Hardy, I.
Amphitruo, Plautus, I; II; III; V.
Amphitryon, Molière, II; III; IV; V.
Amphytrite, Monléon, I; V.
Amsterdam hydropique, P. V. C. H., III.
Amurat, La Clairière, III.
Anatomist, Ravenscroft, III.
Anaxandre, Du Ryer, P., I; III; V.
Andria, Terence, IV.
Andrienne, Baron, IV.
Andromache, Euripides, IV.
Andromaque, Racine, I; II; III; IV; V.
Andromaque, see *Troade*, Sallebray.
Andrómeda, Calderon, I.
Andromède, Corneille, I; II; III; III, 895; IV; V.
Andromire, Scudéry, I; II; III; V.
Andronic, Campistron, IV; V.
Angelica, Fornaris, III.
Angélique et Médor, Dancourt, III; IV; V.
Angélique et Médor, Le Riche, II.
Animaux raisonnables, III, 287; IV, 863, V.
Anne de Bretagne, Ferrier, IV; V.
Annibal, Colonia, IV.
Annibal, Desmaretz, II.
Annibal, Prade, II; IV; V.
Annibal, Riupeirous, IV.
Annibal, Scudéry, II; III.
Annibal, Mort d', Corneille, T., III; IV; V.
Annonce du Grondeur, Palaprat, IV.
Antigone, Boyer, IV, 983.
Antigone, Garnier, II; III.
Antigone, II, 593; Pader d'Assézan, IV; IV, 983.
Antigone, Rotrou, I; II; III; III, 893; IV; V.
Antigone, Sophocles, II; IV; V.
Antioche, Le Francq, I.
Antiochus, Corneille, T., II; III; IV.
Apartemens, Brécourt, III; IV; V.
Apollon berger, Boucher, IV.
Apoticaire devalisé, Villiers, I; III; IV, 983; V.

Apparences trompeuses, Boisrobert, I; II; III.
Apparences trompeuses, Hauteroche, III; IV; V.
Appius, see *Virginie romaine.*
Après-Soupé des auberges, Poisson, III; IV; V.
Arcadie de Messire Philippes Sidney, see *Cour bergère.*
Arétaphile, Du Ryer, P., I; II.
Argel fingido, Lope, III.
Argélie, Abeille, IV; V.
Argénis, Du Ryer, P., I; II; III.
Argénis et Poliarque, Du Ryer, P., I; II.
Ariadne ravie, Hardy, I.
Ariane, Corneille, T., III; IV; V.
Ariarathe, L'Enfant de Saint Gilles, IV.
Aricidie, Le Vert, II; III; V.
Arie et Pétus, Gilbert, II; III; IV; V.
Arimène, Montreux, I.
Aristène, Troterel, I; II; V.
Aristoclée, Hardy, I.
Aristodème, Boyer, II; V.
Aristotime, Le Vert, II; IV; V.
Arlequin Bachus, Denis, IV.
Arlequin Défenseur du beau sexe, Biancolelli, L., IV.
Arlequin Empereur de la lune, Fatouville, IV.
Arlequin esprit aérien, Romagnesi, M.-A., IV.
Arlequin Grapignan, see *Arlequin Procureur.*
Arlequin Homme à bonne fortune, Regnard, IV; V.
Arlequin Jason, Fatouville, IV.
Arlequin lingère du Palais, Fatouville, IV.
Arlequin Mercure galant, Fatouville, IV.
Arlequin Misanthrope, Biancolelli, L., IV.
Arlequin Phaéton, Palaprat, IV; V.
Arlequin Procureur, Fatouville, IV; V.
Arlequin Prothée, Fatouville, IV.
Arlequin Roland, Bordelon, IV.
Arlette, Bazire, I.
Armelina, Lope de Rueda, II.
Armetzar, Chappuzeau, III.
Armilla, Serono, I.
Arminius, Campistron, IV; V.
Arminius, Scudéry, I; II; II, 803; IV.
Arsace, Prade, II; III; V.
Arsacome, Hardy, I.
Artaxate, L'Ecuyer, III.
Artaxerce, Boyer, II; IV; V.
Artaxerce, Magnon, II; III; IV; V.
Art de régner, Gillet de la Tessonerie, I; II; V.
Asba, Brueys, IV.
Asdrubal, Montfleury (Z. Jacob), II.
Asinaria, Plautus, III.
Aspar, Fontenelle, II.
Aspasie, Desmaretz, II.
Astérie, Du Faultrey, IV.
Astrate, Quinault, II; III; IV; V.
Astrée et Céladon, Rayssiguier, I.
Astrólogo fingido, Calderon, II; II, 804.
Atalante, Boyer, III; IV; IV, 983; V.

Athalie, Racine, I; III; IV; V.
Athée foudroyé, see *Festin de Pierre*, Dorimond.
Athée foudroyé, see *Festin de Pierre*, Nouveau.
Athénaïs, La Grange-Chancel, IV; V.
Athénaïs, Mairet, II; V.
Athlette, Montreux, I.
Atrabilaire amoureux, see *Misanthrope.*
Attendez-moi sous l'orme, Dufresny, IV.
Attendez-moi sous l'orme, Regnard, IV; V.
Attila, Corneille, II; III; IV; V.
Augmentation de la Baguette, Regnard, IV.
Auguste, Mort d', see *Agrippa.*
Aulularia, Plautus, III; V.
Ausente en el lugar, Lope, II.
Avantures des Champs Elisées, L. C. D. V., IV.
Avanturier, Visé, IV.
Avare, Molière, II; III; IV; V.
Avare duppé, Chappuzeau, III; V.
Avariés, Brieux, IV.
Aventure de Sémélé, J. M. C. D. L., II.
Aventures amoureuses, see *Salmigundis.*
Aventures de nuit, Chevalier, III.
Aveugle Amante, see *Sœur valeureuse.*
Aveugle clairvoyant, Brosse, II; V.
Aveugle clairvoyant, Legrand, M.-A., II; IV.
Avocat Patelin, Brueys, IV; V.
Avocat sans étude, Rosimond, III; III, 896; IV; V.
Avocat sans pratique, see *Avocat sans étude.*
Avocat sans sac, see *Avocat sans étude.*
Avocat savetier, see *Avocat sans étude.*
Axiane, Scudéry, I; II; II, 803-4; III.
Aymer sans sçavoir qui, d'Ouville, II; III; III, 895.
Azarie, Basin, I.

Bagolins, see *Ombre de son rival.*
Bague de l'Oubly, Rotrou, I; II; V.
Baguette, Bordelon, IV.
Baguette, Dancourt, IV; V.
Baguette de Vulcain, Regnard, IV.
Bailli d'Anières, Regnard, IV.
Bains de la porte S. Bernard, Boisfran, IV.
Bajazet, Racine, I; II; III; IV; IV, 983; V.
Bajazet, Mort de, see *Tamerlan.*
Bal, see *Bourgeois de Falaise.*
Balance d'état, Dubosc de Mont-André, III.
Balde, Jobert, II; III.
Ballet extravagant, Palaprat, IV; V.
Baltazar, Charenton, III.
Banda y Flor, Calderon, III.
Banqueroutier, Fatouville, IV; V.
Barbons amoureux, Chevalier, III.
Baron d'Albikrac, Corneille, T., III.
Baron d'Asnon, Denis de Varennes, IV.
Baron de la Crasse, Poisson, I; II; III; IV; V.

Baron des Fondrières, Corneille, T., IV; V.
Barons, Le Noble, H. N., III.
Barons fléchois, Le Noble, H. N., III.
Bassette, Champmeslé, III; IV; V.
Bassette, Hauteroche, III; IV.
Batteau de Bouille, Jobé, IV; V.
Bavardes, see *Mercure galant*.
Béatitude, Grouchy, I.
Beau Pasteur, Fonteny, I.
Beauté persécutée, see *Orphise*.
Bel Esprit, L. A. P., IV.
Bélinde, Rampale, I; II.
Bélisaire, Desfontaines, II.
Bélissaire, Rotrou, I; II; III; IV; V.
Belle Alphrède, Rotrou, I; II; II, 804; III.
Belle Egyptienne, Hardy, I; II.
Belle Egyptienne, Sallebray, II; III; V.
Belle Esclave, L'Estoile, C. de, II.
Belle Esther, Mainfray, I.
Belle Invisible, Boisrobert, I; III; IV; V.
Belle Lisimène, see *Pyrandre et Lisimène*.
Belle-Mère, see *Force du sang*, Dancourt.
Belle Plaideuse, Boisrobert, I; III; IV; V.
Belle Policritte, Gillet de la Tessonerie, II.
Bellérophon, Quinault, III; IV; V.
Bellissaire, La Calprenède, II; III.
Bellissante, Desfontaines, II; III, 896.
Beral victorieux, Borée, I.
Bérénice, Corneille, T., II; III; IV; V.
Bérénice, Du Ryer, P., I; II; III; V.
Bérénice, Racine, II; III; IV; IV, 984; V.
Berger extravagant, Corneille, T., II; III; V.
Bergerie, see *Parfaits Bergers*.
Bergeries, Racan, I; II; III, 893; V.
Berger inconneu, Bazire, I.
Bestes raisonnables, Montfleury, III; IV.
Bien perdu recouvré, see *Apoticaire devalisé*.
Bigame généreux, see *Adolphe*.
Blanche de Bourbon, Regnault, I; II; III, 895.
Bocages, La Charnays, I.
Bonnet enchanté, Brécourt, V.
Bon Soldat, Dancourt, IV; V.
Bourgeois de Falaise, Regnard, IV; V.
Bourgeoise, Rayssiguier, I; II.
Bourgeoises à la mode, Dancourt, IV; V.
Bourgeoises de qualité, Hauteroche, III; IV; IV, 984; V.
Bourgeoises de qualité, see *Fête de village*.
Bourgeois Gentilhomme, Molière, I; II; III; IV; V.
Boutades, Scarron, II, III, V.
Bout de l'an de Henry le Grand, E. G. C., I.
Bouts-rimez, Saint-Glas, IV.
Bradamante, Corneille, T., IV; V.
Bradamante, Garnier, I; II.
Bradamante, La Calprenède, II.
Bradamante ridicule, II, 76; III, 663.

Brave, Baïf, II.
Bretteur, see *Marthe Le Hayer*.
Britannicus, Racine, I; II; III; IV; V.
Brouilleries nocturnes, Nanteuil, III.
Brute et de Porcie, Mort de, Guérin de Bouscal, I; II; V.
Brutus, Bernard, IV; V.
Burlador, Tirso de Molina, I; III; IV; V.

Caballero, Moreto, III.
Cadenats, Boursault, III; IV.
Cadenats forcé, see *Amour sentinelle*.
Caffé, Rousseau, J.-B., IV; V.
Cajan, F. G. S. B., III.
Camma, Corneille, T., II; III; IV; V.
Cammane, La Caze, II.
Cammate, Hays, I.
Campagnard, Gillet de la Tessonerie, I; II; III; V.
Campagnard dupé, III, 791; IV, 984; V.
Candelaio, Bruno, I.
Capitan Matamore, véritable, Mareschal, I; II.
Capricieux, Rousseau, J.-B., IV; V.
Captifs, Rotrou, I; II; III.
Captivi, Plautus, II.
Cariste, Baro, I; II.
Carline, Gaillard, I.
Carnaval de Lyon, Legrand, M.-A., IV.
Carnaval de Venise, Dancourt, IV; V.
Carrosses à cinq sous, see *Intrigue*.
Carrosses d'Orléans, La Chapelle, III; IV; V.
Cartel, Gaillard, I; II.
Cartel de Guillot, Chevalier, III; IV.
Carthaginoise, Montchrestien, I.
Cartouche, Legrand, M.-A., IV.
Casa con dos puertas, Calderon, II; III.
Cassandre, Boisrobert, I; III; IV.
Cassandre, Boyer, II.
Cassette, Brécourt, III; IV.
Cassius et Victorinus, La Grange-Chancel, IV.
Castelvines y Monteses, Lope, II.
Catharina, Roillet, II.
Cato, Addison, II.
Caton, Abeille, IV.
Caton, Mort de, Auger, II.
Cause des femmes, Delosme de Monchesnay, IV; V.
Cavalier par Amour, Vaumorière, IV.
Ceinture magique, Rousseau, J.-B., IV.
Célénie, Passar, I.
Céliane, Rotrou, I; II, 804; III; III, 893; V.
Célidée, Rayssiguier, I; II; V.
Célie, Rotrou, I; II.
Célimène, Rotrou, I; II; III; IV; V.
Célinde, Baro, I; II; V.
Céline, Beys, I; II.
Céline et Théodore, see *Théodore*, Boisrobert.
Celosa de sí misma, Tirso de Molina, II; IV.
Cenobia, Calderon, II; III; IV.
Céphale et Procris, Dancourt, IV.

Félismène, Hardy, I; IV.
Femme d'intrigues, Dancourt, IV; V.
Femme guerrière, Romagnesi, M.-A., IV.
Femme industrieuse, Dorimond, III; V.
Femme juge, Montfleury, I; III; IV; V.
Femme rusée ou industrieuse, see *Femme industrieuse*.
Femmes à la mode, see *Bourgeoises à la mode*.
Femmes coquettes, Poisson, III; IV; V.
Femmes savantes, Molière, I; II; III; IV; V.
Femmes vertueuses, see *Trompeurs trompez*.
Feste de Chambor, see *Pourceaugnac*.
Feste de Vénus, Boyer, II; III.
Festin de Pierre, Corneille, T., III, IV.
Festin de Pierre, Dorimond, III; V.
Festin de Pierre, see *Don Juan*.
Festin de Pierre, Villiers, I; III; V.
Festin de Pierre, nouveau, Rosimond, III; V.
Fête de village, Dancourt, IV; V.
Fêtes de Thalie, La Font, III.
Fêtes nocturnes du Cours, Dancourt, IV.
Fidalgo aprendiz, Melo, III.
Fidélité reconnue, see *Bellissante*.
Fidelle Bergère, Frénicle, I.
Fidelle Esclave, Vallée, III.
Fidelle Tromperie, Gougenot, I; II.
Filandre, Rotrou, I; II; II, 804; V.
Filippo, Alfieri, IV.
Filis de Scire, Pichou, I; II.
Fille Capitaine, Montfleury, III; IV; V.
Fille de bon sens, Palaprat, IV; V.
Fille Précepteur, Legrand, M.-A., IV.
Fille sage, docte et vertueuse, see. *Athénaïs*, Mairet.
Fille savante, Fatouville, IV.
Filles errantes, Regnard, IV.
Fille supposée, La Grange-Chancel, IV.
Fille Viceroy, Nanteuil, III; IV.
Filli di Sciro, Bonarelli, G., I; II; III; V.
Fillis de Scire, Du Cros, I.
Fils criminel, see *Festin de Pierre*, Dorimond.
Fils criminel, see *Festin de Pierre*, Villiers.
Fils désadvoüé, Guérin de Bouscal, I; II.
Fils exilé, Mouffle, II.
Fils naturel, Dumas, A., IV.
Fils supposé, Boyer, II; III; V.
Fils supposé, Scudéry, I; V.
Finette, see *Famille à la mode*.
Flateurs trompez, see *Timon*.
Flatteur, Rousseau, J.-B., IV; V.
Flavio et Juliette, see *Femmes coquettes*.
Florante, Rotrou, I.
Florentin, Champmeslé, IV; IV, 984; V.
Florice, Passar, I.
Florimonde, Rotrou, I; II; III.
Florivale et Orcade, Joyel, I.
Foire de Besons, Dancourt, IV; V.
Foire de St. Germain, La Pinelière, I; IV.
Foire St. Germain, Dancourt, IV.
Foire St. Germain, Regnard, IV; V.
Foire St. Laurent, Legrand, M.-A., IV.

Folie de Clidamant, Hardy, I.
Folie de Turlupin, Hardy, I.
Folie du sage, Tristan l'Hermite, II; V.
Folie d'Ysabelle, Hardy, I.
Folies amoureuses, Regnard, IV.
Folies de Cardénio, Pichou, I; II; V.
Folle Enchère, Dancourt, IV; V.
Folle Gageure, Boisrobert, I; II; III; IV; V.
Folle Querelle, Subligny, III; IV.
Fonds perdu, see *Notaire obligeant*.
Fontaine de sapience, Biancolelli, L., IV.
Fontanges, Perrault, IV.
Fontanges maltraitées, Baron, IV.
Force du destin, Baro, I.
Force du sang, Brueys, IV.
Force du sang, Dancourt, IV.
Force du sang, Hardy, I.
Forte Romaine, Vallée, III.
Fossiles, Curel, I.
Fou de qualité, see *Fou raisonnable*.
Fou raisonnable, Poisson, III; IV; V.
Fourbe, Lenoble, IV.
Fourbes heureux, Palaprat, IV.
Foux divertissans, Poisson, III; IV; V.
Fragmens de Molière, Champmeslé, III; IV; V.
Francion, Gillet de la Tessonerie, II; III; V.
François Spera, J. D. C. G., I.
Frayeurs de Crispin, Crosnier, IV.
Frégonde, Hardy, I; II.
Frère indiscret, Hardy, I.
Frères Ennemis, see *Thébaïde*.
Frères rivaux, see *Céline*.
Frères rivaux, Chevreau, II; V.
Funestes Amours de Belcar et Méliane, see *Tyr et Sidon*.
Fureur d'Astiages, see *Cyrus triomphant*.
Furieuse Monomachie, see *Cartel*.

Gabinie, Brueys, IV; V.
Galand doublé, Corneille, T., III.
Galán Fantasma, Calderon, III.
Galans ridicules, Chevalier, III.
Galanteries du Duc d'Ossonne, Mairet, I; II; V.
Galantes vertueuses, Desfontaines, II.
Galant Jardinier, Dancourt, IV.
Galerie du Palais, Corneille, I; II; III; IV; V.
Galimatias, Roziers Beaulieu, II.
Galopea, Chiabrera, I.
Garçon insensible, see *Hypolite*, Gilbert.
Garçon sans conduite, Montfleury, IV.
Gardien de soy-mesme, Scarron, II; II, 804; III; IV; V.
Gazette, Dancourt, IV; V.
Gelosie fortunate del Prencipe Rodrigo, Cicognini, III.
Gendre de M. Poirier, Augier, III; IV.
Généreuse Allemande, Mareschal, I; II.
Généreuse Ingratitude, Quinault, III; IV; V.
Généreux Ennemis, Boisrobert, I; III.
Générosité chrestienne, see *Natalie*.
Générosité d'Alexandre, see *Porus*, Boyer.

Hylas, Inconstances d', Mareschal, I; II; III; V.
Hypermnestre, Riupeirous, IV.
Hypocondre, Rousseau, J.-B., IV.
Hypocondriaque, Rotrou, I; III; V.
Hypolite, Gilbert, II; III; IV; V.

Ibrahim, Scudéry, I; II; III; IV; V.
Idolâtre converty, see *Cajan*.
Ile d'Alcine, Regnard, IV.
Illusion comique, Corneille, I; II; III; V.
Illusion grotesque, Néel, IV.
Illustre Amalazonthe, Desfontaines, II.
Illustre Bassa, see *Ibrahim*.
Illustre Berger, Poirier, II.
Illustre Comédien, Desfontaines, II; V.
Illustre Corsaire, Mairet, II; III.
Illustre Désespéré, see *Caton, Mort de*.
Illustre Olympie, see *Saint Alexis*.
Illustre Philosophe, La Chapelle (nun), III.
Illustre Pirate, see *Eurimédon*.
Illustres Ennemis, Corneille, T., III.
Illustres Fous, Beys, I; II; III; IV; V.
Il ne faut jurer de rien, Musset, IV.
Imitables Amours de Théoys et de Carite, see *Béatitude*.
Impériaux et Bohèmes, Coppée, I.
Important, see *Important de Cour*.
Important de Cour, Brueys, IV; V.
Impromptu, Vivonne, IV.
Impromptu de Garnison, Dancourt, IV; V.
Impromptu de l'Hostel de Condé, Montfleury, II; III.
Impromptu de Suresnes, Dancourt, IV.
Impromptu de Versailles, Molière, I; II; III; IV; V.
Impuissance, Veronneau, I; III.
Inavvertito, Barbieri, III.
Inceste supposé, Hardy, I; II.
Inceste supposé, La Caze, II; III; V.
Inconnu, Corneille, T., IV; V.
Inconnue, Boisrobert, I; II; III.
Inconstance punie, Dorimond, III; V.
Inconstance punie, La Croix, C. S. de, I; III; V.
Indégonde, Montauban, II; III; V.
Indian Emperour, Dryden, V.
Indienne amoureuse, Du Rocher, I.
Indiscret, Voltaire, IV.
Inès de Castro, La Motte-Houdart, IV.
Infante Salicoque, Brécourt, III.
Infidèle Confidente, Pichou, I; II, 803; V.
Infidèles fidèles, Calianthe, I.
Injustice punie, Du Teil, II; IV.
Innocence descouverte, see *Marfilie*.
Innocence reconnue, see *Geneviève*, Avre.
Innocence reconnue, see *Soupirs de Sifroi*.
Innocens coupables, Brosse, II.
Innocente Infidélité, Rotrou, I; II; V.
Innocent Exilé, Provais, II.
Innocent malheureux, Grenaille, II.
Ino et Mélicerte, La Grange-Chancel, IV; V.
Interesse, Secchi, II; III.

Intéressé, see *La Rapinière*.
Intrigue des académies, see *Joueuse dupée*.
Intrigue des carosses, Chevalier, III; III, 895; IV; V.
Intrigue des Filous, L'Estoile, C. de, II; III; V.
Intrigues amoureuses, Gilbert, II; III; V.
Intrigues d'Arlequin, Bordelon, IV.
Intrigues de la lotterie, Visé, III; IV; V.
Intrigues de la Vieille Tour, Du Perche, III; IV; V.
Intrigues des hôtelleries, see *Filles errantes*.
Invisible, see *Dame invisible*, Hauteroche.
Ion, Euripides, IV.
Iphigeneia at Aulis, Euripides, II; IV; V.
Iphigeneia in Tauris, Euripides, II; IV; V.
Iphigénie, Le Clerc, II; IV; V.
Iphigénie, Racine, I; II; III; IV; V.
Iphigénie, Rotrou, I; II; IV; V.
Iphigénie, see *Pylade et Oreste*.
Iphigénie en Tauride, Racine, IV; V.
Iphis et Iante, Benserade, I; II.
Ipocrito, Aretino, III.
Irène, Basset, III.
Iris, Coignée de Bourron, I; II.
Irrésolu, Destouches, IV.
Isaac, Rosier, I.
Isabelle, Ferry, I.
Isabelle médecin, Fatouville, IV.
Isolite, La Tour, I.
Israel affligé, Vallin, II.

Jacob, La Poujade, I.
Jalouse d'elle-même, Boisrobert, I; II; III; V.
Jalousie du Barbouillé, Molière, III; V.
Jaloux, Baron, IV; V.
Jaloux, see *Curieux Impertinent*.
Jaloux, IV, 442.
Jaloux désabusé, Campistron, IV.
Jaloux endormy, see *Cadenats*.
Jaloux honteux, Dufresny, IV.
Jaloux invisible, Brécourt, III; V.
Jaloux sans sujet, Beys, I; V.
Janin, Millet, I.
Jeanne d'Angleterre, La Calprenède, II; V.
Jeanne de Naples, Magnon, II; III; IV; V.
Jephté, Boyer, II; IV; V.
Jephté, Brinon, I.
Jephté, Venel, IV.
Jephtes, Buchanan, I; IV.
Jésus-Christ, Coppée, I.
Jeune Bergère, see *Lisimène*, Boyer.
Jeune Célimène, II, 594; III, 387.
Jeune Lisimène, see *Lisimène*, Boyer.
Jeune Marius, Boyer, II; III; IV; V.
Je vous prens sans verd, Champmeslé, IV; V.
Joas, Mort de, La Grange-Chancel, IV.
Jodelet, Feinte Mort de, Brécourt, II; III; V.
Jodelet Astrologue, d'Ouville, II.

13

Marc-Antoine, Garnier, I; II; II, 804.
Marc-Antoine, Mairet, I; II; III, 893; IV; V.
Marchand duppé, Fatouville, IV.
Marchand ridicule, Gillot, IV.
Marcus Curtius, Coppée, I.
Marfilie, Auvray, Jean, I.
Marguerite de France, Gilbert, II; III; V.
Mariage d'Alexandre, see *Roxane*.
Mariage d'amour, Du Ryer, Isaac, I.
Mariage de Bachus, Visé, III; IV.
Mariage de Cambyse, Quinault, II; III.
Mariage de Fine-Epice, Sainte-Marthe, III.
Mariage de la Reine de Monomotapa, Bel-Isle, IV.
Mariage de Rien, Montfleury, III.
Mariage de Tite, see *Aricidie*.
Mariage d'Orphée, see *Descente d'Orphée aux Enfers*, L'Espine.
Mariage d'Orphée et d'Euridice, see *Descente d'Orphée aux Enfers*, Chapoton.
Mariage du Cid, Chevreau, II; V.
Mariage fait et rompu, Dufresny, IV.
Mariage forcé, Molière, II; III; IV; V.
Mariage sans mariage, Marcel, III.
Mariages inopinés, Caillet, IV.
Mariamne, Hardy, I; II; V.
Mariane, Tristan l'Hermite, I; II; III; IV; V.
Maria Stuart, Schiller, IV.
Marido hace mujer, Mendoza, III; V.
Marie Stuard, Boursault, IV, V.
Marie Stuard, Regnault, II; IV.
Marie Stuart, Tronchin, II.
Mari infidèle, see *Apparences trompeuses*, Hauteroche.
Mari retrouvé, Dancourt, IV; V.
Maris en bonnes fortunes, Etienne, III.
Maris infidèles, Visé, III; IV.
Mármol de Felisardo, Lope, I; II.
Marqués de Alfarache, Lope, III.
Marqués del Cigarral, Solórzano, II.
Marquis Bahutier, see *Après-Soupé des auberges*.
Marquis de la Rotonde, Desaci, III.
Marquis friands, see *Costeaux*.
Marquis Paysan, see *Sot toujours sot*.
Marquis ridicule, see *Amant ridicule*.
Marquis ridicule, Scarron, II; III; IV.
Marthe Le Hayer, Blessebois, IV.
Martin Braillart, see *Trigaudin*.
Martyre de Sainct Clair, see *Fils exilé*.
Martyre de Sainte Justine et de Saint Cyprien, see *Saints Amants*.
Martyre de Sainte Ursule, Yvernaud, III.
Martyre de Saint Genest, see *Illustre Comédien*.
Martyre de Saint Sébastien, Jesus Maria, III.
Martyre de Saint Vincent, Boissin de Gallardon, I.
Martyre des SS. Innocens, Jesus Maria, III.
Mary sans femme, Montfleury, III.
Matrone d'Ephèse, see *Arlequin Procureur*.

Maux sans remèdes, Visé, III; V.
Mauzolée, Mareschal, I; II.
Maximian, Corneille, T., III.
Mayorazgo figura, Solórzano, II.
Mayor Imposible, Lope, III; IV.
Mayor Monstruo, Calderon, II.
Medea, Dolce, II.
Medea, Euripides, I; II.
Medea, Seneca, I; II.
Médecin malgré lui, Molière, I; II; III; IV; V.
Médecin par force, see *Médecin malgré lui*.
Médecins, see *Amour Médecin*.
Médecins vengez, see *Elomire hypocondre*.
Médecin volant, Boursault, III.
Médecin volant, Molière, III.
Médée, Corneille, I; II; III; IV; V.
Médée, Longepierre, II; IV; V.
Méléagre, Benserade, I; II; IV; V.
Méléagre, Hardy, I; II.
Méléagre, La Grange-Chancel, IV; V.
Méliane, Croisac, III.
Mélicerte, Molière, III; IV; V.
Mélite, Corneille, I; II; II, 804; III; III, 894; IV; V.
Mélite, see *Bélinde*.
Mélize, Du Rocher, I.
Menaechmi, Plautus, I; II; III; IV.
Ménechmes, Regnard, IV.
Ménechmes, Rotrou, I; II; III; IV.
Menteur, Corneille, I; II; III; IV; V.
Menteurs qui ne mentent point, see *Nicandres*.
Mentirosa Verdad, Villegas, III.
Merchant of Venice, Shakespeare, V.
Mercure, see *Mercure galant*.
Mercure galant (Comédie sans titre), Boursault, III; IV; V.
Mère coquette, Quinault, III; IV; V.
Mère coquette, Visé, III; V.
Mère ridicule, Montfort, IV.
Merlin Déserteur, Dancourt, IV; V.
Merlin Dragon, Desmares, N., II; III; IV; V.
Merlin Gascon, Raisin, J., IV; V.
Merlin peintre, La Tuillerie, IV.
Merope, Torelli, IV.
Mérovée, Billard, I.
Métempsycose des amours, Dancourt, IV.
Mezzetin Grand Sophy de Perse, Delosme de Monchesnay, IV.
Miles gloriosus, Plautus, I; II; III.
Mirad á quién alabáis, Lope, I.
Mirame, Desmaretz, I; II; V.
Miroir de l'union belgique, Lancel, I.
Miroir des veuves, Heyns, I.
Misanthrope, Molière, I; II; III; IV; IV, 984; V.
Mithridate, Racine, II; III; IV; V.
Mithridate, Mort de, La Calprenède, I; II; IV; V.
Mocedades del Cid, Castro, II.
Mocedades del duque de Osuna, Monroy y Silva, I.
Mœurs du tems, Saint-Yon, IV; V.

Momies d'Egypte, see *Suite de la Foire St. Germain.*
Monna Vanna, Maeterlinck, II; IV.
Monsieur Alphonse, Dumas, A., IV.
Montézume, Ferrier, IV; V.
Mort amoureux, see *Hypocondriaque.*
Mort burlesque, Les Isles le Bas, III.
Morti vivi, Sforza d'Oddi, II; III.
Morts vivants, d'Ouville, II.
Mort vivant, Boursault, III; V.
Moscovite, Canu, I.
Mostellaria, Plautus, III; IV; V.
Mots à la mode, Boursault, IV; V.
Moulin de Javelle, Dancourt, IV.
Muertos vivos, Lope, III.
Muerto vivo, Paredes, III.
Muet, Palaprat, IV; V.
Mustapha, Belin, II; IV.
Mustapha, Orrery, V.
Mustapha, Mort de, see *Solyman,* Mairet.
Myrtil et Mélicerte, Guérin, N., III; IV.
Myrtillo, Andreini, Isabella, I.

Naifuetez champestres, see *Nopces de Vaugirard.*
Naissance d'Amadis, Regnard, IV; V.
Naissance du monde, see *Création du monde.*
Natalie, Montgaudier, III.
Naufragio prodigioso, Lope, I.
Négligent, Dufresny, IV; V.
Néron, Mort de, Péchantré, IV; V.
Niais de Sologne, Raisin, J., IV.
Ni amor se libra, Calderon, III.
Nicandres, Boursault, III; IV.
Nicomède, Corneille, I; II; III; IV; V.
Niobé, Frénicle, I; V.
Nitétis, Desjardins, III.
Nitocris, Du Ryer, P., I; II; III; IV; V.
Nitocris, La Tuillerie, IV; V.
Noble imaginaire, see *Riche Mécontent.*
Nobles de province, Hauteroche, III; IV; V.
No hay amigo para amigo, Rojas, III, 896.
No hay burlas, Calderon, III.
No hay peor sordo, Tirso de Molina, II; III, 896.
No hay ser padre, Rojas, I; II.
Nopce de village, Brécourt, III; V.
Nopce interrompue, Dufresny, IV; V.
Nopces de Vaugirard, Discret, II; III; V.
No siempre lo peor, Calderon, III.
No son todos ruiseñores, Lope, I.
Nostre-Dame de Cambron, Coppée, I; II.
Notaire obligeant, Dancourt, IV; V.
Nouveau Marié, see *Ambigu comique.*
Nouveauté, Legrand, III.
Nouvelle Stratonice, Du Fayot, III.
Nouvellistes, Hauteroche, III; IV.
Nouvellistes de Lille, Dancourt, IV.
Nuevo Pitágoras, Du Perron de Castera, III.
Nuit vénitienne, Musset, I.

Obligados y Ofendidos, Rojas, III.
Ocasión perdida, Lope, I.

Occasions perdues, Rotrou, I; II.
Octavia, Seneca, IV.
Œdipe, Corneille, I; II; III; V.
Œdipe, Prévost, I.
Œdipe, Tallemant des Réaux, II.
Œdipe, Voltaire, I; II.
Œdipus, Seneca, I.
Œdipus rex, Sophocles, II; IV; V.
Olimpia, Della Porta, III.
Ombre de Molière, Brécourt, III; IV; V.
Ombre de son rival, Crosnier, IV.
Ombre du Comte de Gormas, Chillac, II.
Omphalle, Grandchamp, I.
Opéra, les, Saint-Evremond, III; IV; V.
Opéra de campagne, Dufresny, IV.
Opéra de village, Dancourt, IV; V.
Opérateur Barry, Dancourt, IV; V.
Opiniâtre, Brueys, IV.
Orante, Scudéry, I.
Oreste, II, 594; Le Clerc, IV.
Oreste et Pilade, La Grange-Chancel, IV; V.
Orestes, Euripides, IV.
Originaux, D. L. M., IV.
Orizelle, Chabrol, I.
Ormisda, Zeno, II.
Oromazes, Cadet, II.
Oroondate, Guérin de Bouscal, I; II.
Oroondate, Mariage d', Magnon, II; IV; V.
Oropaste, Boyer, II; III; V.
Orphise, Desfontaines, II; III.
Osman, Tristan l'Hermite, II; III; IV; V.
Osmar, Mort du grand, see *Osman.*
Ostorius, Pure, III.
Othello, Shakespeare, II.
Othon, Corneille, III; IV; V.
Othon, Mort d', Belin, IV.
Ottone, Ghirardelli, III.
Ottone, Manzoni, L., III.
Oublieux, Perrault, IV.
Ouverture du theatre . . . du Palais Cardinal, see *Mirame.*
Ozmin, Hardy, I.

Pacifique, Sainte Vertu, III.
Palacio confuso, II, 683.
Palemon, Frénicle, I; V.
Palène, Boisrobert, I; II.
Palinice, Rayssiguier, I; V.
Pancrace, Chasteauneuf, III.
Pandoste, Hardy, I.
Pandoste, La Serre, I.
Panégyrique de l'Ecole des femmes, Robinet, III.
Panthée, Billard, I.
Panthée, Durval, I; II.
Panthée, Hardy, I; II.
Panthée, Tristan l'Hermite, I; II; III; V.
Panurge, Montauban, III; IV; V.
Papyre, Mareschal, I; II; III; V.
Paraître, Donnay, III.
Parasite, Tristan l'Hermite, III.
Parecido en la corte, Moreto, IV.
Parfaits Bergers, Croisille, I; II.

Sabinus, Passerat, IV.
Sac de Carthage, La Serre, I; II; IV.
Sacrifice d'Abraham, Dumoret, IV.
Sacrifice d'Abraham, Péchantré, IV.
Sacrifice sanglant, see *Clarionte*.
Sacristán Saguijo, Lope, III.
Sage Gouverneur, see *Art de régner*.
Sage Visionnaire, I. D. B. I., II.
Saincte Aldegonde, Coppée, I.
Saincte Dorotée, Le Ville, III.
Saincte Justine, Coppée, I.
Sainct Lambert, Coppée, I.
Saint Alexis, Desfontaines, II.
Saint Béningne, Caillet, IV.
Sainte Agnès, Troterel, I; II; V.
Sainte Aldégonde, d'Ennetières, II; III, 896.
Sainte Catherine, Boissin de Gallardon, I.
Sainte Catherine, La Serre, I; II.
Sainte Catherine, Poytevin, I.
Sainte Catherine d'Alexandrie, see *Illustre Philosophe*.
Sainte Cécile coronnée, Jean François de Nisme, III.
Sainte Elisabeth, Le Ville, III.
Sainte Elisabeth Reine de Portugal, see *Pacifique*.
Sainte Reine, Blessebois, IV.
Sainte Reine, Le Grand, A., III; IV.
Sainte Reine, Ternet, IV.
Sainte Suzanne Martyre, see *Forte Romaine*.
Sainte Ursule, Le Ville, III.
Saint Eustache, Baro, I; II; III, 893; V.
Saint Eustache, Bello, I.
Saint Eustache, Desfontaines, II; V.
Saint Genest, véritable, Rotrou, I; II; III; V.
Saint Gervais, Cheffault, III.
Saint Herménigilde, Jesus Maria, III.
Saint Herménigilde Royal Martyr, see *Royal Martyr*.
Saint Mammès, Levacher de Lavrigny, IV.
Saint Nicolas, Soret, I.
Saint Remy, Fies, IV, 983.
Saints Amants, Caillet, IV.
Salmigundis comique, Denis, IV.
Sanche Pansa, Guérin de Bouscal, I; II; III.
Sancho Pança, Dancourt, IV.
Sancho Pança, Dufresny, IV; V.
Sanglante Tragédie de la Mort et Passion de Notre Seigneur Jésus-Christ, see *Théandre, Mort de*.
Sapor, Regnard, IV.
Satire des Satires, Boursault, III; IV; V.
Saturnales, see *Prude du temps*.
Satyre du Temps, see *Railleur*.
Saul, Billard, I.
Saül, Du Ryer, P., I; II; III; IV; V.
Saul, La Taille, Jean de, I; II.
Saül, Nadal, II.
Savetier avocat, see *Avocat sans étude*.
Scapin, Fourberies de, Molière, I; II; III; IV; IV, 984; V.

Scédase, Hardy, I; II; V.
Scévole, Du Ryer, P., I; II; III; IV; V.
School for Scandal, Sheridan, III.
Scipion, Desmaretz, II; IV; V.
Scipion, Pradon, IV; V.
Scythes, Voltaire, IV.
Second Chapitre du Diable boiteux, Dancourt, IV.
Secrétaire de Saint-Innocent, L'Estoile, C. de, II; III; V.
Secretario de sí mismo, Lope, IV.
Secret révélé, Palaprat, IV; V.
Seïla, Mort de, see *Jephté*, Venel.
Séjanus, Magnon, II; III; V.
Séleucus, Montauban, III; V.
Sélidore, Quenel, II.
Sélim, Grand, Le Vayer de Boutigny, II.
Semblable à soy-mesme, V, 151; see *Ambigu comique*.
Semejante á sí mismo, Alarcón, III.
Sémiramis, Gilbert, II; IV, 983; V.
Sémiramis, véritable, Desfontaines, II; III, 896; IV.
Sénèque, Mort de, Tristan l'Hermite, II; III; IV; V.
Señor de noches buenas, Cubillo, III.
Sérénade, Regnard, IV; V.
Sertorius, Corneille, II; III; IV; V.
Sésostris, Longepierre, IV; V.
Sésostris, Pascal, Fr., III; V.
Sganarelle, Molière, I; II; III; IV; V.
Sicilien, Molière, III; IV; V.
Sidère, Bouchet d'Ambillou, I.
Sidère, see *Dorise*.
Sidonie, Mairet, II; III; IV.
Siflets, Palaprat, IV.
Sifroy, Blessebois, III; IV.
Sigismond, Gillet de la Tessonerie, II; V.
Silanus, Abeille, IV.
Silence, see *Corine*.
Silla, La Rue, IV.
Silvanire, Mairet, I; II; V.
Siroe, II, 553.
Sir Politick would-be, Saint-Evremond, IV; IV, 984; V.
Six cadenats, see *Cadenats*.
Sœur, Rotrou, I; II; III; V.
Sœur généreuse, Boyer, II; III.
Sœur généreuse, see *Sœur*.
Sœur ridicule, Montfleury, IV.
Sœurs jalouses, Lambert, III; V.
Sœurs rivales, Visé, IV.
Sœur valeureuse, Mareschal, I; II; V.
Sofonisba, Trissino, I.
Soldat malgré-luy, Chevalier, III; V.
Soldat poltron, see *Soldat malgré-luy*.
Soliman, Dalibray, II.
Soliman, Jacquelin, III.
Soliman, II, 409; La Tuillerie, IV; V.
Solimano, Bonarelli, P., I; II.
Solyman, Mairet, I; II; IV; V.
Solyman II, Thillois, V.
Songes des Hommes esveillez, Brosse, II; V.
Sophonisbe, Corneille, I; II; III; IV; V.
Sophonisbe, Garel, I.
Sophonisbe, La Grange-Chancel, IV.

Sophonisbe, Mairet, I; II; III; IV; IV, 983; V.
Sophonisbe, Montreux, I; III.
Sophonisbe, see *Carthaginoise*.
Sophonisbe, Voltaire, I.
Sorella, Della Porta, II; III.
Sortija del Olvido, Lope, I; II; V.
Sot toujours sot, Palaprat, IV; V.
Sot vengé, see *Lubin*.
Souhaits, Delosme de Monchesnay, IV.
Souhaits, Regnard, IV.
Soupçons sur les apparences, d'Ouville, II; III.
Souper mal apprêté, Hauteroche, III; IV; V.
Soupirs de Sifroi, Blessebois, IV.
Sourd, Desmaretz, II.
Souteneurs et Soutenues, see *Marthe Le Hayer*.
Statira, Pradon, II; IV; IV, 983; V.
Stilicon, Corneille, T., II; III; IV; V.
Strange Interlude, O'Neill, II.
Stratonice, Brosse, II; III.
Stratonice, Quinault, II; III; V.
Suite de la Coquette, see *Dame à la mode*.
Suite de la Foire St. Germain, Regnard, IV; V.
Suite de la Mort de César, see *Brute et de Porcie, Mort de*.
Suite de Mariane, see *Enfans d'Hérodes*.
Suite du Menteur, Corneille, II; III; V.
Suitte d'Ibrahim Bassa, see *Perside*.
Suivante, Corneille, I; II; III, 894; V.
Sultane, Bounin, I; II.
Sultan Osman, Coppée, I; V, 50.
Supercherie d'amour, Ch. de, I.
Superstitieux, Dufresny, IV.
Suppositi, Ariosto, III.
Suréna, Corneille, I; III; IV; V.
Susanna, Jourdan, IV; V.
Suzanne, Louet, IV.
Sylvanire, d'Urfé, I; IV; V.
Sylvie, Mairet, I; II; III; V.

Tableau tragique, see *Florivale et Orcade*.
Talestris, Lenoble, IV.
Tamerlan, Pradon, II; IV; V.
Tamerlan et Bajazet, Magnon, II; IV.
Tancrède, Scarron, III.
Tapisserie vivante, Romagnesi, G., IV.
Tarquin, Pradon, IV; V.
Tartuffe, Molière, I; II; III; IV; V.
Teatro senza commedie, Romagnesi, M.-A., IV.
Téléphonte, Gilbert, II; III; IV; V.
Téléphonte, La Chapelle, II; IV; V.
Teodora, Bartolommei, II.
Téofile, Sérizanis de Cavaillon, IV.
Théagène, Gilbert, II; III; IV, 983.
Théagène et Cariclée, Hardy, I; II, 803; V.
Théagène et Chariclée, Racine, III.
Theandrathanatos, Stoa, II.
Théandre, Mort de, Chevillard, II.
Théâtre de Neptune, Lescarbot, I.
Thébaïde, Boyer, IV.
Thébaïde, Racine, I; II; III; IV; V.

Thebais, Seneca, II.
Thémistocle, Du Ryer, P., I; II; III; IV; V.
Théocris, Troterel, I.
Théodat, Corneille, T., III; IV; V.
Théodore, Boisrobert, I; II; III.
Théodore, Corneille, I; II; III; IV; V.
Theophilus, Sérizanis de Cavaillon, IV.
Thèse des dames, Biancolelli, L., IV.
Thésée, La Fosse, IV; V.
Thésée, La Serre, I; II.
Thobie, Ouyn, I.
Thomas Morus, La Serre, I; II; III.
Thuilleries, Rayssiguier, I; II.
Thyeste, Monléon, I; II; V.
Thyestes, Seneca, I; II.
Tía y Sobrina, Moreto, III.
Tibérinus, faux, see *Agrippa, roy d'Albe*.
Tigrane, Boyer, II; III; V.
Timoclée, Hardy, I; II; III.
Timoclée, Morel, III.
Timocrate, Corneille, T., III; IV; V.
Timoléon, Saint-Germain, II.
Timon, Brécourt, III; IV; V.
Tiridate, Campistron, IV; V.
Titapapouf, see *Voleur*.
Tite, Magnon, II; III; V.
Tite et Bérénice, Corneille, III; IV; V.
Toison d'or, Corneille, III; IV; IV, 984; V.
Toison d'or, see *Arlequin Jason*.
Tombeau de maître André, Biancolelli, L., IV; V.
Tomyre, Borée, I.
Tonaxare, faux, see *Oropaste*.
Torrismon, Dalibray, I; II.
Torrismondo, Tasso, I; II.
Tragédie sainte, Davesne, II.
Trahison punie, Dancourt, IV.
Trahizons d'Arbiran, d'Ouville, II; III.
Traición busca el castigo, Rojas, II; III, 896; IV.
Traistre trahi, see *Veuve*, Corneille.
Traître puni, Lesage, IV.
Trasibule, Montfleury, III; IV; V.
Tres mujeres en una, Remon, II.
Trésorière, Grévin, I; II.
Trigaudin, Montfleury, IV.
Triomphe d'Amour, Guerrini, III.
Triomphe d'amour, Hardy, I.
Triomphe de Colombine, see *Thèse des dames*.
Triomphe de la chasteté, see *Eugénie*, Le Febvre.
Triomphe de la foy, see *Alphonce*.
Triomphe de la Foy et de la Constance, see *Thomas Morus*.
Triomphe de la Foy sur les Chaldéens, see *Josaphat*, D. L. T.
Triomphe de la Ligue, Nerée, I.
Triomphe de l'amour et de l'amitié, see *Damon et Pythias*.
Triomphe de la Vertu, see *Climène*, La Serre.
Triomphe des Bergers, Donnet, II.
Triomphe des cinq passions, Gillet de la Tessonerie, II; III.

GENERAL INDEX OF PARTS I, II, III, IV, AND V [1]

Abderrahmen, III, 181-2.
A. B. D. S., I, 398.
Abeille, II; IV; IV, 983; V, 7, *Argélie,
Coriolan, Lyncée,* 94.
Abélard, IV, 698.
Abigail, IV, 328-30.
Abimelech, IV, 314.
Ablancourt, I, 734.
Abry, *Histoire de la litt. fr.,* I, 714.
Accius, IV, 895.
Accursius, II, 289, 442.
Achab, I, 65, *681-3.*
Acta Sanctorum, I; II; III; III, 894.
Adam, IV, 538.
Adam, Antoine, V, 150-2; *Théophile,* IV, 983.
Adam, Maître, IV, 895; *Chevilles,* IV, 689.
Adams, J. Q., I; II.
Addison, *Cato,* II, 594.
Adon, III, 415.
Advantures de Thyrsis, II, *249-50,* 765.
Adversa fortuna de . . . Cabrera, II, 544.
Advertissement au Besançonnois, I, 243, 575; II, 204.
Advielle, *Théâtre à Arras,* IV, 200, 578.
Ælian, II, 289.
Æschylus, II; IV; V, 26.
Æsop, I; II; III; IV; V, 124.
Agilulphe, III, 418-9.
Agnan Sarat, I, 15, 17, 727-8, 731.
Agnès, IV, 278.
Agreda, I, 53, 62; V, 28-9.
Agrippa, Cornelius, III, 273; IV, 702.
Aigaliers, d', I.
Aigue d'Iffremont, III, 15.
Aiguillon, d', I, 476; II.
Aimable Comtesse, IV, 414.
Aimé-Martin, III, 105, 230, 519; IV, 94.
Alain Chartier, see Chartier.
Alais (daughter of Louis VII), II, 387.
Alamanni, II, 155.
Alarcón, II; III; V, 29.
Alard, IV, 933-4.
Alba, Duke of, IV, 252.
Albigny, III, 286.
Alboin, II, 194-5, 701-4.
Albucasis, II, 426.
Albumazar, II, 426.
Albret, Alain d', IV, 181.
Albret, maréchal d', III, 555; IV, 474.
Albret family, IV, 707.
Alciati, IV, 442.
Alcidamas, II, 425.

Alécis, see *Patelin.*
Alemán, *Guzmán,* I, 62, 327; V, 29.
Alembert, d', IV, 306.
Alexandre et Annette, I, 146-7.
Alexis Angelus, II, 634-5.
Alexis Comnenus, II, 634-6.
Alfieri, I, 708; IV, 275, *Filippo,* 257.
Alfonso XI, II, 403.
Algazel, II, 426.
Ali el-Abbas (Haly), II, 426.
Alizon, I; II.
Al Kinde (Aliquinde), II, 426.
Allacci, III; IV, 251.
Allainville, IV, 567.
Allard, I, 465.
Allatius, *Apes Urbanae,* I, 526.
Alleaume, I, 168, 352; II, 49.
Allen, J. T., *Stage Antiquities,* I, 8, 715, 718.
Allier, *Cabale des dévots,* III, 8, 623.
Alliot, II, 345.
Almanach de Milan, IV, 683.
Alonso, see Alfonso XI.
Alphonse de Naples, IV, 181.
Amadis, I; III; IV; V, 29, 70.
Amadis Cuisinier, IV, 617.
Amalasunta, II, 383; III, 148-9, 602-3, 665.
Amalon, III, 182-3.
Amalthée, III, 132.
Amans rusés, see *Amour combatuë.*
Amant douillet, III, 701-2.
Amaulry, IV, 461, 864.
Ambition trop insolente, see *Hérodes.*
Ambrose, Saint, II; III, 405.
Ambrun, d', *Discours,* IV, 537.
American Journal of Philology, I, 60.
Amescua, see Mira de Amescua.
Ammianus Marcellinus, II, 401; IV, 342-3.
Amour clandestin, see *Axiane.*
Amour combatuë, II.
Amour déguisé, II, 474.
Amoureux brandons, I, 26.
Amour Médecin, I, 141.
Amours de la fille de l'amour, II, 427.
Amours de Louis le grand, IV, 938.
Amours de polichinel, IV, 934.
Amurat II, III, 145.
Amurat IV, IV, 78.
Amy du Cid, I, 582, 591.
Amyot, I, 46; IV.
Anacreon, II, 485; III; IV.
Anan, d', II, 208.

---

[1] When a Roman numeral is followed immediately by a period or a semicolon, it refers to the index of the Part indicated; when it is followed by a comma and an Arabic numeral, it refers to the Part of which the page is indicated by the Arabic number. This index repeats in full short items listed in the indices of Parts I, II, III, IV; this also longer items, but, instead of giving them in full, it refers the reader to an earlier index or to earlier indices. It includes the index of Part V, made according to the principles on which the index of Part IV is based, and the index of the supplements to Parts I, II, III, IV, none of which has been previously indexed.

14

15